It is obvious that the subject of the Secc nated the Rev. Ernest B. Gentile for 58 years, as he says. This book enables us to participate in a distillation of his years of research. It gripped me as extremely timely, scholarly, exhaustive, authoritative and logical. Before I finished the book I could almost hear the sound of Gabriel's trumpet heralding Christ's return.

Dr. Judson Cornwall
Pastor, teacher, author of 50 books, traveling minister

It is indeed a high honor to be asked to endorse any writings published by Ernest Gentile because his life is the walking Word manifested by his mannerisms, spirit, and scholarly presentation of the experienced revelation he possesses of the living Word. Whatever the reader's personal view of Christ's Second Coming—and there are several—Ernest Gentile's presentation will provoke him or her to search the Scriptures regarding this important event.

Fuchsia T. Pickett
Conference speaker, popular author

Ernest Gentile desires to see that the biblical teaching regarding the Second Coming of Christ be given its rightful place in both the thoughts and the actions of Christians. In his view it should neither be ignored as an irresolvable riddle nor promoted merely for intellectual debate. It should rather be a source of great hope and an encouragement toward godly living.

In this book Ernest is able to take a fresh look at this subject while showing appropriate respect for traditional views. He is passionate without being polemic in his approach. I believe this book to be an important contribution because Ernest brings to this subject a unique combination of scholarly integrity, pastoral concern and prophetic passion.

Ken Malmin
Dean of Portland Bible College and textbook author

With the renewed interest in the return of Jesus Christ, this book is timely. To say it is well-written is to minimize Ernest Gentile's incredible ability to impart deep revelation in simple terms and readable form. All content is carefully documented by Scripture, both Old and New Testaments. Although his position on the end times is clear, he allows that the readers may differ in interpretation. Reading the book left me with an intense desire for Christ's return and a prayer that I may be ready.

This book is an excellent resource for teachers and all seekers who hunger to understand the future in light of God's Word and in relevance to today. I highly recommend it.

Iverna Tompkins
Prominent traveling minister, author, founder of Iverna Tompkins Ministries

In a day when everybody seems interested in fictional accounts of the end times, Ernest Gentile's book is a breath of fresh air. It is definitely nonfiction! My acquaintance with Ernest came at the invitation of my pastor, a long-time friend of the Gentile family. He said, "Tommy, you have to meet this man." My advice to you would be the same, except to say, "You have to read this man." His relationships span a huge network of friends. It seems that everybody either knows Ernie Gentile or knows about him. It's time the world at large met him. You may not agree with his well-thought-out approach to the end times, but you will be forced to admit he knows what he's talking about. Drawing on years of ministry experience, a wealth of biblical knowledge and a huge bank account of credibility, Ernest Gentile makes this book a must-read for anyone interested in the last days.

Tommy Tenney
Author of *The God Chasers,* founder of the God Chasers Network

The recent worldwide interest in the Second Coming of Christ has been accelerated by the events in the Middle East. The emphasis of Ernest Gentile on a final triumph and victory over the powers of evil frees us to live in hope.

Robert Webber
Northern Baptist Theological Seminary, prolific author on worship

For serious students in the realm of eschatology, *The Final Triumph* is a must-read kind of text. Excellent research has been done and the work is well-documented. *Simple, clear, easy reading* and *succinct* describe this book. Beyond this, Ernest's book is *unique.* Of the eighty to ninety books I have read on eschatology, of all millennial views, none deals with end-time events in the unique manner that Ernest's does. This is the only text I have read that specifically deals with the some 453 references to Christ's Second Coming. Ernest also presents some distinctive alternatives to the various millennial schools of thought. This book is highly recommended and worthy of a place in every minister's library.

Kevin J. Conner
Australian Bible scholar, author and teacher

THE FINAL TRIUMPH

What Everyone Should Know About Jesus' Glorious Return

Ernest B. Gentile

Published by Chosen Books
A division of Baker Book House Company
P.O. Box 6287, Grand Rapids, MI 49516-6287

Printed in the United States of America

Library of Congress Cataloging-in-Publication Data

Gentile, Ernest B.
The final triumph : what everyone should know about Jesus' glorious return / Ernest B. Gentile.
p. cm.
Includes bibliographical references and index.
ISBN 0-8007-9284-X (pbk.)
1. Second Advent. I. Title
BT886.3 .G46 2001
236'.9—dc21 00-065840

For current information about all releases from Baker Book House, visit our web site:
http://www.bakerbooks.com

CONTENTS

TABLES

To Joy Dove
To mark 51 wonderful years together

INTRODUCTION

The Second Coming of Christ is of profound interest to Bible-believing Christians everywhere. More than an intriguing topic or academic exercise, this subject is vital to the Christian's belief system. Jesus' Second Coming is classified by most churches as a principal tenet of their creed of faith. In the short Apostles' Creed we read: "He ascended into heaven, and is seated at the right hand of the Father. He will come again to judge the living and the dead." The Athanasian Creed adds, "At whose advent all men are to rise again with their bodies and render an account of their own deeds."

The entire Christian Church, in spite of variations in detail, has always agreed on the great themes of the end times: the Second Coming of Christ, the resurrection from the dead, the day of judgment, and heaven and hell. Unlike the other world religions, Christendom believes that her Founder is presently alive and that He will return personally to this earth. The Church universal awaits this grand happening!

In June 1999 I listened to popular TV host Larry King interviewing evangelist Billy Graham. In the course of an interesting discussion on the late President John F. Kennedy, Dr. Graham mentioned the President's fascination with spiritual things and with what the Bible had to say. President Kennedy had particularly asked Billy about the Second Coming of Christ and whether the Bible said much about it. Billy endorsed this great event enthusiastically and emphasized that the Bible was specific that it would take place. The President was deeply interested but also frustrated, asking if his Church believed in the Second Coming and why he had not heard about it. Billy hastened to assure him that this doctrine was indeed part of the tenets of faith of the Roman Catholic Church. The President, a devout believer in the Bible, a consistent churchgoer and one who believed in Christ, was deeply disturbed by this news, for he felt caught in inexcusable ignorance on a serious subject.

Many people today feel the same way. They want to know more about this important topic.

The glorious return of Jesus will be the greatest, grandest event in human history, the climax of the running battle between God and Satan that has persisted throughout biblical history. The title of this book, *The Final Triumph,* is exactly what Christ's Second Coming will be. You can share in this ultimate victory over sin, Satan and death. My prayer is that, as you read, you will gain a renewed interest in this wonderful event and assume a spiritual wakefulness so this occurrence will not catch you unprepared.

The seven New Testament experts on the subject—Jesus, Paul, Peter, John, Luke, James and Jude—make a fascinating presentation of this important event. A remarkable clarity, unity and urgency flow through their writings. In Appendix B I have recorded all their New Testament material on the Second Coming, with partial quotations for quick reference. The 453 verses (my personal count) yield a total of 159 essential ideas on the overall subject. These verses and basic concepts shape the Church's belief in Christ's return, and they are the foundation of this book.

I have divided the New Testament into six divisions, devoting one or more chapters to each division. The ideas and verses of each division are arranged in a narrative style. Chapter 13 combines these fascinating points of information and verses (of the six sections) into one continuous narrative.

The effort to extricate relevant verses in the New Testament and then assemble them in narrative form has been a delightful venture. This uncommon approach, I feel, challenges us to honesty and clarity. The subtitle of this book, "What Everyone Should Know About Jesus' Glorious Return," may seem somewhat ambitious, but it is based on this use of *all* the New Testament references. These verses indeed cover all you and I should know on the subject!

The four major schools of thought on the Second Coming of Christ are presented without bias in chapter 3. The basic components of each viewpoint are listed, along with helpful diagrams; appropriate books for further reference are also suggested. These approaches are presented in one convenient place in the book for both information and future reference.

The chapters of Part 2 will concentrate on a straightforward reading of the seven biblical experts. Their clear ideas will be given prominence, but contemporary interpretations—with terminology and information that Paul would not recognize—are put in a secondary position.

Slightly more than two chapters are dedicated to "The Olivet Discourse." This is appropriate for the *one* prophetic message of Jesus given in the gospels (although the material is controversial). Dealing with the destruction of Jerusalem in A.D. 70 and His Second Coming at an undisclosed future time, Jesus gave some of His most important teaching on this subject.

Some principles and concepts in the book of Revelation are evident, whereas others will become clear only with the passage of time. The Old Testament prophets often said things clearly, such as Micah foretelling that the Messiah would be born in Bethlehem, but the actual awareness of how, when and where did not occur until the time of fulfillment. It happened as the prophet said it would, but as an amazement and wonder to all who observed the literal realization. My concentration will be confined to the Second Coming verses rather than to a detailed study of the whole book of Revelation.

Jesus, Paul and the other five spoke of only *one* Second Coming—one glorious coming, at which time the righteous will be resurrected from the dead and the living remaining saints will be caught up together to meet the Lord in the air. Jesus, I contend, will not first come secretly to remove His Church out of the world to escape tribulation, and then later, publicly and gloriously, to the world. Such conclusions, most authorities admit, can come only by personal inference, not from clear-cut Scripture. My approach here is to show what the New Testament verses say and to present the conclusions I perceive are self-evident.

I promote a literal Millennium that is Christian in nature, devoting Appendix D to that subject. Also, I believe that the Church will triumphantly undergo a last-days tribulation.

The Second Coming of Christ is a fascinating subject. While doing research, I have been humbled to read the scholarly presentations of many fine authors. Although there is not total agreement, their tremendous effort to make this information available to the Church is a gift that cannot be ignored. I hope we will draw closer together as we prayerfully seek clarification.

The final, ultimate, glorious coming of Jesus Christ is our heritage. Let's be charitable with each other concerning secondary issues, and profit from sincere, agreeable conversation on the subject. As one family let us possess and proclaim our one blessed hope, the Second Coming of the Lord Jesus Christ.

PART 1

THIS BACKGROUND STUFF IS IMPORTANT

ONE

IT'S LATER THAN YOU THINK!

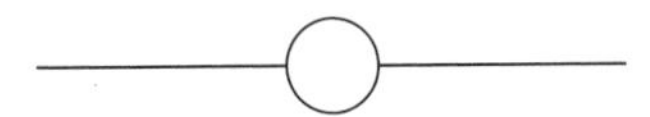

One morning I decided to check out the accuracy of my newly acquired hourglass. My brother Joe had sent me this beautiful decorative piece—probably as a gentle reminder about the length of my sermons! I decided to spend the waiting time in prayer.

The hourglass is an instrument for measuring time, consisting of a vessel with two bulbs of glass joined by a narrow passage through which a quantity of fine white sand runs from one bulb to the other in just an hour.

The tiny granules of sand began to flow through the narrow aperture in a steady stream. I glanced up several times out of curiosity. Because the hourglass was sitting on a coffee table, and I was bowed in prayer, my casual glance upward was on the same level as the upper glass. My watch told me that half an hour had passed. A small heap of sand now reposed in the lower bulb, but it appeared that no sand had emptied from the higher bulb. Drawing closer, I looked into the upper container and made an unexpected discovery. The sand emptied from inside the cone of sand! Later I observed that after about two minutes a small hole appeared in the middle of the upper pile of sand. The sand closest to the hole drained first, while the sand against the glass wall remained stationary.

Scientists call this principle "the coefficient of friction." The particles against the glass are less prone to move because the glass wall is stationary, whereas the central granules completely surrounded by other free-to-move grains are inclined to free movement or erosion.

Looking into the upper bulb, I perceived that the inner core of the sand cone had been draining steadily. A thin wall of sand remained against the glass wall, causing me to think that more sand (or time) remained than was actually the case. I squinted hard through my trifocals but could not see the sand in motion. Grabbing my magnifying glass, I focused on the upper rim, but could see no movement on the fringes of the wall of sand. Would the sand empty by the deadline? My watch gave notice that only four minutes remained! The hourglass looked as though at least another fifteen minutes remained. Once again the thin layer of sand against the glass fooled me.

Then, in the closing moments, the remaining sand plunged in a miniature avalanche. I blinked in amazement. All the sand had shifted from the upper glass to the lower in exactly one hour. In spite of appearances, the hourglass had functioned perfectly.

It occurred to me that I had just seen a remarkable illustration of the Second Coming of Christ. Each grain of sand represented an event or divinely appointed prophecy that must take place before Christ's Second Coming. Jesus will return when all is fulfilled. Note these references:

> "But all this was done that the Scriptures of the prophets might be fulfilled."
>
> Matthew 26:56

> "All things that are written by the prophets concerning the Son of Man will be accomplished."
>
> Luke 18:31

> ". . . that all things must be fulfilled which were written in the Law of Moses and the Prophets and the Psalms concerning Me."
>
> Luke 24:44

> ". . . that He may send Jesus Christ, who was preached to you before, whom heaven must receive [*retain*, Williams] until the times of restoration of all things, which God has spoken by the mouth of all His holy prophets since the world began."
>
> Acts 3:20–21

At times the world and the Church have thought things were not moving very fast on the prophetic timetable. Actually the rate of fulfillment has been active, consistent and continuous. Now, as we approach the end, many feel that much more time remains because they are looking at the stationary sand against the glass, but they really see only a thin layer *that is about to slide*.

It is later than we think! Prophetic destiny rests on the Church and the nations of the world. Even as you read, the sand is flowing and every grain is well performing its divine function. When the last grain of prophetic destiny has passed into history, the peoples of planet earth "will see the Son of Man coming on the clouds of heaven with power and great glory" (Matthew 24:30).

The Second Coming of Christ

Our Lord Jesus Christ will personally and publicly return to earth, and it will be the greatest happening in human history—the final triumph for Christ and His Church. Although the Bible itself does not use the expression *the Second Coming*, it is compatible with biblical teaching. Jesus said, "I will come again. . . . I will come to you. . . . I am going away and coming back to you" (John 14:3, 18, 28). The book of Hebrews speaks of Jesus' first appearance, in order to die on the cross, then adds, "To those who eagerly wait for Him He will appear a second time" (Hebrews 9:28).

Jesus made several appearances to His disciples after being raised from the dead. In His final visit He told them to wait in Jerusalem for the empowerment of the Holy Spirit, which would enable them to be witnesses throughout the world. Then, defying gravity, His body began to ascend from the earth.

Awestruck, the disciples gaped at the soaring figure. Suddenly two white-robed messengers appeared and gently reproved the bewildered disciples: "Men of Galilee, why do you stand gazing up into heaven? *This same Jesus,* who was taken up from you into heaven, *will so come in like manner as you saw Him go into heaven*" (Acts 1:11, emphasis added).

The doctrine of Christ's coming occupies 453 of the 7,957 verses in the King James Version of the New Testament. In other words, approximately one verse in eighteen deals with the Lord's return—certainly a dominant theme that colors the entire New Testament.[1]

Six chapters are traditionally understood to give the most complete explanation on the subject: Matthew 24 and 25, Luke 21, 1 Thessalonians 4 and 5 and 2 Peter 3. Only three of the 27 books of the New Testament do not refer to the Second Coming (Philemon and 2 and 3 John).

No one knows exactly when Christ will return. "Of that day and hour no one knows, no not even the angels of heaven, but My Father only. . . . Watch therefore, for you do not know what hour your Lord is coming. . . . Watch therefore, for you know neither the day nor the hour in which the Son of Man is coming" (Matthew 24:36, 42; 25:13; see also Luke 12:39–40; Acts 1:7). Mark 13:32 says that "of that day and hour no one knows, neither the angels in heaven, *nor the Son,* but only the Father" (emphasis added).

We see, then, that mortal man, immortal angels and even the Son of Man while He lived on earth did not know the exact day of His coming. Jesus was clearly not frustrated by this lack of information; it had no immediate importance to His ministry on earth.[2]

An Explosion of Glory

Jesus, our beloved Lord and Master, will return to earth soon. His second advent will be more glorious than words can describe or Hollywood's sophisticated technology could possibly depict. Try to imagine the combined energy and excitement of the greatest celebrations we humans have experienced: the Allied troops marching into Paris at the end of the Second World War, New York tickertape parades, an explosive Fourth of July celebration, centennial observances, the exciting climax of a Super Bowl, the worldwide celebration of the new millennium. The result makes not even a blip on the scale of comparison with Christ's return.

Astronomers tell us of colossal eruptions of fiery energy in the outer reaches of space. Huge sections of the ethereal skies flame with light whose blazing essence is so intense that it cannot be measured by earthly standards. Stars explode and nebulae burst with light intensity beyond our ability to comprehend. Yet Jesus' coming will be greater than these epic proportions of power and glory!

The time will arrive when the last prophetic grains have passed, and our God will declare all things fulfilled. The hosts of heaven will mass in blazing garments of light behind Him who is the dazzling brightness of God's glory. Like robed faculty and dignitaries assembling to make a grand entry at a graduation ceremony, the hosts of heaven will gather in regal splendor to make entrance to planet earth.

As Spurgeon preached:

> He cometh with hosts of attendants, and these of a nobler sort than earthly monarchs can summon to do them homage. With clouds of angels, cherubim and seraphim, and all the armies of heaven he comes. With all the forces of nature, thundercloud and blackness of tempest, the Lord of all makes his triumphant entrance to judge the world. The clouds are the dust of his feet in that dread day of battle when he shall ease him of his adversaries, shaking them out of the earth with his thunder, and consuming them with the devouring flame of his lightning. All heaven shall gather with its utmost pomp to the great appearing of the Lord, and all the terrible grandeur of nature shall then be seen at its full. Not as the Man of sorrows, despised and rejected of men, shall Jesus come; but as Jehovah came upon Sinai in the midst of thick clouds and a terrible darkness, so shall he come, whose coming shall be the final judgment.[3]

Jesus the Christ, who has been "held" in the heavens until all things are fulfilled, will initiate the glorious descent. Heaven will empty as all the mighty angels and all spirits of the deceased saints form a royal entourage of spectacular size and magnificence.

The Lord's victorious voice will roar like a million nuclear explosions, the sound booming and crashing throughout all creation with incalculable speed. This thunderclap will fulminate from one universe to another, like a stone skipping along the surface of a lake. The triumphant shout of Jesus will instantly apprehend every living and created thing in the total vastness of all space.

Some say that when Jesus cried, "Lazarus, come forth!" (John 11:43), He specifically identified His friend by name so the whole graveyard would not awaken. Probably so! *This* triumphant shout, however, does awaken and resurrect all those who died in Christ. In spite of how Christian men and women have died—consumed by fire, eaten by sharks, blown apart in explosions, rotted by plague, or simply having expired quietly—their energized earthly particles shall miraculously reassemble as the gloriously beautiful, incorruptible bodies of the righteous in the resurrection of the just. The Holy Spirit will quicken or enliven or bring back to life all those who have died in Christ.[4]

Other great sounds will also be heard. Gabriel the archangel will issue his clarion command to gather all saints. The great trumpet of heaven will sound to proclaim the coming of the Son of Man and to gather all saints. The angels of God will suddenly break rank and scatter to invade every place on earth where saints have died, ushering these newly resurrected, redeemed ones into the living presence of their omnipotent Savior.

Jesus will return as King of kings and Lord of lords. All powers, principalities and potentates, both natural and spiritual, will bow before Him. Leading the brilliant, shining armies of heaven, the Son of Man will make His bold entrance into earth's atmosphere. What a procession it will be! The radiant Christ and His followers will descend to earth like an orbiting spacecraft circling the globe in reentry, waiting until the conflagration of melting elements has finally subsided and a new, shining earth has emerged.[5] As when all floodlights are switched on in a darkened stadium, the luminous splendor of His meteoric coming will instantly light up the atmosphere and stratosphere of the earth. The whole universe will be illuminated by the glory of God.

Resurrection change will occur instantly at the shout and trumpet call. Glorious, incorruptible, imperishable bodies shall spring forth from the dark graves of this earth to meet the Lord in the lightened skies. The living Church, those members of the spiritual Body of Christ who have not died previous to Jesus' coming ("we who are alive and remain," 1 Thessalonians 4:17), will joyfully discover their bodies wondrously changed by the power of God. Corruptible, hurting, dying bodies transformed—reconstructed in a split second—into the same state as Jesus' glorified, resurrected body! These living saints will soar upward to meet the Lord in the air.

Jesus' comeback will be reminiscent of the triumphant return of the Roman general from his wars. All Rome would mass along the parade route to watch as the conquering hero reentered the royal city in his shining chariot drawn by milk-white horses. The frenzied crowds shouted and cheered as the mighty conqueror and his troops marched exultantly in all the glory that Rome was capable of bestowing. In stark contrast behind the magnificent conqueror, the stripped, dispirited captives shuffled along in chains.

Paul uses this graphic illustration to make clear the accomplishment of Christ on the cross—how He triumphed over sin and all spiritual powers (2 Corinthians 2:14; Ephesians 4:8; Colossians 2:15; 1 Peter 3:22). The Second Coming will be the literal reenactment of what has already been accomplished spiritually through Calvary; it will be a magnificent public display for the whole world to see.

Just prior to Jesus' return, world systems will come together in a unified one-world government. The supreme leader, known as the Antichrist, the lawless one or the anarchist, will be the very embodiment of all that is evil and corrupt. Although unrealized by himself, his appearance in history will be one of the grains of sand that will slip through heaven's hourglass during the closing minutes.

Godly people will suffer a difficult and trying time—the ultimate persecution of all ages. Nevertheless a remnant of overcomers will persevere to the end. Paul said specifically that some will be alive when Jesus returns. The conquerors of that hour will experience God's preserving grace and presence in a remarkable way. They will be the finest and best of the Church's elite spiritual warriors.

Peter and Paul describe the Second Coming as a time of awesome judgment. The Antichrist will be destroyed by the brightness of Christ, the ultimate darkness overcome by the supreme Light. The heavens and earth will burst into fire and the elements will melt with fervent heat. All that is evil and corrupt will be put to the torch of God's wrath. Evil destroyed! The earth transformed! God's people safely with Jesus! The physical bodies of the saints will be glorified and immortalized, and the physical earth and its components redeemed from the curse.

A Logical Approach

I just completed reading the entire New Testament four times during a brief period. Using a new, unmarked edition of the New King James Version with no cross-references or notes, I sought to locate all the verses referring to the Second Coming of Christ, which I then identified with a marking pen. This was a pleasant and conclusive way to crystallize my ideas on a subject that has fascinated me for 58 years. Appendix B lists all the marked references—an amazing 453 verses!

My original list, gleaned from previous readings, the concordance and various commentaries, was considerably enlarged. More verses came from each new reading of the New Testament. Certain references, previously overlooked, seemed to cry out for inclusion.

My new list includes verses about the day of Christ's coming; i.e., "the Day of the Lord," "day of judgment," "that Day," etc. (*Day* is sometimes capitalized in the NKJV). References to the resurrection also seem appropriate. Two well-known texts in Revelation, chapters 14 and 19, merit inclusion in the list, although I avoid including controversial or unclear passages, such as the one verse in Revelation mentioning Armageddon.

The clear-cut statements provide us with the basic outlook of the apostolic Church. Certain verses, however, do refer to Christ's coming but are somewhat unclear—for example, Romans 2:16: "in the day when God will judge the secrets of men by Jesus Christ." I included such verses.

The teaching of the seven experts I mentioned in the introduction—Jesus, Paul, Peter, John, Luke, James and Jude—will be our focus. Their statements stand as the uncontested foundation of the doctrine.

The six sections of this book—the gospels, the Acts, 1 and 2 Thessalonians, other Pauline epistles, general epistles and Revelation—feature verses on the Second Coming of Christ. From all these verses I draw the 159 basic ideas that are used in the final narration (chapter 13).

Summary of New Testament Verses on the Second Coming

Section	Number of NT Verses	% of Total Verses
1. Gospels	238	53%
2. The Acts	16	3%
3. 1 & 2 Thessalonians	29	6%
4. Other Pauline epistles	84	19%
5. General epistles	42	9%
6. Revelation	44	10%
Total	**453**	**100%**

Two Great Prayers

Modern Christians tend to be overly involved with mechanics and technicalities, even in our doctrinal discussions. The Second Coming is a case in point. Our focus tends to be, "Will we go through the Tribulation?" or, "Who is the Antichrist?" or, "How much time do I have to get ready?"—rather than simply living in the joyful hope of Jesus' return.

The early Christians, perhaps because of heavy persecution, seemed to long for the literal presence of Jesus. Their belief was one of the heart as well as the head. Stephen, the first martyr, as he lay dying, called out, "Lord Jesus, receive my spirit" (Acts 7:59). They yearned for the *parousia* (presence) of their Savior, "and they loved not their lives unto the death" (Revelation 12:11, KJV).

The apostles Paul and John exemplified this same spirit in two sincere mini-prayers. Only three words each, these ring out as prophetic, passionate cries that resonate in the spirit of every sincere Christian. Paul and John both knew that Jesus would return when He could, and they probably knew He would not come back until after they were gone. They were not afraid of tribulation or persecution or the spirit of Antichrist. They served God with a burning fervency. Their prayers involved the great hope and passion of the Church.

As Paul finished his first epistle to the Corinthians, having provided helpful answers for a number of church problems, and undoubtedly feeling somewhat weary, he cried out the ultimate solution for every situation: "O Lord, come!" (1 Corinthians 16:22). In Aramaic this is *Maranatha!*

John, having just witnessed heaven's prophetic panorama of awesome events to come, closed the great Apocalypse (22:20) with a prayer that captures the heart attitude of Christians everywhere: "Come, Lord Jesus!"

These poignant prayers illustrate that the early Church focused more on Jesus' return, and on what was expected of them, than on secondary issues that often occupy modern minds. They possessed a doctrine of the heart, not the head. Certain things, they sincerely believed, would evolve on their own. The Church should concentrate on the essential task left to them.

Peter's advice, in this light, makes much sense:

> You must not forget, dear friends, that a day is like a thousand years to the Lord, and a thousand years is like a day. The Lord isn't really being slow about his promise to return, as some people think. No, he is being patient for your sake. He does not want anyone to

> perish, so he is giving more time for everyone to repent. But the day of the Lord will come as unexpectedly as a thief. Then the heavens will pass away with a terrible noise, and everything in them will disappear in fire, and the earth and everything on it will be exposed to judgment. Since everything around us is going to melt away, what holy, godly lives you should be living! You should look forward to that day and hurry it along—the day when God will set the heavens on fire and the elements will melt away in the flames. But we are looking forward to the new heavens and new earth he has promised, a world where everyone is right with God.
>
> 2 Peter 3:8–13, NLT

Let's keep the two apostolic prayers ever in mind: "O Lord, come!" and "Come, Lord Jesus!" Perhaps we can even add our own cry: "Come quickly, Lord Jesus!"

TWO

WHY ALL THESE STRANGE WORDS?

Seven words are very important in the study of the Second Coming. Three are Greek terms—*parousia, epiphaneia* and *apokalypsis*—which refer to the advent, manifestation and revelation of Jesus Christ in His Second Coming. Noted British scholar F. F. Bruce comments, "They are three alternative designations of one and the same event."[1] The fourth word, *Rapture,* now an accepted English word, is derived from a Latin term and generally refers to Christ's Second Coming. The fifth word is the English word *imminent,* used by some to describe the possible immediacy of His coming. The last two words, *Millennium* and *Tribulation,* refer to periods of time usually associated with the Second Coming.

1. *Parousia:* Advent, Coming, Arrival, Presence

Appearing 24 times in the Greek New Testament, the noun *parousia* refers to the arrival of a person at a certain place. More specifically it "denotes both an arrival and a consequent presence with."[2] The word is composed of *para,* "alongside, beside," and the substantive form of the verb *eimi,* "to be." "It basically means 'being along-side of' and conveys the sense of the English word 'presence.' It is used in the New Testament of a person's presence as contrasted with his absence."[3]

For instance, Paul described how "the coming of Titus" made him extremely happy (2 Corinthians 7:6–7). Paul trusted that his own coming to the Philippians would also be an encouragement (Philippians 1:26). Three other references, 1 Corinthians 16:17, 2 Corinthians 10:10 and Philippians 2:12, allude to a person's arrival or presence. The remaining occurrences of *parousia* refer seventeen times to the future coming and presence of Christ and once to the coming of the Antichrist, the lawless one (2 Thessalonians 2:9).

Paul also had a more technical meaning of *parousia* in mind when discussing Christ's coming. As Greek scholar W. Bauer explains, "*[Parousia]* became the official term for a visit of a person of high rank, especially of kings and emperors visiting a province."[4] The gathering of taxes or payments to make preparations for the special occasion sometimes preceded such royal visits. One record shows that contributions were made for a crown to be presented to a king on his arrival.[5]

Parousia had a twofold meaning, therefore, for the New Testament Christian. It was a warm, loving description of intimate fellowship (the return, arrival and presence of a friend), and it also depicted the glorious arrival of the supreme Ruler of the universe.

Parousia is used seventeen times in reference to the Second Coming:

- Once the disciples asked, "What will be the sign of Your coming?" (Matthew 24:3).
- Three times Jesus referred to "the coming of the Son of Man" (Matthew 24:27, 37, 39).
- Five times the apostles referred to "His coming" (1 Corinthians 15:23; 1 Thessalonians 2:19; 2 Thessalonians 2:8; 2 Peter 3:4; 1 John 2:28).
- Seven times the Word describes "the coming of the [our] Lord" or "Lord Jesus Christ" (1 Thessalonians 3:13; 4:15; 5:23; 2 Thessalonians 2:1; James 5:7–8; 2 Peter 1:16).
- Once it is called "the coming of the day of God" (2 Peter 3:12).

2. *Apokalypsis:* Revelation, Disclosure, Unveiling, Uncovering

This word appears eighteen times in the Greek New Testament and means "an uncovering, a laying bare, making naked." It refers to events "by which things or states or persons hitherto withdrawn from view are made visible to all."[6]

The meaning can be illustrated by the unveiling of a statue. Imagine this scene: A war hero is to be memorialized by the proud citizens of his hometown. A statue is commissioned, completed and installed in a local park, where it is temporarily covered with a shroud. On the day of dedication, as proud townsfolk gather, a city dignitary speaks glowingly of the hero, then pulls the restraining cord. The covering drops off and the magnificent statue suddenly appears to all. An unveiling, a public *apokalypsis* has just taken place.

Apokalypsis is used four ways in the New Testament:

- Three times to describe the revelation of truth (Luke 2:32; Romans 16:25; Ephesians 1:17).
- Eight times to describe spiritual revelations through visions, etc. (1 Corinthians 14:6, 26; 2 Corinthians 12:1, 7; Galatians 1:12; 2:2; Ephesians 3:3; Revelation 1:1).
- Twice to describe what happens at the Second Coming (Romans 2:5; 8:19).
- Five times to describe the glorious Second Coming (1 Corinthians 1:7; 2 Thessalonians 1:7; 1 Peter 1:7, 13; 4:13).

3. *Epiphaneia:* Manifestation, Appearing, Visibility

Ancient secular Greek writers use *epiphaneia* in their mythology to portray the visible manifestation of an invisible deity, and how such a god might intervene in human affairs or bring help. The word also appears in the Septuagint, the Greek Old Testament, to describe manifestations of God's glory. The basic meaning is to bring to light, to make visible, as an enemy is made visible to an army in the field. In a medical sense the word described symptoms. Our English word is *epiphany,* meaning literally "a shining forth." J. Rodman Williams comments: "The Greek word also contains the idea of brightness, radiance, even splendor."[7]

Epiphaneia occurs six times in the New Testament, five times in the pastoral epistles and once in 2 Thessalonians. It is used in two ways:

- Of Jesus' first appearance on the earth (2 Timothy 1:10).
- Of Jesus' coming in judgment (2 Thessalonians 2:8; 2 Timothy 4:1, 8; Titus 2:13).

Jesus' coming will be no secret, hidden event, but a breaking into history of the glory or splendor of God.

4. *Rapture:* Caught Up

The word *rapture* is derived from the Latin word *rapio,* which is found in the Latin Bible text of 1 Thessalonians 4:17 and translated "caught up." It refers to the time when the Church of God is taken out of this world:

> The Lord Himself will descend from heaven with a shout, with the voice of an archangel, and with the trumpet of God. And the dead in Christ will rise first. Then we who are alive and remain shall be *caught up* together with them in the clouds to meet the Lord in the air. And thus we shall always be with the Lord.
>
> 1 Thessalonians 4:16–17 (emphasis added)

The question for modern Christians is whether Paul meant what a simple reading of the text implies: that Jesus will come publicly in glory, with the whole Church caught up at that time. Or does Paul refer to a special, secret catching away of Christians just before the great Tribulation begins, which will *later* be followed by the glorious coming of Christ?

This second interpretation, by common acknowledgment, is one that originated about 170 years ago but that has a very strong following.[8] To read this much into the obvious meaning of the verse raises important questions that deserve answers. For instance, did Jesus and Paul have a two-phase coming in mind when they taught on the Second Coming? Is it possible that an evolution in thought about these matters has occurred that has brought today's Church to a belief not held by the early Church?

Good insight on the real focus of the Rapture is given by George Ladd: "The Rapture has as its first objective the union of the living Church with her returning Lord. . . . The second significance of the Rapture is the transformation of the bodies of the believers."[9]

5. *Imminent:* At Any Moment

Sometimes religious ordination or membership on a faculty or in a church requires signing a statement that you believe in an "imminent" coming of Christ. It is easily misunderstood. In English usage *imminent* suggests something ready to take place, especially something hanging threateningly over one's head.

The way the word is used in religious context means that Christ may come at any moment, not that His coming is necessarily immediate. One author defines it as "an ever-present possibility."[10] Imminence by this definition means that no event predicted by Scripture must yet occur, and no prophesied event stands in the way, before Christ can return to rapture the Church. Did Jesus, Peter and Paul believe that Jesus might come back at any time—that nothing remained to be fulfilled? Did the apostles live out their ministries expecting an any-moment secret coming of Christ that would rapture out the Church?

The belief in an imminent Rapture is usually designated as *pretribulationism* because such a Rapture would take place before the Tribulation. Indeed it enables the Church to escape the Tribulation. Closely connected with this belief is the strongly emphasized teaching in the New Testament of "watching" and "waiting" for the Second Coming. The idea, which I feel can be effectively debated, is that "we can watch for His coming only if it is imminent."[11]

Those who believe that Christ will come after (or at the end of) the Tribulation are designated *posttribulationists.*

One of the best critiques I have seen on imminency (specifically addressing why Jesus told us to watch and wait) is that by Douglas J. Moo, professor at Trinity Evangelical Divinity School. Although he is a dispensationalist, his study has led him to a posttribulation position. He says that "none of the many words used to describe the nearness of the Parousia, or the believer's expectation of it, requires an 'any moment' sense of imminency."[12]

Is it true that we can watch for His coming only if it is imminent? We will see in chapters 4 through 7, where we discuss Jesus' own teaching, that the New Testament use of *watch* does not mean "to look for," but rather "to be wakeful" in a spiritual and moral sense.[13]

Consider for the moment that Jesus, Peter and Paul did *not* believe in an imminent coming.

What Jesus Believed

Jesus did not believe He could come back at any moment, because He foretold:

- Delay before His return (Luke 19:11–27; Matthew 24:45–51; 25:5, 19).
- The destruction of Jerusalem in A.D. 70 (Matthew 24; Luke 21).
- The treading down of Jerusalem until "the times of the Gentiles are fulfilled" (Luke 21:24).
- The disciples' witness "in Jerusalem, and in all Judea and Samaria, and to the end of the earth" (Acts 1:8).
- The martyrdom of Peter as an old man (John 21:18–19).
- The evangelization of all nations before the end (Matthew 24:14).[14]
- The reaction of the sun and moon (Matthew 24:29).

What Peter Believed

Peter did not believe Jesus would come back in his lifetime because:

- Jesus told Peter he would grow old and be martyred (John 21:18–19).
- Peter told the Church how to live after his death (2 Peter 1:13–15).
- Peter believed that Jesus must remain in heaven until all things spoken by the prophets were fulfilled (Acts 3:20–21).

What Paul Believed

Paul did not believe that Jesus would come back at any moment because:

- Paul felt he had an apostolic commission to fulfill (Acts 9:15).
- Paul knew he yet had to appear before kings (Acts 9:15).
- Paul was informed that he had a great ministry ahead in Corinth, which continued eighteen months (Acts 18:9–11).
- Paul knew he would preach the Gospel in Rome (Acts 23:11; 27:24), which occurred two full years later.
- Paul knew that false leaders would arise after his death (Acts 20:29;[15] 2 Timothy 4:3–6).
- Paul taught that Jesus would come after the Antichrist was revealed (2 Thessalonians 2:3).[16]

Some feel that Paul was speaking of himself and any others who might survive until the Lord's return when he said in 1 Thessalonians 4:17, "We who are alive and remain shall be caught up together with them in the clouds to meet the Lord in the air." One commentator, basing his conclusion on this text and the use of *we* in 1 Corinthians 15:51–52, says that "there was to [Paul's] mind the possibility of His coming in his lifetime: in fact, he seems to have an expectation that he would not pass through the gates of death at all, that he would live to see the Lord in His glorious return. . . ."[17] I feel, in contrast, that Paul's use of *we* is more a simple literary device to show that all sincere believers are included in this hope. Paul himself (as I already stated) apparently expected to die before Christ's return.

Jesus, Peter, Paul and all the rest of the apostolic Church believed in a quick, soon coming—but not a coming that could be at any moment. Consider that Jesus really wants to return and that He would come at any moment if He could. But all things must be fulfilled; all the grains of sand must pass through the prophetic hourglass (Acts 3:21). His coming is not arbitrary, but rather set by the will of the Father.

The "imminent" interpretation is based on the "any moment" Rapture theory that Christ can secretly come at any time for the Church, and then return later in a glorious Second Coming after a period of great tribulation. Careful readings of the New Testament cause me to doubt seriously that such a secret coming to the Church and a glorious coming to the world—in other words, a two-phase coming—will occur. Also, this approach necessitates dividing the resurrection into at least three parts (Rapture, Resurrection of the righteous, Resurrection of the ungodly), and such interpretation rudely complicates the Bible's straightforward presentation. Our seven biblical experts give the impression that only one coming will occur, the glorious return of Jesus after all has been fulfilled.

I like this statement by J. Rodman Williams, professor at Regent University: "'Impending' is a better term than 'imminent.' 'Imminent' implies the idea of an any-moment return; 'impending' implies the idea of approaching, or being near at hand."[18]

Four of the seven key words we are examining in this chapter concur: Christ's one-and-only coming will be an *arrival*, a *revelation*, a *manifestation*, a *catching up*—when all things are fulfilled.

6. *Millennium:* One Thousand Years

This term is derived from two Latin words: *mille*, meaning thousand, and *annum*, meaning year. The word *millennium* is a good

English word, but it does not actually appear in the Bible. Since *thousand years* does appear six times in a text of six verses (Revelation 20:2–7), the capitalized word *Millennium* is used in a religious sense when discussing this much-debated period.

Some feel that this period will be a literal thousand-year earthly reign of Christ, a period introduced by His Second Coming. Others see no precedent for it in previous Scripture, so they feel it must have a figurative or spiritual application to the present Church age, the era of Gospel proclamation that was introduced by Christ's first advent and will be ended by His second.

From such a small text—generally recognized as the *only* biblical statement on such a one-thousand-year period of time—the Millennium rises to dominate, shape and define the systems of eschatology. Every school of thought grapples with the role of the Millennium in God's Kingdom program. Neither Jesus nor Paul specified a thousand-year period, so this concept introduced at the end of the canonized New Testament raises legitimate questions in the minds of thoughtful readers of the Bible: Did Jesus and Paul believe in a Millennium? Is the Millennium possibly "the age to come," which Jesus and Paul both taught? Was belief in a Millennium common in the early Church? Does it have a literal or symbolic meaning? When does it begin and when will it end? Put more simply, every approach must answer one question: When *is* the Millennium?

Some contend that Jesus will come *before* a literal Millennium, hence the term *premillennialists.* Others who believe He will come *after* a spiritualized Millennium here on earth concludes the Church age are classified as *postmillennialists.* Those who spiritualize the Millennium as the Gospel age and believe we are experiencing it at present are called *amillennialists.* Admittedly this summary is too simplistic, but for now it serves our purpose.

More millennial discussion is given in Appendix D.[19] There I will list my reasons for believing in a literal one-thousand-year period of time in which the saints will live and reign with Christ on earth. Why will this happen, and can it be justified scripturally?

7. *Tribulation:* A Time of Great Trouble

The Tribulation refers to a time of earthly troubles (three and a half years, seven years or an indeterminate time) occurring just previous to the glorious Second Coming. God will pour out judgment and even wrath on the world.

Some do not believe there will be a specific Tribulation of prescribed duration; others believe there will be one of seven years' duration. One interpretation says there will be three and a half years of extreme human tribulation followed by three and a half years of divine wrath (concluded by the Second Coming).[20]

Those who believe in a Tribulation usually interpret it to be the last three and a half years (half a week) or seven years (one week) of the last week of Daniel's famous seventy-weeks prophecy (Daniel 9).[21] See Appendix C.

The next chapter summarizes briefly the four major interpretations of the events of Christ's coming. Before we analyze the New Testament references, it seems reasonable to survey the basic directions that commentators have taken. The four presentations are straightforward, unbiased accounts, accompanied by reading suggestions if further research is desired.

THREE

WHAT DO THE INTERPRETERS SAY?

Although all Christians believe in Christ's Second Coming, opinions on the details surrounding that great event continue to vary. The branch of theology dealing with the future is called eschatology (from *eschatos*, the word for "the last"), and it is an important aspect of our Christian belief system.

Of greater importance, however, is our understanding of the clear, fundamental doctrines of Christianity. Our eschatology should evolve out of a good grasp of those points that are the clearest and least mysterious in the Bible. The fact of Christ's Second Coming is a cardinal doctrine of Christianity and part of our doctrinal foundation. The speculative aspects of the events associated with Christ's return need to be studied, but they must not be made issues that divide us from other Christians. They are neither tests of orthodoxy nor facets of absolute truth on which our theological faith rests.

This chapter is meant to be a helpful survey and source of reference of the four major schools of thought on the Second Coming of Christ. The names commonly used to classify these broad categories are based on the place that the Millennium—the thousand-year period mentioned in Revelation 20:2–7—holds within each belief system:

1. Historic premillennialism
2. Amillennialism
3. Dispensational premillennialism
4. Postmillennialism

Most of us find *millennium* hard enough to spell, let alone interpret! The word, suddenly popular through secular promotion (movies, TV, books and the arrival of the year 2000), has tended to assume farfetched meaning, so the topic for Christians takes on new significance.

You may find, as I have, that each system of interpretation, when left unchallenged, tends to oversimplify the biblical data, even when presenting certain worthwhile biblical insights. Each approach has strengths and weaknesses; no one school, regrettably, answers every question fully and satisfactorily. Many Christians hold beliefs that combine the thoughts of several different schools.

Some years ago I attended a conference on eschatology in which two capable scholars presented their views and debated the Millennium. One represented the viewpoint of a literal thousand-year period; the other presented the amillennial approach, which says that the thousand-year reign of Christ is an invisible, spiritual reality rather than a literal, earthly Kingdom. All the schools of interpretation were considered and the two debaters did credible jobs. I found myself giving consideration to certain points just because of my esteem for and relation to the speakers. I also found it amusing that, after the conference, it appeared that no one had changed his or her mind! Because we all esteemed each other, however, we have remained good friends and have developed a healthier respect for the opinions of others.

Professor F. F. Bruce, attempting to answer an inquirer's question about the Millennium, said, "If we are content to follow the relevant passages of Scripture as they come, we can dispense with interpretative labels; I for my part would not care to wear any of them."[1]

As much as I sympathize with Bruce's statement, I do feel that it is both honest and important to point out the different interpretations of the Millennium and how Christ's coming relates to it. The good news of this study is that, in spite of differences, we all believe in the glorious, literal return of Jesus Christ!

1. Historic Premillennialism

A Basic Definition. "The view first articulated in the early church: Christians endure the Tribulation (not necessarily seven years), after which Christ returns. Many who adhere to this view today believe a 'rapture' will accompany the Second Coming."[2]

Historic Premillennialism

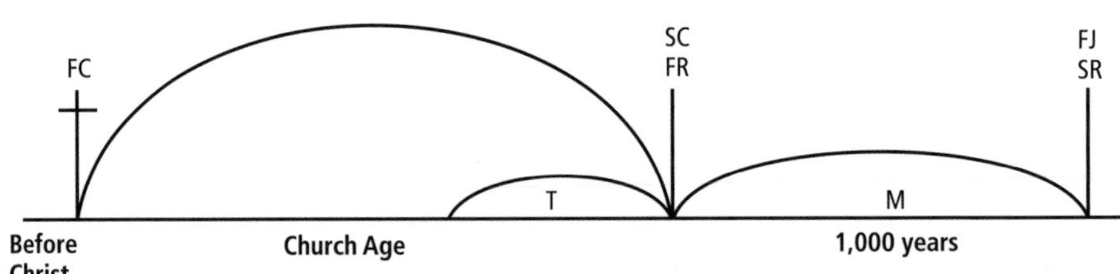

Notations: FC=First Coming; FR=First Resurrection; FJ=Final Judgment; M=Millennium; T=Tribulation; SC=Second Coming; SR=Second Resurrection

Comments. The historic premillennialist believes in only one glorious Second Coming of Christ. This coming will inaugurate a literal thousand-year reign of Christ on earth, during which time the powers of Satan will be completely bound, and all saints, Jew and Gentile, will reign with Christ. There will be two literal, bodily resurrections, first, of the righteous, at the beginning of the Millennium when Christ returns, and second, of the unsaved, at the end of the thousand years.

This school of thought finds no biblical support for the idea that the return of Christ will be divided into two phases—one before the Rapture and one after the Tribulation. Most historic premillennialists believe that the Rapture of the Church will occur at the Second Coming of Christ at the end of the Tribulation. Nor does this position find Scripture to substantiate that the Church will *not* go through the Tribulation, which is generally thought to be just before the Millennium.

The late George E. Ladd summarized this position in *The Blessed Hope,* a book considered the classic statement of this approach:

> The vocabulary of the Blessed Hope knows nothing of two aspects of Christ's coming, one secret and one glorious. On the contrary, the terminology points to a single indivisible return of Christ. Scripture says nothing about a secret coming of the Lord.[3]

The historic and dispensational premillennialist positions both believe in a literal Millennium. The dispensational position makes the Millennium a time of renewing national Judaism; the historic position, in contrast, sees this period as the glorious expression of the full redemption of God's people (both Jew and Gentile believers), society and the natural creation.

Historic premillennialism stresses the present and future aspects of the Kingdom of God. Christ now sits on the throne of David, the Kingdom of God is now active in the spiritual life of the Church (composed of both Jews and Gentiles), and the propagation of the Gospel is the Church's present agenda. Yet, the full, literal expression of the Kingdom will take place in the Millennium or the age to come. The Church is considered the present-day expression of the people of God, and it is composed of all Jews or Gentiles who believe in Jesus Christ.

Reading That Promotes the Historic Premillennial (and Posttribulational) View

- Beasley-Murray, George R. *Jesus and the Last Days: The Interpretation of the Olivet Discourse* (Hendrickson, 1993). A thorough discussion of the Olivet Discourse as presented by Mark.
- Conner, Kevin J. *The Foundations of Christian Doctrine* (Bible Temple, 1980). Conner believes in a literal Millennium that is Christian rather than Jewish in nature.

- Gundry, Robert H. *The Church and the Tribulation* (Zondervan, 1973). This classic book touting a posttribulation position is now out of print, but Gundry has updated his material and added some arguments in a new book, *First the Antichrist* (Baker, 1997), that appeals to the lay leader.
- Katterjohn, Arthur. *The Tribulation People* (Creation House, 1975).
- Ladd, George E. *The Blessed Hope* (Eerdmans, 1956). Ladd believed that the great Tribulation is still future and that it must occur before the Rapture and second advent of Christ (aspects of the same event).
- Mounce, Robert H. *The Book of Revelation: The New International Commentary on the New Testament* (Eerdmans, 1977).
- Payne, J. Barton. *Encyclopedia of Biblical Prophecy* (Harper & Row, 1973). Barton believes in imminency, a premillennial Second Coming and a posttribulational point of view that spiritualizes the Tribulation.
- Reese, Alexander. *The Approaching Advent of Christ* (Marshall, Morgan & Scott, 1937). Reese presented one of the most comprehensive defenses of posttribulationism. He believed that the Church is the true Israel and includes saints of all ages.

Well-Known Historic Premillennialists. G. R. Beasley-Murray, W. J. Erdman, Frederic L. Godet, Irenaeus, Justin Martyr, George Eldon Ladd, Robert H. Mounce, Papias, J. Barton Payne, Tertullian, R. A. Torrey and Theodor Zahn.

2. Amillennialism

A Basic Definition. "The view of Augustine and Roman Catholicism (and in most respects, mainline traditions like Presbyterian, Lutheran, etc.): The current age is the 'Millennium' in that Christ rules in His Church and in the hearts of Christians, though the world becomes increasingly evil."[4]

The amillennial interpretation does not deny the Millennium of Revelation 20, but interprets it as taking place right now, rather than in the future. It is identified with the present spiritual reign of Christ at the right hand of God, where by faith His people are raised and seated with Him; thus there will be no literal millennial Kingdom. Christ's advent will be *after* the Millennium (or Church age). Satan is presently bound through Christ's ministry. Some see Christ's reign as beginning in His earthly ministry or at His resurrection. Amillennialists view the Kingdom promises to Israel as symbolic and apply them either to the Church age or to eternity.

Amillennialism

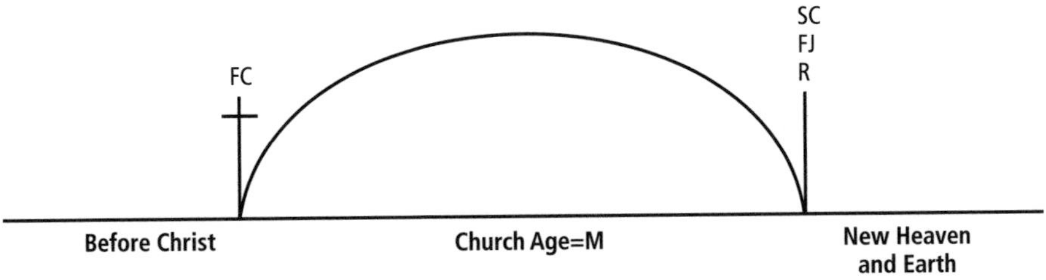

Notations: FC=First Coming; FJ=Final Judgment; M=Millennium; SC=Second Coming; R=Resurrection (general)

Comments. Anthony A. Hoekema, in presenting the case for amillennialism, writes:

> The term *amillennialism* is not a happy one. It suggests that amillennialists either do not believe in any millennium or that they simply ignore the first six verses of Revelation 20, which speak of a millennial reign. Neither of these two statements is true. Though it is true that amillennialists do not believe in a literal thousand-year earthly reign which will follow the return of Christ, the term *amillennialism* is not an accurate description of their view. . . . "Amillennialists" believe that the millennium of Revelation 20 is not exclusively future but is now in process of realization.[5]

Hoekema proceeds to explain, using the principle of "progressive parallelism," how the thousand years is to be interpreted: "According to this view, the book of Revelation consists of seven sections that run parallel to each other, each of which depicts the church and the world from the time of Christ's first coming to the time of his second." Revelation 20–22 constitutes the last of these seven sections and does not describe, therefore, what follows the return of Christ. "Revelation 20:1 takes us back once again to the beginning of the New Testament era."

It is generally understood that the first serious effort to interpret Revelation 20 in a non-literal (nonmillenarian) way was by Augustine in the beginning of the fifth century. Since he was convinced that the thousand-year period of Revelation 20 was the period between the first and second advents of Christ, he became disillusioned because the real world did not match the Bible's description of the Kingdom. He then came to feel that the Kingdom must be spiritual, not literal. In his treatise *The City of God,* he described the thousand years as the period between the first advent and the final conflict.[6]

William E. Cox, one of the leading exponents of amillennialism, quotes Walvoord's definition favorably while attempting to define his own position:

> A good definition of amillennialism comes from the pen of one of its severest critics. "Its most general character is that of denial of a literal reign of Christ upon the earth. Satan is conceived as bound at the first coming of Christ. The present age between the first and second coming is the fulfillment of the millennium. Its adherents are divided on whether the millennium is being fulfilled now on the earth (Augustine) or whether it is being fulfilled by the saints in heaven (Kliefoth). It may be summed up in the idea that there will be no more millennium than there is now, and that the eternal state immediately follows the second coming of Christ."[7]

The amillennialist believes that the binding of Satan in Revelation 20 occurred at the cross. God has now curtailed, but not annihilated, the influence of Satan during the Gospel age. This means Satan cannot prevent the spread of the Gospel to the nations by deceiving them, and that the nations cannot conquer the Church.[8] The Millennium, therefore, is an indefinite time period (the present age) between the first and second comings of Christ. Between these two comings Christ reigns over a spiritual Kingdom in the hearts of mankind.

Amillennialism teaches that there is one general, bodily resurrection of all the dead, not two last-days resurrections. The first resurrection is a spiritual one, the new birth. The second resurrection is a physical raising of all the dead, both the wicked and the righteous, when the final judgment of all will occur and each enters his or her final state.

Reading That Promotes the Amillennial View

- Allis, Oswald T. *Prophecy and the Church* (Presbyterian and Reformed, 1945). Allis, a prominent amillenarian, believed that the Church is the true Israel, that she includes saints of all ages and that she will go through the Tribulation.
- Bavinck, Herman. *The Last Things: Hope for This World and the Next* (Baker, 1996). Bavinck, a leading Dutch theologian at the turn of the century, "was probably one of those theologians who was most responsible for the rise of Reformed amillennialism in the twentieth century" (Mathison).
- Berkhof, Louis. *Systematic Theology* (Eerdmans, 1941). A systematic theology from a standard Reformed position.
- Berknouwer, G. C. *The Return of Christ* (Eerdmans, 1972).
- Cox, William E. *Amillennialism Today* (Presbyterian and Reformed, 1966).

Also, *An Examination of Dispensationalism* (Presbyterian and Reformed, 1971). His *Biblical Studies in Final Things* (Presbyterian and Reformed, 1967) gives an introductory explanation of this position.

- Hendriksen, William. *More than Conquerors* (Baker, 1939).
- Hoekema, Anthony A. *The Bible and the Future* (Eerdmans, 1979). "The best and most comprehensive explanation of amillennialism in print" (Mathison).

- Mauro, Philip. *The Seventy Weeks and the Great Tribulation* (Bible Truth, 1944). Also, *The Gospel of the Kingdom* (Grace Abounding, 1988).

Well-Known Amillennialists. Jay E. Adams, Oswald T. Allis, G. C. Berknouwer, Louis Berkhof, William Hendriksen, Anthony A. Hoekema, Abraham Kuyper, Philip Mauro, Bruce Waltke and Edward J. Young.

3. Dispensational Premillennialism

A Basic Definition. "The view of many modern fundamentalists and conservative evangelicals. The Rapture plays a key role and occurs before the seven-year Tribulation (or in the middle of the Tribulation—and for some, at the end). The 'church age' is really a 'parenthesis,' in which God's dealings with Israel are put on hold while he builds the Gentile church."[9]

Dispensationalism has become popular because of its distinctive teachings on the end times, such as the imminent, pretribulation Rapture of the Church. *Imminent* means, in this case, that no Scripture prophecy remains unfulfilled to keep Christ from coming at any time. The Rapture, occurring before the Tribulation, is the secret catching away of the Church so she will not endure judgment and divine wrath.

The glorious Second Coming of Christ will occur after the Tribulation and inaugurate a literal thousand-year Millennium here on earth at a time yet future. During this time Christ will reign on earth, ruling the world from Jerusalem. All the promises made to national Israel will be fulfilled literally at this time, and there will be a virtual restoration of the Old Testament economy. All believers will be resurrected bodily at Christ's coming to share in His millennial reign. Revelation 20 yet remains future.

This school of thought divides all history into seven dispensations, or periods of time. We are now in the sixth dispensation, characterized by grace, and called the Church age—the era of

Gospel proclamation between the first and second advents of Jesus Christ.[10]

Dispensational Premillennialism

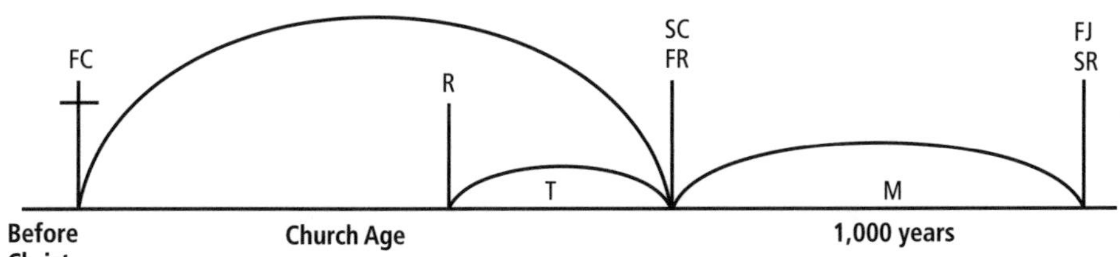

Notations: FC=First Coming; FJ=Final Judgment; FR=First Resurrection; R=Rapture; SC=Second Coming; SR=Second Resurrection; T=Tribulation; M=Millennium

Comments. Those who advocate this approach prefer to be known as premillennialists, for the literal Millennium is a major component of their belief. The Second Coming of Christ will introduce the Millennium. John F. Walvoord made this strong (and controversial) statement about the importance of this belief system: "It is not too much to say that millennialism is a determining factor in Biblical interpretation of comparable importance to the doctrines of verbal inspiration, the deity of Christ, substitutionary atonement, and bodily resurrection."[11]

For the dispensationalist the Millennium is a literal thousand-year period in which the historic Davidic kingdom is revived and continued with a real king sitting on a material throne.[12] This literal fulfillment of Old Testament prophecies about Kingdom and land is an important feature of dispensationalism. "Into the millennium is placed the fulfillment of virtually all Old Testament prophecies not fulfilled by the time of Christ, or at least by Pentecost."[13] There is a strong Jewishness connected with this concept of a millennial Kingdom: The Temple is rebuilt and the entire Old Testament sacrificial system is restored.[14] There is uncertainty about the spiritual state of the people who live during this time.

This literal approach brings the ultimate conclusion that "the basic premise of Dispensationalism is two purposes of God expressed in the formation of two peoples [Israel and the Church] who maintain their distinction throughout eternity."[15] The Church is not prophesied about or even mentioned in the Old Testament. Since Israel rejected the Kingdom, which Jesus offered her, God then offered the Kingdom to the Church. The Church was a substitute for Israel, but the Kingdom will again be offered to Israel after the time of the Gentiles is complete. The Church is considered a set of parentheses, appearing momentarily in history between the sixty-ninth and seventieth weeks of Daniel's prophecy. The Old Testament prophetic clock has not ticked since Pentecost, and no prophecy has been fulfilled since the time of Christ.[16]

Zola Levitt, well-known messianic Jewish teacher, says:

> . . . The Premillennial/Dispensational view is that, while the Church is the new creation of the Lord that proclaims the Gospel in this age, the Church does not replace Israel in its national covenant relationship with God. The covenant with Israel does not guarantee personal salvation for all Jews. It does, though, guarantee personal salvation for the "remnant" of Jewish people in all ages, including the Church Age. Also, it guarantees the preservation and restoration of Israel to the Land in preparation for the Tribulation and the second Coming of Christ.[17]

The late Dr. M. R. DeHaan, the famous voice of the Radio Bible Class in the 1950s and 60s, was a strong dispensationalist. He said of the Second Coming:

> . . . When everything is black and dark for the world, the "Lord himself shall descend from heaven . . ." (1 Thess. 4:16–17). This we call the "Rapture" of the Church, which is the secret sudden coming of Christ for His own. Immediately after the Church is raptured, the Antichrist will be revealed, the time of the world's greatest sorrow and anguish will begin and for seven years the Tribulation will last, when the world will experience the greatest period of sorrow, warfare, bloodshed and destruction in its history. . . .

During this period of tribulation on earth the Church will be with the Lord in the air. Then, at the close of this brief but intense period of tribulation, the Lord will come again publicly on the clouds of heaven with His glorified Church which was caught away before the Tribulation.[18]

Charles Caldwell Ryrie, prolific author on the subject, gives the following summary of dispensational premillennialism:

Premillennialists believe that theirs is the historic faith of the Church. Holding a literal interpretation of the Scriptures, they believe that the promises made to Abraham and David are unconditional and have had or will have a literal fulfillment. In no sense have these promises made to Israel been abrogated or fulfilled by the Church, which is a distinct body in this age having promises and a destiny different from Israel's.[19]

Reading That Promotes the Dispensational Premillennialist View

- Archer, Feinberg, Moo and Reiter. *Three Views on the Rapture* (Zondervan, 1984).
- Chafer, Lewis Sperry. *Dispensationalism* (Dallas Seminary, 1936).
- DeHaan, M. R. *The Second Coming of Jesus* (Zondervan, 1944).
- Larkin, Clarence. *Dispensational Truth* (Larkin, c. 1920).
- LaHaye, Tim and Jerry B. Jenkins. *Are We Living in the End Times?* (Tyndale, 1999).
- Levitt, Zola. *Broken Branches: Has the Church Replaced Israel?*
- Lindsey, Hal. *The Late Great Planet Earth* (Zondervan, 1970).
- MacArthur, John F. *The Second Coming.*
- Ryrie, Charles C. *Dispensationalism Today.*
- Scofield, C. I., ed. *The Scofield Reference Bible* (Oxford University Press, 1967).
- Walvoord, John F. *The Blessed Hope and the Tribulation* and *The Millennial Kingdom*. Also, *The Rapture Question.*

Some Well-Known Dispensational Premillennialists. Gleason L. Archer, Donald G. Barnhouse, Lewis Sperry Chafer, J. N. Darby,

Charles L. Feinberg, Norman L. Geisler, Dave Hunt, Tommy Ice, Harry A. Ironside, Grant Jeffrey, Walter C. Kaiser, Tim LaHaye, Hal Lindsey, John F. MacArthur, J. D. Pentecost, Charles C. Ryrie and John F. Walvoord.

Reading That Critically Investigates the Origin of Dispensationalism

- Cox, William E. *An Examination of Dispensationalism* (Presbyterian and Reformed, 1971).
- Katterjohn, Arthur. *The Tribulation People* (Creation House, 1975).
- Ladd, George E. "The Rise and Spread of Pretribulationism," *The Blessed Hope* (Eerdmans, 1956), chapter 2.
- MacPherson, Dave. *The Incredible Cover-Up: The True Story of the Pre-Trib Rapture* (Logos, 1975).
- Reiter, Richard R. "A History of the Development of the Rapture Positions," *Three Views on the Rapture* (Zondervan, 1984), chapter 1.

Progressive Dispensationalism

Millard Erickson comments on some new developments within the dispensational ranks:

> Since about the middle of the twentieth century, dispensationalism has been undergoing some modifications, leading to the emergence of a group of theologians and Biblical scholars calling themselves "progressive dispensationalists." Among the more prominent of these are Darrell Bock of Dallas Seminary, Craig Blaising of Southern Baptist Seminary, and Robert Saucy of Talbot School of Theology. While redefining or even abandoning some of the tenets of traditional dispensationalism, they maintain that they preserve the distinctive features of that system of thought.[20]

Here is a simplistic summary of the present redefinement taking place in dispensationalism:

- The Kingdom of God is the unifying theme of biblical history.
- The messianic/Davidic reign has been initiated in heaven by Christ.
- The new covenant is already in force, with the full blessings to be realized in the Millennium.
- Many promises formerly relegated to the millennial Kingdom are currently seeing fulfillment because of Jesus' reign on the Davidic throne in heaven (as, forgiveness of sins and Holy Spirit ministry), with complete fulfillment at the Second Coming.
- The importance of Israel and her future in Palestine is downplayed, and far more emphasis given to the Church and her present and future roles in the plan of God.
- The Church is not just a new people group, but redeemed humanity, including both Jews and Gentiles. There is still place, however, for God's special promises to literal Israel.
- Prophecies referring to the nation and land of Israel are interpreted literally, and the Millennium will have a distinctively Jewish character.
- The customary dispensations of biblical history have been restructured into four periods: the patriarchal (Adam to Sinai), Mosaic (Sinai to the ascension of Christ), ecclesial (the ascension to the Second Coming) and Zionic (part 1, the Millennium; part 2, the eternal state).
- All the dispensations are related to the final dispensation, and the gradual development toward that goal is what gives progressive dispensationalism its name.[21]

Reading That Promotes the Progressive Dispensational Approach[22]

- Blaising, Craig A. and Darrell L. Bock. *Progressive Dispensationalism* (Victor/BridgePoint, 1993).
- ———, eds. *Dispensationalism, Israel and the Church: The Search for Definition* (Zondervan, 1992).

- Saucy, Robert L. *The Case for Progressive Dispensationalism* (Zondervan, 1993).

4. Postmillennialism

A Basic Definition. "The view of most nineteenth-century evangelicals and some Reformed people today: Christians, with God's help, will gradually convert and reform society into a blessed, though not perfect, state."[23]

The advent of Christ will take place *after* (post-) the Millennium (i.e., after the millennial kingdom concludes). Some postmillennialists believe that "the Millennium spans the entire period between Christ's first and second advents," while others "argue that the Millennium refers to either the last thousand years of the present age or to a long period of time immediately preceding the Second Coming."[24] Keith A. Mathison, in a recent apologetic for this position, says:

> Fundamental to postmillennial eschatology is the doctrine that the messianic kingdom has been inaugurated, and that Christ has been given this kingdom in connection with the events of the First Advent. Because Satan has been bound and the saints are now reigning with Christ, postmillennialism identifies the "thousand years" of Revelation 20 with the entire period between the two advents of Christ. There is no need for the church to "bring in the kingdom" because the kingdom already exists.[25]

This millennial period is one of peace and righteousness on earth, the final and most glorious part of the Church age. Some postmillennialists believe this golden age has already begun, although they cannot give an exact starting time. It will result from the worldwide dissemination and acceptance of the Gospel. Kenneth L. Gentry Jr., a leading exponent, says, "Christ will return to the earth after the Spirit-blessed Gospel has had overwhelming success in bringing the world to the adoption of Christianity."[26] Some feel that "the present age has been and will continue to gradually merge into the millennial age as an increasing proportion of the world's inhabitants turn to the Christian faith."[27] Although Christ will not have returned bodily, the Kingdom of God will be on earth. Christ will reign, and reigns now, over a literal, earthly Kingdom from a heavenly throne. Finally He will return to earth and pronounce final judgment.

Postmillennialism

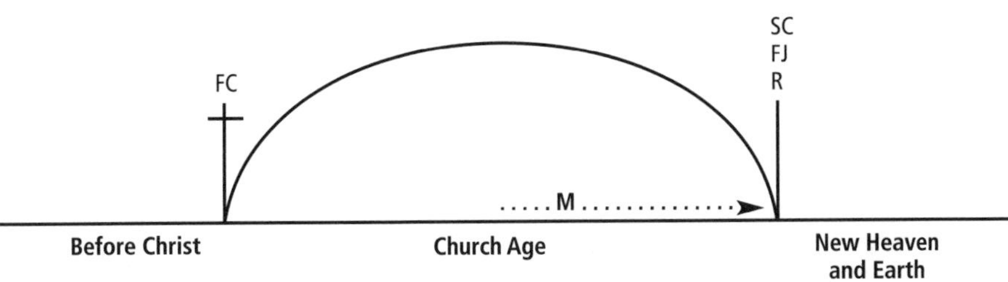

Notations: FC=First Coming; FJ=Final Judgment; M=Millennium; SC=Second Coming; R=Resurrection (general)

Comments. J. Marcellus Kik, a leading spokesman, has written a classic statement of this position. His book *An Eschatology of Victory* is an optimistic view of Christianity's ultimate triumph in society. He says:

> The *postmil* looks for a fulfillment of the Old Testament prophecies of a glorious age of the church upon earth through the preaching of the gospel under the power of the Holy Spirit. He looks forward to all nations becoming Christian and living in peace one with another. He relates all prophecies to history and time. After the triumph of Christianity throughout the earth he looks for the second coming of the Lord.[28]

Postmillennialism is called by Kik the "Historic Reformed Eschatology"; it is the historic position of Princeton Theological Seminary.

Another strong advocate of this position is Loraine Boettner:

> Postmillennialism is that view of the last things which holds that the kingdom of God is now being extended in the world through the preaching of the gospel and the saving work of the Holy Spirit in the hearts of individuals, that the world eventually is to be Christianized and that the return of Christ is to occur at the close of a long period of righteousness and peace commonly called the millennium. It should be added that on postmillennial principles the Second Coming of Christ will be followed immediately by the general resurrection, the general judgment, and the introduction of heaven and hell in their fullness.[29]

The Puritan scholars of the seventeenth century were strong postmillennialism advocates. Those preachers, their sermons and their writings fanned amazing revival in Scotland, England and America. It has generally been overlooked that the main features of this movement are all the effects of revival. They believed firmly in revivals of religion as the great means by which the Church advances in the world and by which she will ultimately triumph.[30]

R. C. Sproul, in his recent book *The Last Days according to Jesus,* summarized postmillennialism by listing seven of the key features as advocated by Kenneth L. Gentry Jr.:

- The messianic Kingdom was founded on earth during the earthly ministry of Christ in fulfillment of Old Testament prophecy. The Church became the "Israel of God."
- The Kingdom is redemptive and spiritual rather than political and physical.
- The Kingdom will exercise a transformational sociocultural influence in history.
- The Kingdom of Christ will gradually expand in time and on earth through Christ's royal power but without His physical presence on earth.
- The Great Commission will succeed—the virtual Christianization of the nations.
- There will be an application of biblical law in society. *Pietistic* believers deny the total transformation of culture while *theonomic* believers affirm total transformation.

- An extended period of spiritual prosperity may endure for millennia, after which history will be drawn to a close by the personal, visible, bodily return of Christ. His coming will be accompanied by a literal resurrection and a general judgment.[31]

Reading That Promotes the Postmillennial View

- Boettner, Loraine. *The Millennium* (Presbyterian and Reformed, 1957).
- Chilton, David. *Paradise Restored: A Biblical Theology of Dominion* (Dominion, 1987).
- Gentry, Kenneth L. Jr. *He Shall Have Dominion* (Dominion, 1991).
- Hodge, Charles. *Systematic Theology,* Vol. IV (Scribner's, 1871).
- Kik, J. Marcellus. *An Eschatology of Victory* (Presbyterian and Reformed, 1971).
- Mathison, Keith A. *Postmillennialism* (Presbyterian and Reformed, 1999).
- Russell, J. Stuart. *The Parousia: The New Testament Doctrine of Our Lord's Second Coming* (Baker, 1999). This is a reprint of the 1887 original edition, a classic presentation of original thought. I think he goes too far with his "full preterism," but every serious student should be aware of his unique handling of the Olivet Discourse and the destruction of Jerusalem in A.D. 70.
- Shedd, W. G. T. *Dogmatic Theology* (Scribner's, 1888).
- Strong, Augustus H. *Systematic Theology* (Griffith & Roland, 1907).

Well-known Postmillennialists. Oswald T. Allis, Athanasius, St. Augustine, John Calvin, Jonathan Edwards, Kenneth L. Gentry Jr., A. A. Hodge, J. Marcellus Kik, J. Gresham Machen, Iain H. Murray, John Owen, R. J. Rushdoony, W. G. T. Shedd, Augustus H. Strong and B. B. Warfield.

An Appeal for Charity

The one great hope of the Church is the glorious Second Coming of Jesus Christ. Paul calls it "the blessed hope and glorious appearing of our great God and Savior Jesus Christ" (Titus 2:13).

The devotion of all the above servants of God to His Word is very apparent, and they agree on one essential: Jesus is coming again! As our thoughts about the Rapture, Tribulation and Millennium open for discussion, let's display liberty and charity in our attitudes. An extreme position limits fellowship, demands an unbiblical test of orthodoxy and requires undivided allegiance to questionable elements in Christian doctrine. I am delighted to see a more open attitude these days among Christians and ministers as they discuss these important events.

Some may feel that my presentation has oversimplified the four schools of interpretation, and this is probably so. Certainly each approach has other features. My review here is not meant to defend or discredit, but rather to provide a quick overview that covers the essentials. I have been challenged to think harder and reflect more deeply because of the dedicated scholarship to which I have referred. May the Lord guide us all into greater perception of His will, purpose and intention.

And now consider: 55 percent of all the verses in the New Testament on the Second Coming are found in the gospels. Our next chapter, therefore, will introduce the abundant teaching of Jesus on this subject.

PART 2

GOOD NEWS! JESUS WILL RETURN

FOUR

JESUS TALKED A LOT ABOUT HIS COMING BACK

A number of significant ideas about the Second Coming of Christ, some very startling, are woven into the four gospels. Looking through this amazing window, we view Jesus' thinking about His future, that of His people and how this present age will end.

Jesus describes His return as sudden, public, glorious and universally visible. His graphic, true-to-life stories tell what we must do to be ready for this awesome event, and what the consequences are *if we do not prepare*.

Approximately 65 of the 159 main thoughts on the subject in the New Testament are found in the gospels. (Some of these ideas are not unique to the gospels.)

The ten chapters of Part 2, "Good News! Jesus Will Return," supply all the information on Christ's return presented in the New Testament. To provide better form and sequence, I have divided the New Testament into six sections: the gospels, Acts, Thessalonians, other Pauline epistles, other epistles and Revelation. Each section presents a summary record of the Second Coming in narrative (or story) form, utilizing only the verses and ideas presented in that part of the New Testament. A final narrative in chapter 13 summarizes all the material in the previous smaller narratives—in other words, all the information presented in the entire New Testament on the subject of Christ's triumphant return.

Since this chapter introduces the gospel information, the first narrative record will set forth the 238 verses of the gospels in 65 key ideas. I have numbered each concept and grouped the narrative into paragraphs of compatible thoughts, with the lead concept appearing in bold type.

The Gospel Record

Everything Jesus Wanted His Disciples to Know About His Glorious Return

1. **Jesus Christ Himself will return**	John 14:3
2. with power and great glory	Matthew 6:13; 24:3, 27, 30; Mark 13:26; Luke 21:27
3. —the great glory of His Father	Matthew 16:27; Mark 8:38
4. and His own glory.	Matthew 25:31; Luke 9:26
5. He will come with all His holy angels	Matthew 16:27; 24:31; 25:31; Mark 8:38; Luke 9:26; John 1:51
6. in, on and with the clouds of heaven	Matthew 24:30; 26:64; Mark 13:26; 14:62; Luke 21:27
7. sitting at the right hand of the Power	Matthew 26:64; Mark 14:62; Luke 22:69
8. and everyone will see Him.	Matthew 24:30
9. **He will come with a great sound of a trumpet**	Matthew 24:31
10. and the sound of His voice.	John 5:25–29
11. He will send forth His angels	Matthew 24:31; Mark 13:27
12. who will gather His elect from the farthest part of earth.	Matthew 24:31; Mark 13:27; Luke 13:28–30
13. The angels will separate the wicked from the just.	Matthew 13:39–42, 49–50
14. **He will sit on His glorious throne,**	Matthew 19:28; 25:31
15. and He will judge cities and nations	Matthew 12:18; 25:31–46; Luke 10:14
16. and the generations.	Luke 11:31, 51
17. All tribes of the earth shall mourn.	Matthew 24:30; Luke 21:35

18. We shall be "repaid" at the resurrection of the just. — Luke 14:14
19. The apostles will sit on twelve thrones and judge the twelve tribes of Israel. — Matthew 8:12; 19:28
20. **He shall reward every person according to his works.** — Matthew 15:13; 16:27; Mark 10:30–31; Luke 13:30
21. We will be judged by Jesus' words. — John 12:48
22. Nothing is secret that will not be revealed. — Matthew 18:35; Luke 8:17
23. He will come and serve His followers — Luke 12:37–40
24. and drink the fruit of the new vine with them and eat the Passover. — Matthew 26:29; Luke 22:16, 18, 29–30
25. He has prepared a place for us and will receive us, — John 14:3
26. but He will judge unbelievers and the disobedient. — Matthew 7:23; 12:32, 41–46; 24:37–41
27. **This will initiate the "regeneration."** — Matthew 19:28
28. **The resurrection of the just will take place on that last day.** — Matthew 22:28, 30–32; Mark 12:25–26; Luke 20:33–38; John 6:39–40, 44, 54; 11:23–26
29. **Christ's coming will be the day of the Son of Man** — Matthew 25:13; Luke 17:24, 30
30. —in that day — Luke 10:12
31. —until that day — Matthew 26:29; Mark 14:25
32. —that day — Matthew 7:22; 24:36; Luke 21:34
33. —day of judgment. — Matthew 11:22; 12:36
34. **His coming will be preceded by astronomical signs** — Matthew 24:29–30; Mark 13:24–25; Luke 21:25–26
35. and perplexing earthly signs — Luke 21:25
36. which will cause believers to know that their "redemption draws near." — Luke 21:28
37. **His coming will be fully expected and eagerly awaited by the Church,** — Matthew 24:42
38. the people who do understand the season or signs of the times — Matthew 24:32–33; Luke 21:29–31
39. and who note "when these things begin to happen." — Luke 21:28

40. **His coming will be sudden, abrupt and startling—not foreseen, anticipated or looked for by people of the world (Luke 17:28, 30)—as portrayed in the following fourteen illustrations. His coming will be like**
41. —a flash of lightning — Matthew 24:27; Luke 17:24
42. —the snap of a snare or trap — Luke 21:34–36
43. —the appearance of eagles [vultures] over a carcass — Matthew 24:28; Luke 17:37
44. —the arrival of summer (a blossoming fig tree) — Matthew 24:32–33
45. —the flood in the days of Noah — Matthew 24:37–39; Luke 17:26–27
46. —the judgment in the days of Lot — Luke 17:28–30
47. —a person taken from a task or sleep — Matthew 24:40–41; Luke 17:34–36
48. —the burglarizing of a household by a thief — Matthew 24:43; Luke 12:37–40
49. —a master checking up on slaves — Matthew 24:45–51; Luke 12:42–48
50. —an owner inspecting his slaves' activities — Mark 13:35–36; Luke 12:35–37
51. —a returning nobleman — Luke 19:12–27
52. —a bridegroom's arrival — Matthew 25:1–13
53. —a returning slave owner who appears and demands an accounting — Matthew 25:14–30
54. —the sudden pain and joy of childbirth. — John 16:21
55. **No one knows the specific day or hour of His coming.** — Matthew 24:36, 42; 25:13; Mark 13:32–37
56. Watch (be alert) therefore. — Matthew 24:42; Mark 13:35, 37
57. **He will come when "you" (that is, Jerusalem, the Jews) say, "Blessed is He who comes in the name of the Lord,"** — Matthew 23:39; Luke 13:35
58. when the whole world will have heard the Gospel witness. — Matthew 24:14; Mark 13:10

59. **When He comes, will He find faith on the earth?** Matthew 28:20; Luke 18:8
60. We are not to be worried about the dedication of others, but serve Him until He comes. John 21:22–23
61. He will receive believers. John 14:3, 18, 28–29; 16:16–22
62. There will be a harvest. Mark 4:29

Note: The following references require special attention.

63. Disciples will not finish going through the cities of Israel before He comes. Matthew 10:23
64. Some then living will not die until they see the Son of Man coming in His Kingdom. Matthew 16:28; Mark 9:1; Luke 9:27
65. This generation will not pass away until all things take place. Matthew 24:34; Mark 13:30; Luke 21:32

Jesus and Paul Agree on the Basics

Jesus' description of His return is much like that given by Paul in his epistles: Christ will come in spectacular glory, with a great shout, with the trumpet of God, with mighty angels and on billowing clouds. Both Jesus and Paul strongly emphasize that, when Christ returns, every person will be rewarded according to his or her works, and that the followers of Jesus must live lives of holiness, dedication and watchfulness.

The following chart shows the harmony and similarity of Jesus and Paul in their basic teaching on the Second Coming.[1]

How Did He Get This Information?

Where did Jesus get His ideas? The Hebrew Scriptures were a strong influence, naturally, yet the written Word of His day did

Comparison of Jesus and Paul

John 14:3	1 Thessalonians 4:16–17
• "I will come again" • "and receive you to Myself" • "that where I am, there you may be also."	• "The Lord Himself will descend" • "Then we . . . shall be caught up . . . to meet the Lord in the air." • "And thus we shall always be with the Lord."
Matthew 24:30–31	**1 Thessalonians 4:16–17**
• "They will see the Son of Man coming" • "with a great sound of a trumpet, on the clouds of heaven" • "with a great sound of a trumpet" • "and they will gather together His elect."	• "The Lord Himself will descend from heaven" • "in the clouds to meet the Lord" • "and with the trumpet of God." • "...[We] shall be caught up together with them"

not contain the specific explanation that Jesus Himself declared with such authority.

One unique reference He certainly knew was Daniel 7:13–14, a text similar to His own description of the Second Coming and considered by some commentators as a direct prediction:

> "I was watching in the night visions, and behold, One like the Son of Man, coming with the clouds of heaven! He came to the Ancient of Days, and they brought Him near before Him. Then to Him was given dominion and glory and a kingdom, that all peoples, nations, and languages should serve Him. His dominion is an everlasting dominion, which shall not pass away, and His kingdom the one which shall not be destroyed."[2]

Through prayer Jesus received marvelous biblical insight into both His earthly ministry and His future return. He experienced a wonderful consciousness of God and a sharper focus on His ministerial commission. Jesus fulfilled literally the messianic text of Isaiah 50:4–6—that is, He learned to awaken each morning to the instructive voice of His Father and then carry out the inspired spiritual directives of that day. His sagacious understanding of the Second Coming is best traced to those times in God's presence and the revelation that was a natural consequence of it.[3] Isaiah's prophecy seems to capture the essence of Jesus' experience:

> "Behold, the former things have come to pass, and new things I declare; before they spring forth I tell you of them."
>
> Isaiah 42:9

> "I have made you hear new things from this time, even hidden things, and you did not know them. They are created now and not from the beginning; and before this day you have not heard them, lest you should say, 'Of course I knew them.'"
>
> Isaiah 48:6–7

The Greatest Concern of Christ

Several concerns characterize Christ's teaching. He particularly assured His disciples about the resurrection of God's people (Luke 20:33–38; John 5:25–29; 6:39–40, 44, 54; 11:23–26). Death will be overcome by life! Jesus called this raising of the righteous dead "the resurrection of the just" (Luke 14:14), which will occur at the Second Coming.

Jesus stressed that He will come quickly, unexpectedly, and will reward every person according to his works. He showed a strange disregard for explaining the mechanical details of His coming and the resurrection, choosing rather to call emphatic attention to the importance of the spirituality and readiness of His followers. *The Interpreter's Bible* gives this summary: "Jesus expects his followers to be ready at every moment (Matthew 24:43–44), prepared in every way (25:4), making use of their talents (25:14–30) and actively engaged in works of mercy (25:31–46)."[4]

A series of fourteen true-life illustrations (see numbers 40–54 above) particularly warn the disciples that His Second Coming will be sudden, abrupt, startling—and unforeseen, unanticipated and unsought by the people of the world. Jesus' followers must be prepared. Presented with white-hot intensity and pointed frequency, the statements of Jesus force us to conclude that *readiness is the chief emphasis that the Teacher wished His students to grasp.*

When the Plane Takes Off, Will You Be on Board?

Jesus spent much time explaining His coming in terms of human preparedness and responsibility. His fourteen illustrations teach us at least four important lessons:

1. Like the Snap of a Mousetrap: The **Suddenness** *of the Second Coming*

- A flash of lightning (Matthew 24:27; Luke 17:24)
- The snap of a snare (Luke 21:35)
- The sudden appearance of vultures in the sky at the death of an animal (Matthew 24:28; Luke 17:37)

Jesus said we should not go out looking for Him since we will find only false Christs and false prophets. Jesus' actual coming will be too sudden for us to get ready and travel somewhere. We will not have to travel to Him; He will come to us. Ladd says, "The Second Coming of Christ is to be no secret event recognizable only by a few, but like a flash of lightning, evident to all."[5]

2. Like the Break-In of a Cat Burglar: The **Unexpectedness** *of the Second Coming*

- A thief robbing a house (Matthew 24:43; Luke 12:37–40)
- A slave owner returning and demanding an accounting (Matthew 25:14–30)
- Working people suddenly removed from their tasks or beds (Matthew 24:40–41; Luke 17:34–36)

We must live knowing the event will possibly occur in our lifetimes, but it could happen when we do not expect it. Live as though Jesus may come today; plan and work as though you have your whole life before you.

3. Like a Confirmed On-Time Arrival: The **Expectedness** *of the Second Coming*

- A blossoming fig tree when summer has arrived (Matthew 24:32–33)
- The flood of Noah that came when the ark was finished (Matthew 24:37–39; Luke 17:26–27)
- The judgment on Sodom and Gomorrah when Lot had left (Luke 17:28–30)

The world will be unprepared for Jesus' advent, for they have no belief or concern in its appearance. The Church, by contrast, is to be aware of the approach of the Second Coming, staying alert to the signs of the times and continuing the work of ministry. While the society of Noah's day relentlessly pursued its deadly moral plunge, Noah and family patiently, tirelessly and fervently continued building their ship of salvation. The Church will not know the exact day or hour, but the season will indicate its proximity.

We must all be prepared personally. Jesus illustrated this by referring to the blossoming of a fig tree; we know this happens in summer. Jesus also said, "When these things begin to happen, look up and lift up your heads, because your redemption draws near" (Luke 21:28).

4. Like the Final Report on an Income Tax Audit: The **Accountability** *of the Second Coming*

- A master checking up on his slaves (Matthew 24:45–51; Luke 12:42–48)

- An owner inspecting his slaves' activities (Mark 13:35–36; Luke 12:35–37)
- A nobleman returning to his home (Luke 19:12, 15)
- A bridegroom arriving for bridesmaids who are expected to be prepared (Matthew 25:1–13)
- A woman experiencing the sudden pains and joy of childbirth (John 16:21)

We are to live in a state of watchfulness, which keeps us busy doing the work and will of God, rather than being caught up in the busyness of worldly living.

The importance of being watchful and prepared is highlighted in the parable of the ten virgins (Matthew 25:1–13). Five were wise and five foolish, "but the wise took oil in their vessels with their lamps" (verse 4). Lacking oil for their lamps, the negligent, unwise virgins could not enter and participate in the wedding. The obvious meaning is that those waiting for Christ's return must be spiritually prepared (filled with the oil of the Holy Spirit) as well as watchful. It is our personal responsibility to be ready, for there is "the absolute untransferability of the oil"[6]—no person can rely on the preparedness of another in order to ensure his or her own preparedness.

Jesus followed with another parable. He clearly stated—emphasized—that we will give an accounting of what we have done for the Lord (Matthew 25:14–30). The Master has put "talents"[7] into our hands and expects that we will use these abilities and giftings to bring fruit and blessing to the Kingdom of God. For the diligent who have wisely exercised their gifts to make more for the Master, there will be wonderful, satisfying reward . . . and, in stark contrast, a frightful reckoning for the negligent (Matthew 24:44–51). In the parable the "severe punishment inflicted on the unfaithful servant is striking."[8]

Did Jesus Overlook Anything About His Return?

Jesus did not cover this entire subject, but He did *not* leave out certain aspects because of ignorance, oversight or disregard. It is obvious that a progressive understanding took place in the early Church, at least in terms of the written record. During His earthly ministry Jesus taught what was appropriate and essential at the time for His followers to know: "As My Father taught Me, I speak these things" (John 8:28). Later the other writers (particularly Paul, Peter and John), inspired by the Spirit, added certain pieces to the puzzle to fill out the picture. Finally Jesus gave the closing teaching to John that would cap all previous teaching and seal the record.

The omissions by the various authors are easily observed in chapter 13 in "The New Testament Record" (see p. 207), by comparing each concept presented with the reference(s) cited. The entries with no gospel references are obvious and represent thoughts not included by Jesus in His teaching. The numbers after each omission in the following listing are the reference numbers used in "The New Testament Record" for easier identification.

Jesus did *not* mention:

1. *His coming in terms of hope,* whereas Paul calls the Second Coming "the blessed hope" (#8).
2. *The appearance of the Antichrist* as a precursor of the Second Coming, but Paul did mention it to the Thessalonians (#30).
3. *"The last trump"* or "the seventh angel," but they are mentioned by John in Revelation and Paul in Corinthians (#31, 54).
4. *"The voice of the archangel,"* but it is mentioned in Thessalonians (#55).
5. *An entourage of saints* at His return, but Jude stated that Christ will be accompanied by "ten thousands of His saints" (#42) and Paul specified "all His saints" (#43).
6. *That "those who pierced Him" would see Him,* as John later said (#45, 46).
7. *That He would return in the same body,* but the messengers present at His ascension stated this emphatically (#47).
8. *That He would appear sinless,* but later references do (#59).
9. *The expression "flaming fire"* or reference to the "slaying of the man of lawlessness," as Paul did (#63, 64).

10. *Earth change and meltdown.* Peter stated this, but he may have gotten some of his ideas from Jesus (#66–68).
11. *The changing of our bodies* in the resurrection and the catching up, but Paul mentioned them (#70–72).
12. *The Judgment Seat of Christ* (although He did speak of judgment and a day of judgment). Paul did use this expression (#117–24).
13. *Crowns as rewards,* although He did speak of rewards (#117, 121). This expression is used in the epistles (#123).

Sometimes the statement is made (and I have said this myself) that we should not teach what Jesus did not teach. But now I find that anything taught anywhere in the New Testament is meant for instruction to the Church. The above thirteen points indicate that, according to the written account, Jesus did not teach every facet of the Second Coming. By the same token Paul, Peter, John, James, Luke and Jude taught things not recorded in the gospels. For the full picture we must have the information from all seven of our expert witnesses!

The argument is often made that Jesus did not teach on or refer to a one-thousand-year Millennium, so the information in Revelation 20 must therefore be figurative or spiritual language. This important thought deserves an immediate, brief answer here, and a more extended explanation in Appendix D.

I maintain that Jesus did refer to a literal Millennium; He simply did not call it by that name. Because He spoke to a Jewish audience, He used terms and descriptions they could understand and relate to. Jesus spoke of "the age to come" (Matthew 12:32), a term well-known to the Jews. He also used another familiar term, *the regeneration* (Matthew 19:28), and then described that time in terms similar to Revelation 20:4.

The identification of the time frame for this coming period was taught to John by Jesus, even if it was done after His ascension (Revelation 1:1). This post-ascension teaching to John should be considered as reliable as teaching from the gospels. It would have been counterproductive during His earthly ministry for Jesus to teach a specific time frame, with all that pertained to it. Later, after the Church opened to include the Gentiles, Jesus did expand the

Church's knowledge of the subject by teaching John the specifics listed in Revelation 20.

The next three chapters will continue the teaching of Jesus on His glorious return. Interpretations will be given for a number of the references in the above listing. And in the opening section of the very next chapter, we will address three most bewildering statements of Jesus.

FIVE

HOW JESUS DESCRIBED HIS SECOND COMING

Jesus is the number-one expert on His Second Coming. Naturally we also consult the biblical writings of James, John, Jude, Luke, Paul and Peter, but Jesus Himself remains our chief witness. He said, "I am One who bears witness of Myself" (John 8:18) and, ". . . I have come into the world, that I should bear witness to the truth" (John 18:37). John calls Him "the faithful witness" (Revelation 1:5) and "the Faithful and True Witness" (Revelation 3:14).

Although Jesus said He did not know the exact time of His return (I believe He meant during His earthly ministry), He did have the most profound and personally real understanding of the Second Coming of any of the seven witnesses. When Jesus was transfigured, for instance, He experienced the brilliant glory of God to such an extent that His face blazed like the sun and His garments glistened with intense light.

As Jesus remained in intimate relationship with His heavenly Father, a marvelous consciousness of His earthly and heavenly ministry developed within Him. A unique prophetic awareness of the Second Coming gradually filled His mind, finally bursting forth during the last week of earthly ministry in words that astounded His disciples.

Not all Jesus' teaching is easy to understand; it requires a prayerful, thoughtful approach. We begin our study by considering three statements that have been a continuing puzzle to Bible students.

Three Bewildering Statements

The narrative given in the last chapter ended with three hard-to-interpret statements by Jesus (#63–65). Did He really mean to say He would return to earth within about forty years—just one generation?

> "When they persecute you in this city, flee to another. For assuredly, I say to you, you will not have gone through the cities of Israel before the Son of Man comes."
>
> Matthew 10:23

> "Assuredly, I say to you, there are some standing here who shall not taste death till they see the Son of Man coming in His kingdom."
>
> Matthew 16:28

> "Assuredly, I say to you, this generation will by no means pass away till all these things are fulfilled."
>
> Matthew 24:34

Jesus did not return within that time frame, personally and literally, in the glorious manner predicted. This glaring inconsistency between prediction and historical fact has caused a flurry of activity among Bible interpreters to explain what Jesus meant. The seeming discrepancy, as R. C. Sproul points out, has brought the credibility of Christ into question. Sproul contends that the very prophecy—Jesus' discourse on the Mount of Olives—that should "confirm both the credentials of Jesus and the inspiration of Scripture is, ironically, the prophecy used by critics like [Bertrand] Russell to debunk both Jesus and the Bible. . . . The main problem with Jesus' predictions in the Olivet Discourse is that they include not only predictions regarding Jerusalem and the temple, which did come to pass with astonishing accuracy, but also prediction of his own coming in glory, or his parousia."[1]

The three statements of Jesus, as well as the Olivet Discourse, can be approached in any one of four ways:

1. Jesus was mistaken about the time of His return.
2. The time frame references are to be taken figuratively and the *parousia* references literally.
3. The time frame references are literally true and the *parousia* and associated events are to be taken figuratively.
4. Two literal time frame periods and two literal happenings are involved: one, the literal destruction of Jerusalem, which was to occur within a generation's time; and two, the glorious Second Coming, which was to occur within an unspecified time. Additional events precede both happenings and pervade the Church age.

Number 4 will be my approach, but I want to discuss number 3 briefly, as it has bearing on our study.

This approach is called the *preterist* interpretation, named after the grammatical term meaning "past tense." In the case of the three references above (and the use of *the end of the age* in the Olivet Discourse), the preterist interprets the time frame references *literally* in the past, since they are expressed in a seemingly straightforward manner. The time frame definition determines the whole interpretation since it appears to be so clearly and unequivocally stated. This approach suggests that the references to Christ's coming must automatically be made symbolic or figurative, and refer not to the final, glorious advent of Christ but to some historical situation within the clearly stated time frame.

This situation, for the preterist, is the destruction of Jerusalem in A.D. 70. Occurring about a generation after Jesus' sayings, it is considered a fitting, dramatic conclusion to the "Jewish age." Christ did come, it is claimed, in judgment to destroy the Temple and all it stood for. The cosmic signs and glorious coming He mentioned were mere apocalyptic imagery to symbolize judgment.[2]

Amillennialists and postmillennialists, as well as some historic premillennialists, use this preterist approach, but in varying degrees. Some conclude that the three controversial verses teach that the entire Olivet Discourse is already fulfilled, including the Second Coming, while others feel that only the destruction of Jerusalem is fulfilled.

This interpretation about the destruction of Jerusalem, as foretold by Jesus, is logical and well made. A thoughtful reader can accept the *literal* language about Jerusalem and the Temple (as discussed in the next two chapters) but will be disturbed by the strained effort to make the clear language about Christ's *parousia* or coming simply *figurative*.

I find it plausible to accept Jesus' language about His coming (along with the cosmic upheaval) in as straightforward a manner as His description of Jerusalem's destruction. It seems most sensible to accept a literal destruction of Jerusalem *and* the literal coming of Jesus in glory, as described. Jesus undoubtedly expected certain statements to be wisely and appropriately interpreted.

A main thrust of preterism is that "the Kingdom of God is a present reality." I applaud this emphasis on the Kingdom of God here and now among us, over which Christ is reigning, *but I do not feel we must bring Jesus' clear teaching on His coming under question just to obtain this goal.* Without question the New Testament presents a present, active, spiritual Kingdom at work *now*. Equally obvious, the Kingdom of God needs greater expression, which (as Jesus said) will occur in the future. The Lord's reference to the Kingdom *now* and yet *later* seems the balanced approach and reasonable solution to such discussion. More on this as we proceed to discuss the various references.[3]

Now let's look at the three cryptic verses more closely.

1. At the Commissioning of the Twelve

This "very difficult verse" (Tasker), found only in Matthew, is included as part of Jesus' commissioning sermon when He sent out His twelve disciples two by two. He told them they would have a hard time, then added this thought-provoking statement:

> "When they persecute you in this city, flee to another. For assuredly, I say to you, *you will not have gone through the cities of Israel before the Son of Man comes.*"
>
> Matthew 10:23 (emphasis added)

Was Jesus saying that before He returned to earth, they would not have preached in (or "gone through") all the cities in Israel? Could this statement indicate that He was expecting His coming to occur in their foreseeable future?

To begin to answer this question, consider this sequence of Jesus' earthly ministry:

- Jesus began His ministry without help from others (Matthew 4:17, 23).
- Jesus began gathering disciples about Him and exposing them to His methods (Luke 8).
- Jesus authorized twelve of His followers to represent Him in the ongoing, expanding ministry of the Kingdom of God.
- Jesus deputized another seventy to help in the propagation of the Good News. Jesus' instructions were for them to go only to the Jews, not to the Gentiles.
- Finally, in the Great Commission of Matthew 28, Jesus sent forth His followers with the Kingdom message *to all nations.*

The disciples reached the small nation of Israel during Jesus' earthly ministry, which acted as a prototype of Kingdom expansion. After that all nations were to be reached in similar fashion.

Notice this important fact: Before Jesus appointed and commissioned both the Twelve and the seventy (while the disciples were still in their introductory stage of ministry), He had *already* reached all the cities in Israel. This has a direct bearing on the interpretation of our text.

> Jesus went about *all Galilee,* teaching in their synagogues, preaching the gospel. . . . Great multitudes followed Him—from Galilee, . . . Decapolis, Jerusalem, Judea, and beyond the Jordan.
>
> Matthew 4:23, 25 (emphasis added)

> Jesus went about *all the cities and villages,* teaching in their synagogues, preaching the gospel of the kingdom, and healing every sickness and every disease among the people.
>
> Matthew 9:35 (emphasis added)

> He went through *every city and village,* preaching and bringing the glad tidings of the kingdom of God. And the twelve were with Him. . . . And when a great multitude had gathered, and others had come to Him from *every city,* He spoke. . . ."
>
> Luke 8:1, 4 (emphasis added)

The Matthew 10 commissioning involved Palestinian evangelism, with the disciples at that time sent only to the Jews. But Jesus planted the seed in their hearts for the apostolic influence eventually to extend beyond those immediate borders. In verse 18 He said, "You will be brought before governors and kings . . . as a testimony to them and to the Gentiles." This is a strong argument that the period climaxing at the destruction of the Temple was not the entire time frame for Jesus' statement.

The commission is followed by this statement in Matthew 11:1: "When Jesus finished commanding His twelve disciples, . . . He departed from there to teach and to preach *in their cities*" (emphasis added). To reach all the cities of Palestine at that time would not have been a difficult task. George M. Lamsa, expert on Palestine and the Aramaic language, says of our verse in question, "Jesus did not mean the disciples were merely to go over the cities of Palestine because all the cities of Palestine could be covered in a few months." Also, Lamsa points out, "The Eastern text reads, 'You shall not finish converting all the cities of the house of Israel until the Son of man returns.'"[4]

Luke's account of the commissioning (Luke 9:1–5) is followed immediately by this statement: "So they departed and went through the towns, preaching the gospel and healing *everywhere*" (verse 6, emphasis added). The verses quoted seem to confirm that *all* the cities and towns of Palestine were reached in Jesus' day.

Our verse in question, then, could not refer to Jesus' glorious coming as being in the disciples' immediate future—simply because the then-existing cities of Palestine were all reached with the message of the Kingdom during the Lord's earthly ministry.

The text itself offers no clear meaning of Matthew 10:23. Greek scholar A. T. Robertson comments, "Moffatt puts it 'before the Son of man arrives' as if Jesus referred to this special tour of Galilee. Jesus could overtake them. Possibly so, but it is by no means clear."[5] Albert Schweitzer, famous theologian and medical missionary, made the second part of this verse the focal point for his controversial and unfortunate eschatology. He felt this verse meant that Jesus looked for great spiritual results from His disciple-missionaries, who failed to achieve them. He expected Israel to turn to God in repentance, thereby allowing the Kingdom of God to come before they had finished their mission. Supposedly Jesus was dejected because it did not materialize and He had failed.[6] R. V. G. Tasker, general editor of the *Tyndale New Testament Commentaries,* feels this verse "is best understood with reference to the coming of the Son of man in triumph immediately after His resurrection, when He appeared to the apostles and commissioned them to make disciples of all nations."[7]

Various interpreters believe that Jesus referred not to the glorious Second Coming but to His coming in judgment to destroy the Temple. (Two such interpreters are Jewish historian Alfred Edersheim[8] and postmillennialist David Chilton.[9]) D. A. Carson in *The Expositor's Bible Commentary* writes, "They will not have finished evangelizing the cities of Israel before the Son of Man comes in judgment on Israel."[10]

Amillennialist William E. Cox, in contrast, believes this verse refers to neither the final coming of the Son of Man in the clouds of heaven nor the destruction of Jerusalem. He gives the verse a more practical explanation: "The Lord was sending out the Twelve on an earthly mission, and promised them that he would personally join them before they finished the assignment."[11]

George Ladd claimed: "The present verse says no more than that the mission of Jesus' disciples to Israel will last until the coming of the Son of Man. It indicates that in spite of her blindness, God has not given up Israel. The new people of God are to have a concern for Israel until the end comes."[12] F. F. Bruce says, similarly: "It means, simply, that the evangelisation of Israel will not be completed before the end of the present age, which comes with the advent of the Son of man."[13]

Each interpretation (except Schweitzer's) has certain appeal and logic. I have no ironclad interpretation myself, but I tend to agree with Ladd and Bruce. The cities mentioned are not limited to Palestine, but represent the cities worldwide where Israelites are to be found. Because the literal cities of Israel (in Palestine) in Jesus' time were all reached with His message within His earthly ministry, it seems to me that He must have had a broader mission in mind.

Notice that the comments of Jesus in Matthew 11:20–24 agree with the statement in the commission of Matthew 10:15. Jesus "began to upbraid the cities in which most of His mighty works had been done, because they did not repent" (Matthew 11:20). He specifically condemned Chorazin, Bethsaida and Capernaum, saying they would suffer "in the day of judgment" (verse 22). Thus, every city in which the Gospel of the Kingdom has been preached will give an accounting for its response in the day when Christ returns. This will happen, I believe, before the evangelization of all of Israel's far-flung locales.

2. On the Road to Jerusalem

In bold, fanatical manner, Jesus called His followers to take up their crosses and follow Him without compromise. If a person is ashamed of Jesus Christ and His words in this world, Jesus declared, He Himself will be ashamed of that person at His return. At this time Jesus gave the first direct prediction of His rejection, crucifixion and resurrection. Then He spoke of His return, making the following perplexing statement:

> "Assuredly, I say to you, there are some standing here who shall not taste death till they see the Son of Man coming in His kingdom."
>
> Matthew 16:28

Jesus' comments about His return were made in the area near Caesarea Philippi and probably within sight of Mount Hermon

(9,200 feet high). Many believe that within a week or so, Jesus and several of His disciples ascended partway up that mountain, where the Lord was transfigured with dazzling light, interviewed by Moses and Elijah and confirmed by a heavenly voice.

His statement was the ultimate manifesto of personal identity as He described His coming in the glory of God, His Father. Jesus' bold use of *Father* was a constant bone of contention with the religious authorities. He claimed His God to be a loving, personal Father, thereby revealing an intimate relationship that the scribes and Pharisees found unbelievable and impossible.

Our English meaning of the word *glory* hardly does justice to Jesus' description. He will return in the glory of His Father, and His own glory, and the glory of the holy angels (Matthew 24:30; Luke 21:27). Ordinarily this word *glory* suggests certain philosophical values—honor, power, good standing, prestige, reputation and acclamation (based on human credentials). *Glory* can refer to the authority, recognition and acknowledgment given to kings and dignitaries. This glory (essence) of God can also refer to a physical, tangible, observable presence best described as a splendor or luminous cloud. The Hebrews called the divine manifestation or theophany the *shekinah*.

At Jesus' coming this glory will break forth in a visible, physical manifestation of divine light, radiance or splendor. The ultimate, unrestrained, glorious self-manifestation of God, His Son and His angels will occur when Jesus returns.[14] Both aspects—the physical splendor and the public acknowledgment of His majesty—will blend in the greatest cosmic expression of glory ever expressed!

But in the statement from Matthew that has baffled many students of the Bible, Jesus gives the impression to the casual reader that He was promising to return within His disciples' lifetimes. The two other synoptic writers record it as follows:

> "Assuredly, I say to you that there are some standing here who will not taste death till they see the kingdom of God present with power."
>
> Mark 9:1

"... who shall not taste death till they see the kingdom of God."

Luke 9:27

Jesus did return, following His death and resurrection, and appeared to His disciples. But the glaring historical fact is that none of those present to hear this promise lived to witness His return in the visible glory of which He had spoken, making His statement troublesome for interpreters. Various theories have been developed to explain the meaning. This coming of the Son and His Kingdom has been variously identified with:

- Christ's resurrection and ascension
- The Day of Pentecost and the advent of the Holy Spirit
- The spread of Christianity
- The internal development of the Gospel
- The destruction of Jerusalem in A.D. 70

The famous nineteenth-century preacher Charles H. Spurgeon admitted that he had "passed it [this verse] over rapidly because I did not understand it clearly." Finally he came to what he felt was the plain meaning: "At the glorious appearing of Christ there are some [the unrighteous] who will taste death." Spurgeon felt that "the tasting of death" was "a reference to the second death, which [unrighteous] men will not taste of till the Lord comes." When referring to those who were standing there, He was "perhaps singling out Judas as he spoke. . . ." Spurgeon concluded, since Jesus said, "If a man keeps my saying, he shall never taste of death," that the Lord was referring not to physical death but to the divine wrath awaiting every unrepentant sinner.[15]

Another interpretation stresses that the Kingdom of God was indeed manifested with power during the disciples' lifetimes. David Chilton says:

> . . . The Kingdom was not some far-off millennium thousands of years in the future, after the Second Coming. Jesus announced: *"The time is fulfilled, and the Kingdom of God is at hand;* repent and believe in the gospel" (Mark 1:15). Jesus clearly told Israel to repent

> *now,* because the Kingdom was coming *soon*. The Kingdom was *at hand*. He was bringing it in right before their eyes (see Matt. 12:28; Luke 10:9–11; 17:21), and soon would ascend to the Father to sit on the throne of the Kingdom.[16]

Chilton's ideas about the Kingdom now represent solid New Testament thinking, but I fear that some evangelicals today tend to ignore this significant insight. For the text at hand, however, such an interpretation must also provide a credible explanation for the Son of Man's coming. Chilton's explanation that this statement finds fulfillment in the A.D. 70 destruction of Jerusalem seems to underplay the first and plain reading of the context.

One approach, in my estimation, satisfies the facts of history, the conditions of the text and an observation made by Peter: "We did not follow cunningly devised fables when we made known to you the *power and coming* of our Lord Jesus Christ, but were *eyewitnesses of His majesty*" (2 Peter 1:16, emphasis added).

Jesus' statement was a reference to His Transfiguration that was shortly to take place. Notice that all three synoptic accounts of the Transfiguration follow closely, without a break with the prediction, *indicating that event is related to the saying.*[17] Notice, too, how this declaration fits a pattern of special revelation that unfolds within that one week of time:

- Peter's confession of Jesus as the Christ
- The first prediction of the Church
- The first prediction of crucifixion and resurrection
- A visible manifestation of the glory of Jesus Christ as at His Second Coming

For the three disciples who accompanied Jesus, the Transfiguration was an overwhelming spectacle. They saw their Master swathed in the resplendent, bright-light brilliance of the glory of God. His face changed, blazing like the sun, and His garments gleamed radiantly white with heaven's light. Luke records that "they saw His glory" (9:32). Apparently the three later realized they had seen a preview of Jesus' Second Coming.

The apostle Peter, one of the three disciples, confirms this interpretation in 2 Peter 1:16 (quoted above). These key leaders of the Church did not rely on other sources of information about Christ's return; they had seen a personal preview. No wonder they were so fervent about the Second Coming!

An additional thought is inserted into the Matthew account about what will happen at Jesus' return: "He will reward each according to his works [deeds or doing]" (16:27). This will fulfill Psalm 62:12 and Proverbs 24:12. Other references indicate that a judging and rewarding of God's servants for their faithfulness will occur when Jesus returns.

3. On the Mount of Olives

This third statement of Jesus has also provoked much discussion; in fact, it could easily be considered the most controversial verse in the Olivet Discourse:

> "Assuredly, I say to you, this generation will by no means pass away till all these things are fulfilled."
>
> Matthew 24:34

The explanation depends on the meaning of *this generation* and *all these things*.

The verse is best interpreted as making clear that the generation then alive would see the destruction of Jerusalem and the events associated with it, described by Jesus in Matthew 24. (We will consider this in more detail in chapter 7.) Some commentators, I know, feel that the word *generation* should be enlarged in its time frame, but I think this argument has been answered effectively, and we can accept the fact that Jesus was referring to those alive at that time. It is not necessary to change the plain meaning of the word to accommodate a certain interpretation. In fact, to apply the verse to a future generation that lives through the first half of the seven-year Tribulation does radical violence to the text.

The *all these things* refers to the happenings before the city's destruction. Approximately forty years remained between the time that Jesus spoke these words and the time that the Romans, under the crown prince Titus, actually destroyed the Temple. (Note from Psalm 95:10 that a biblical generation equals forty years.) The *things* referring to the Second Coming clearly belong to another time frame—one that is indefinite in time fulfillment and should not be confused with the *things* connected with the city's destruction.

I am convinced that Jesus' disciples would have understood Him to mean that within approximately forty years (the literal time of a generation), the events leading up to and including the destruction of Jerusalem would have taken place. More explanation of this thought is given in chapter 7. The fact that Paul and others used the same descriptions of a future, glorious coming of Christ indicates that Jesus *did* mean for His descriptions of His coming to be future to that generation, and obviously beyond the destruction of Jerusalem in A.D. 70.

Jesus' Descriptions of the Second Coming

The passages in the chart below list the best material Jesus shared on the actual glorious return of the Son of Man. We will discuss the fourth and fifth items on the chart, the fascinating Olivet Discourse (Matthew 24, Mark 13 and Luke 21), in the next two chapters.

Jesus' Descriptions of the Second Coming

The Occasion	Matthew	Mark	Luke	John
1. Bethany beyond the Jordan	———	———	———	1:51 (NASB)
2. Near Caesarea Philippi	16:27–28	8:38–9:1	9:26–27	———
3. Judea beyond the Jordan	19:28	———	———	———

The Occasion	Matthew	Mark	Luke	John
4. On the Mount of Olives	24:27, 30–31	13:26–27	21:27	———
5. Conclusion on the Mount of Olives	25:31–32	———	———	———
6. Before the high priest	26:64	14:62	22:69	———

Since all four gospels were inspired by the Holy Spirit and written by men looking from different vantage points, I contend that the various accounts, properly understood, are their own best commentary on each other. No more authoritative interpretation for Scripture can be found than Scripture itself. I will try as much as possible, then, to seek Jesus' basic, uncomplicated meaning at the moments in which He spoke. Every commentator would like to accomplish this, but it will happen only if we remember that, in Chilton's words, "we must not interpret the Bible as if it dropped out of the sky in the twentieth century. The New Testament was written in the first century, and so we must try to understand it in terms of its first-century readers."[18]

Some of the passages under consideration are not easy to understand, so don't be alarmed if you experience a degree of uncertainty. In some cases I have suggested alternate interpretations to broaden our possible choices.

Now let's look at two of the listings from the chart.

1. Bethany Beyond the Jordan

One interesting verse, John 1:51, has no exact parallel anywhere, and could refer to the Second Coming, or at least lend input to the subject. The episode took place as Nathaniel was called as the fifth disciple. Introduced by Philip, Nathaniel was surprised by Jesus' opening remarks, which apparently he found prophetic in nature. F. F. Bruce gives an accurate (but uncommon) translation:

> Jesus said to him in reply, "Do you believe because I told you that I saw you underneath the fig tree? You will see greater things

than these. Indeed and in truth I tell you," he went on to say to him, "*you will all* see heaven opened and the angels of God ascending and descending on the Son of Man."[19]

(emphasis added)

The imagery recalls Jacob's vision at Bethel when he saw that "a ladder [stairway, staircase, ramp] was set up on the earth, and its top reached to heaven; and there the angels of God were ascending and descending on it" (Genesis 28:12). Jesus, like the ladder, is the bridge between heaven and earth, the Mediator between God and the human race (1 Timothy 2:5). Rotherham adds the significant insight on our text, above, that "the messengers ascend and descend, not 'upon,' but 'unto,' their Lord."[20]

Jesus' words parallel the synoptic passages describing how the Son of Man will be manifested with great power and glory riding on the clouds of heaven and *accompanied by angels*.[21] The Greek text, in saying, "You will all see," points to the great climax of the Gospel age when Jesus returns and every eye will see Him, along with *His holy angels*.

Christ stated clearly that He will return with His holy angels (Matthew 16:27; 24:31; Mark 8:38; Luke 9:26)—in fact, with *all* His angels (Matthew 25:31). Paul later affirmed this fact by describing "the Lord Jesus . . . revealed from heaven with His mighty angels" (2 Thessalonians 1:7), another indication that the angels are literal, not figurative.

Jesus' coming will be a spectacular display of all heavenly beings, fully visible and glorious in appearance.[22] As a dazzling entourage they will escort Jesus, then break ranks and speed forth in blazing glory to gather the redeemed from every quarter of the earth. Jesus explained that the Son of Man "will send His angels, and gather together His elect from the four winds, from the farthest part of earth to the farthest part of heaven" (Mark 13:27). This scene is incomprehensible to our human minds, but it is more than apocalyptic imagery; it is reality in the deepest sense of the word.

The heavenly hosts were always at Jesus' service. A multitude of angels was present at His birth (Luke 2:9, 13–15). They revived and strengthened Him after His arduous forty-day fast and ensuing bout with the devil (Matthew 4:11). An angel strengthened

Him during His greatest moment of prayer agony in the Garden of Gethsemane (Luke 22:43).

And here is another marvelous picture of angels accompanying Jesus. As He finished His Garden intercession, a gang of armed men arrived from the high priest and elders. Impetuous Peter, attempting to protect His Master with drawn sword, struck a blow to the head of Malchus, the high priest's servant. The poor man's ear was sliced off, which Jesus promptly restored and healed. "Then Jesus said to [Peter], 'Put your sword in its place, for all who take the sword will perish by the sword. Or do you think that I cannot now pray to My Father, and He will provide Me with more than twelve legions of angels?'" (Matthew 26:52–53). A legion equaled six thousand troops, so Jesus could have had 72,000 angels on hand at that moment!

We do not know how many angels there are in total, but when Jesus returns they will *all* participate in the grand convoy through the skies. I am a literalist when it comes to the angels at the Second Coming. We will see them, they will gather us to Jesus and we will join them in the exaltation of our Lord![23]

2. *Judea Beyond the Jordan*

The young man walked away from Christ and His followers very dejected. He had just been told that, to be perfect, he must sell all, give to the poor and follow Jesus. Sorrowfully he could not accept the Master's challenge to dispose of his wealth. After he left, Jesus made the astounding statement that "it is easier for a camel to go through the eye of a needle than for a rich man to enter the kingdom of God" (Matthew 19:24).

The amazed disciples found an able mouthpiece in Peter, who (apparently contrasting the disciples with the rich young man) asked what *their* reward would be, since they had left all to follow Jesus. His answer:

> "Assuredly I say to you, that in the *regeneration*, when the Son of Man sits on the throne of His glory, you who have followed Me will also sit on twelve thrones, judging the twelve tribes of Israel."
>
> Matthew 19:28 (emphasis added)

This verse has no direct parallel in the other gospels (although Luke 22:28–30 is the closest in thought). At the "regeneration" Jesus will sit on His glorious throne, and the disciples will each have a throne of his own—an awesome reward! What and when is this regeneration?

Regeneration is the translation of the Greek word *palingenesia*, which can mean "new birth" (*palin*, meaning "again," and *genesis*, "birth"). Used only twice in the Greek New Testament, this word also appears in Titus 3:5 as "the washing of regeneration." T. W. Manson, in his well-known commentary, points this word out as "a technical term in Stoic philosophy, where it signifies the beginning of a new cycle in the cosmic process. . . ." He explains that "the Jewish expectation was different. They also expected the end of the existing order and the beginning of a new one. But the new order would be really new and not a mere repetition of what had gone before. . . . The important thing is that it will be a new era that is new."[24]

In Matthew 19:28 the word *regeneration* is used in the sense of the "restoration of all things," as in Acts 3:21.[25] The meaning here also includes the "renewal" of all things.[26] Friedrich Büchsel comments, "The Jewish faith in the resurrection of the dead and renewal of the world is clothed in this term."[27]

Jesus refers, I believe, to His Second Coming and to the inauguration of His millennial reign on earth. It is the consummation and glorious demonstration of the spiritual Kingdom of God in a literal, actual, earthly fulfillment. Christ will sit on His throne, and the twelve apostles on their twelve thrones, judging the twelve tribes of Israel.

Matthew 25:31 pinpoints the *time* of Christ's throne: "When the Son of Man comes in His glory, and all the holy angels with Him, *then* He will sit on the throne of His glory" (emphasis added). At that time Christ will separate the nations "one from another, as a shepherd divides his sheep from the goats" (verse 32). The regeneration will involve not just Israel but all the nations of the world.

Christ now sits on His messianic throne, of course (Ephesians 1:20–22; Revelation 1:5; 3:11), but when He comes, His glorious reign will go public on a cleansed earth in which righteousness is exalted and satanic influence eliminated. Our text certainly sounds like the Millennium of Revelation 20, particularly since the ideas of thrones and reigning with Christ are mentioned in both places.

Some feel that the Millennium actually refers to the Church age now, since Christ is reigning now, and therefore the "regeneration" is actually the Church age—that is, in effect now.[28] I completely agree that Christ now rules; Paul teaches that we are seated with Him in heavenly places (Ephesians 2:6). In emphasizing this all-important concept, however, we must not overlook the significance of the Kingdom of God finding its fullest and ultimate expression as a literal, uncontested realm on planet earth. The literal, millennial expression of the Kingdom of God is a necessary and appropriate climax to the Kingdom of Christ as we now know it.

Some reject this concept because of the dispensational emphasis on a Jewish Millennium. But Jesus' statement about the apostles judging the twelve tribes of Israel need not lock our interpretation into this Jewish focus. The Millennium will involve *all* God's people, just as in His present reign. Not only the apostles, but *all* overcoming saints will reign with Him (not an uncommon idea in the New Testament; see 1 Corinthians 6:2).

"Judging," as Manson points out, may be taken in the literal sense, "in which case the saying means that the Twelve are to be assessors at the Last Judgement (cf. Mt. 25:31ff; I Cor. 6:3)." Also, the word may be taken in a wider sense, "common in the Old Testament, of 'ruling,' 'administering.'"[29] Perhaps the best solution is a combination of both approaches.

It will be a bright new day when Christ's throne of glory is set up on the earth, the new birth of the world, as a cleansed earth and a perfected Church bask in the splendor of the unrestrained effulgence of the Kingdom of God. Christ will be present with the redeemed of all ages from every nation, Jews and Gentiles alike, in a victorious occupation of our former battle zone.

The next chapter will introduce the longest answer session Jesus ever gave. The disciples' questions formed the launching pad for an awesome prophetic discourse. Jesus' nine "birth pangs" may startle you, but they are as significant and relevant for people today as they were for the disciples of Jesus on the Mount of Olives.

SIX

BIRTH PANGS COMING

His final statement to Jerusalem was made. His call to Jewry's capital was consummated. The last seeds of His public teaching had been cast onto the hard, stony soil of Israel. Jesus, therefore, the rejected Messiah, strode solemnly and resolutely from the den of robbers, leaving it desolate. "He came to His own, and His own did not receive him" (John 1:11). As His last day of public ministry came to a close, Jesus and His disciples left the Temple, crossed the Kidron and slowly climbed the Mount of Olives.

Making a sudden turn in the road, the disciples gazed in awe at the spectacle behind them. This glorious Temple complex in Jerusalem "was probably the most awesome building in the ancient world,"[1] and appropriately filled every Jewish heart with bursting pride. Alfred Edersheim, esteemed historian specializing in that era, describes the sight:

> Just then the western sun was pouring his golden beams on tops of marble cloisters and on the terraced courts, and glittering on the golden spikes on the roof of the Holy Place. In the setting even more than in the rising sun, must the vast proportions, the symmetry, and the sparkling sheen of this mass of snowy marble and gold have stood out gloriously. And across the black valley, and up

> the slopes of Olivet, lay the dark shadows of those gigantic walls built of massive stones, some of them nearly twenty-four feet long. . . . It was probably as they now gazed on all this grandeur and strength that they broke the silence imposed on them by gloomy thoughts of the near desolateness of that House, which the Lord had predicted.[2]

The glittering vision overwhelmed these common men. Unable to contain their admiration, and possibly in a mild effort to temper the Master's previous strong denunciation of city and Temple, they pointed excitedly to the various buildings of the Temple. One of them exclaimed, "Teacher, see what manner of stones and what buildings are here!"

Jesus' stern reply was terrifying: "Do you see these great buildings? Not one stone shall be left upon another, that shall not be thrown down" (Mark 13:2).

Their excitement died instantly, punctured by the hard words of their solemn leader. How could such gigantic buildings be destroyed and such immense stones overthrown? Giovanni Papini says sympathetically:

> They would not understand that those great massive stones, quarried out patiently from the mountains, drawn from afar by oxen, squared and prepared by chisels and mallets, put one upon another by masters of the art to make the most marvelous Temple of the universe; that these stones, warm and brilliant in the sun, should be pulverized into ruins.[3]

Jesus referred to the stones of the Temple, but previously He had described the devastation of the city in identical terms. During His triumphal entry into Jerusalem, as the disciples celebrated with abandon, the sorrowing Christ on His humble donkey saw the city as a people who had missed their spiritual opportunity. Weeping He said:

> "Days will come upon you when your enemies will build an embankment around you, surround you and close you in on every side, and level you, and your children within you, to the ground;

> and they will not leave in you one stone upon another, because you did not know the time of your visitation."
>
> Luke 19:43–44

The judgment of God would come upon Temple, city and people. Jesus was using the Temple, the focal point of their religious life and the visible symbol of God's presence, to introduce His discussion.

Some of those disciples lived to see the day (a scant forty years later) when the entire city and Temple were viciously demolished. Josephus, the first-century Jewish historian, tells us that the great wall of the city "was so thoroughly laid even with the ground by those that dug it up to the foundation, that there was left nothing to make those that came thither believe it had ever been inhabited."[4]

Opening Questions

Serious and reflective, Jesus settled Himself on the Mount of Olives with His inner circle of four, Peter, James, John and Andrew. (Apparently they were the initial inquirers, but the other disciples were probably present during the latter part of the discourse.) Beasley-Murray describes the situation as given in Mark:

> . . . What a superb context it gave for a full-scale eschatological address: Jesus seated on Olivet, with the panorama of Jerusalem, dominated by its temple, before him! It was an ideal setting for the one great discourse of Jesus in his Gospel, placed at the end of his account of the ministry and forming the transition to the passion narrative.[5]

Jesus had already lamented over Jerusalem: "See! Your house is left to you desolate." Then He added the surprising words: "For I say to you, you shall see Me no more till you say, 'Blessed is He who comes in the name of the LORD!'" (Matthew 23:38–39).[6]

Now they sat in plain view of the Temple, a setting that prompted three anxious questions. The disciples were concerned about the impending destruction of the great Temple spread before them, for this would imply that Israel was no longer the covenant nation. It would seem to signify that God had divorced Israel as a nation from Himself. Also, the question of Jesus' *parousia* troubled their minds. Here are the disciples' questions as recorded by each of the synoptic writers:

> "Tell us, when will these things be? And what will be the sign of Your coming, and of the end of the age?" (Matthew 24:3)
>
> "Tell us, when will these things be? And what will be the sign when all these things will be fulfilled?" (Mark 13:4)
>
> "Teacher, but when will these things be? And what sign will there be when these things are about to take place?" (Luke 21:7)

The naïve disciples did not realize that their simple inquiries involved events of major proportion. Their questions provided Jesus with the setting for a major prophetic discourse. From these questions He proceeded to fashion three answers:

- How they will know when the destruction of the Temple and city is about to take place
- What the sign of His coming will be
- What the sign of the end (or consummation) of the age will be

Unfortunately some interpreters relate the Temple comments to some future Temple,[7] while Jesus was specifically addressing the main concern of His disciples, which was the Temple visible before them. It was incomprehensible to them that God would destroy *that* Temple. Was it not to be the world's worship center in the messianic age?

Matthew records one of their questions as, "What will be the sign of Your coming?"—which is the equivalent of Luke's "sign . . . when these things [the Temple's destruction] are about to take place." The disciples apparently expected the destruction of the

Temple to occur at the Second Coming *(parousia)* of the Lord, which in their minds would be the end of the age.

It was a natural conclusion. Kik observes, "They thought that the Saviour would not destroy Jerusalem and its Temple until he came to put an end to the present state of the world at the Day of Judgment."[8] Their biggest concern was to know *when* these things would come about and *what signs* would alert them, so that preparation or escape would be possible.

In spite of Jesus' emphasis on a Kingdom of spiritual dimensions, the Jewish disciples remained mentally bonded to an earthly Temple that would last until the end of time. They failed to realize that the kingly structure before them was only a symbolic type of the spiritual Temple, Christ and His Church.

What Was the Message? Who Was the Audience?

Before we plunge into the specific predictions of the Olivet Discourse, let's step back for a moment and look at it in context. It is one of five significant discourses in the book of Matthew (which is also interspersed with narrative sections). The entire book presents Jesus as the Messiah promised in the Old Testament, the One who will bring the Kingdom of God to men. Each discourse presents one phase of the Kingdom of God:

1. Righteousness of the Kingdom (5:1–7:29)
2. Proclamation of the Kingdom (10:1–42)
3. Mystery of the Kingdom (13:1–58)
4. Fellowship of the Kingdom (18:1–35)
5. Future of the Kingdom (24:1–25:46)[9]

Seated on the Mount of Olives with His disciples, Jesus offered some remarkable predictions about two major events—the destruction of Jerusalem and His own glorious Second Coming. This Olivet Discourse, the fifth major discourse mentioned above, was given toward the end of His passion week ministry. Matthew's record is the most complete, but the abbreviated accounts in Mark

13 and Luke 21 are also significant. The synoptic gospels devote fully 160 verses to this prophecy.

The discourse, a private message to Jesus' disciples, is the second-longest of His recorded sermons. (The longest is the Sermon on the Mount, a message to the general public.) Jesus told the disciples that certain obvious signs would alert His people to each of the momentous events being discussed, and other happenings would characterize the tenor of the Church age.

The Olivet Discourse was Jesus' answer to three questions about the future. His intense and meticulous response ranks as the longest answer session recorded in the gospels. The statements seem literal and straightforward, precluding the possibility that He was trying to cloak His responses in mystery or symbolic imagery. It seems apparent that there was no hidden agenda. Admittedly the text is controversial with a disparity of interpretation, but this does not necessarily mean that He sought to cloak His answers. The mystery arises, I feel, because modern readers cannot fully relate to the emotion-charged setting and the Jewish thinking of that day. Also, in reading the discourse, we are not aware of Jesus' pauses, inflections and emotional expression. Some suggest that not all His words are available to us, and that seems likely.

The late Wilbur M. Smith, world-renowned Bible scholar, author and editor, commented in 1957 (in a statement equally true today) that "there is hardly any passage in the New Testament, outside of the Book of Revelation, so demanding close study for the day in which we live."[10]

The Message

The following outline gives the most natural and logical divisions.

The Olivet Discourse

Divisions	Matthew	Mark	Luke
1. Prediction and opening questions	24:1–3	13:1–4	21:5–7
2. Birth pangs predicted	24:4–14	13:5–13	21:8–19
3. Desolation of Jerusalem	24:15–22	13:14–20	21:20–24

Divisions	Matthew	Mark	Luke
4. False Christs, false prophets	24:23–28	13:21–23	———
5. The coming of the Son of Man	24:29–31	13:24–27	21:25–28
6. The unknown day and hour	24:32–41	13:28–37	21:29–36
7. Closing parables	24:42–25:30	———	———
8. Judgment at the Son of Man's coming	25:31–46	———	———

This discourse contains two main time frames: one for its first-century listeners and one for the end times. The first, involving the destruction of the Temple and Jerusalem, was dramatically fulfilled in A.D. 70, within a generation's time, just as Jesus said. Now we await the second time frame, the return of our Lord, which will occur at an unspecified period at the end of the age. A confluence of spiritual events will consummate this age with Christ's coming, introducing the millennial age to come.

Because the first prediction, the destruction of Jerusalem, came to pass exactly as foretold, the Church can have confidence that the second prediction, the *parousia* of Christ, will also come to pass flawlessly.

Areas of special interest in the discourse:

- The three appearances of "tribulation" as regarding the persecution of the Church, the destruction of Jerusalem and the events at the end of the age.
- The three most thought-provoking verses in Matthew 24: verse 14 ("gospel . . . preached in all the world"); verse 29 ("immediately after the tribulation"); and verse 34 ("this generation will by no means pass away till. . .").
- Jesus' words—should they be taken literally or figuratively (as with "clouds," verse 30)?
- The "most crucial question," according to Sproul: What does Jesus mean by "the end"?[11]

The Text Itself

Compare carefully the records of Matthew, Mark and Luke; they are unequal in length and not always identical in wording (though they may be in meaning). The sequential outline given above is a good guide, studied best in a harmony of the gospels with the three accounts in parallel columns. This allows the reader to see at a glance all the facts presented.[12]

Do the three gospel accounts of the Olivet Discourse agree or disagree in their details and important points? A close reading discloses that the writers use different words and expressions to discuss the same things, and Luke omits some points that are included by Matthew and Mark.[13]

In retelling Jesus' narrative, each of the synoptic writers writes accurately and inspirationally from his unique vantage point and to his select audience. Luke concentrates mainly on the fall of Jerusalem, whereas Matthew focuses on the whole Gospel age. Luke does not refer to Daniel's "abomination of desolation," since it would have little appeal to a Greek-speaking audience. Matthew, on the other hand, writes to Jews who value the ancient Hebrew Scriptures, so the reference to Daniel is significant. Each narrative is true, inspired and meaningful, with the wording geared to a specific readership.

In *The Life of Christ in Stereo*, Johnston M. Cheney has masterfully interwoven the four gospels in such a way as to incorporate all the details into a single chronology, without repeating any parts. He claims—and I must delightfully confirm—that "this minute combination displays the fact that they agree so completely and minutely that they fit together into a single, coherent story, without the addition or omission of a single detail."[14] When so presented, the seeming discrepancies or inconsistencies simply melt away.

The Audience

We know that Jesus spoke to His disciples. Also, it seems logical that Jesus knew future generations would be reading His words and listening to His teachings. He gave His message with caution, undoubtedly perceiving by the Holy Spirit that future followers would consider His words. Jesus had an acute consciousness of the "now-later" theology. He knew, for instance, that the Kingdom was then in existence, yet He spoke of its coming later. Surely it is possible that He was prophetically aware that His words would be studied by later generations.[15]

We can identify at least three possible audiences for Jesus' discourse on the Mount of Olives: first, the disciples with Jesus who might live to see the destruction of Jerusalem; second, generations of Christians who would live throughout the Church age; and third, believers who would be alive when He returned. The discourse contains special words for all three audiences.

The Olivet Discourse is not a close-knit, edited piece of literature like a presidential statement or a meticulously crafted article for *Reader's Digest,* even if it has developed the greatest audience of avid readers that any sermon has ever enjoyed. Jesus spoke spontaneously out of His emotion and immediate spiritual experience—a heart statement filled with concern and hope rather than a prepared academic lecture. His biggest consideration was not to impart apocalyptic secrets, but to strengthen His followers for the difficulties that lay ahead.

Speaking to a handful of tough working men rather than polished theologians, Jesus shared the simple thoughts the Father had given Him. With neither notes nor projection aids, He spoke words so sincere, convincing and astounding that His listeners, like sponges, drank in every word. His passion mesmerized the wide-eyed group. Later, astounded, they would recall with amazing accuracy the powerful thoughts and descriptive language.

Three great concerns filled the mind of Jesus:

1. Jerusalem and the Temple would soon be devastated by the Romans. Within a generation's time legions would surround the city and His followers be forced to flee or perish.
2. The end of the age would just as surely come to pass, but at a distant and unspecified time. The events were clear in Jesus' mind. He described the glorious scene as though angels and trumpet sound were then taking place! Yet the Father had not revealed the actual date of that return. Cosmic events and celestial signs would appear, to the consternation of all earth-dwellers, while believers

would take these happenings as joyful signs of the nearness of His return.

3. Nine "birth pangs" would occur throughout the Church age. These awesome events would introduce and interweave two major events—the destruction of Jerusalem and Jesus' own glorious Second Coming. His followers were to be aware, wakeful and watchful, looking for His return.

Let's take a moment to look at each of the nine birth pangs and examine some of the reasons for the terrible signs that will take place. Then, in the next chapter, we will focus on what Jesus prophesied concerning the destruction of Jerusalem.

The Nine "Birth Pangs"

In the opening section of His teaching, Jesus introduced nine types of events, or "birth pangs" (Matthew 24:4–14), that would occur shortly before Jerusalem's destruction, continue throughout the Church age and climax in even more astounding fashion just before His Second Coming. These significant signs are described as "the beginning of sorrows" (Matthew 24:8; Mark 13:8) or, literally, "the beginning of birth pangs or birth-woes" [Greek, *odin*]. Their combined worldwide intensity presently grows steadily worse and more frequent, like the pains of childbirth leading to delivery:

1. False messiahs
2. Continuing wars
3. Natural disasters
4. Celestial signs
5. Heavy persecutions
6. Lawless apostasy
7. Enduring triumph
8. Worldwide proclamation
9. Miraculous testimony

Within a few years after the death of Christ, the predictions began their dramatic fulfillment.

1. False Messiahs

"Many will come in My name, saying, 'I am the Christ,' and will deceive many" (Matthew 24:5). If anything could be more tragic than those who deceive, it must be the gullibility of the people who are deceived. Paul prophesied in 2 Timothy 3:13 that "evil men and impostors will grow worse and worse, deceiving and being deceived." The ultimate mistake is to accept someone as a divine authority—a Christ, even—without discerning the error. The false messiah does not claim authority as a *representative* of Jesus Christ, but rather the very name that belongs to Him alone. Paul warned, "Let no one deceive you by any means" (2 Thessalonians 2:3).[16]

George R. Beasley-Murray has written a thorough commentary on the Olivet Discourse as presented in the gospel of Mark. He sees in three word groupings (Mark 13:5–6, 7–8, 21–22) "a series of warnings not to be led astray by claims that the end of the age has already begun and the parousia of the Christ is immediately at hand."

He points out that the opening Greek word in the discourse is *blepete* ("Watch!"), and that this is "the most characteristic term of the discourse [as it appears in Mark], and more than any other points to the nature of the discourse."

The word *blepete* carries the basic meaning of "look," but as used in Mark it is infused with urgency and warning. "Through his use of the term *blepete* Mark has emphasized a feature which was already embodied in the material of the discourse and has given to the whole the character of a call to spiritual discernment and alertness."[17]

In recent years we have observed the tragic march of notorious cult messiahs and their bedraggled followers. Some examples: Father Divine, Charles Manson and Sun Myung Moon. Recently the media has given graphic coverage of duped disciples who followed their messiahs even into death: Marshall Applewhite ("Do" of the Heaven's Gate cult) and Jim Jones, who led his followers from the Bay Area of California to death in the jungles of Guyana. People well grounded in the good Word of God will not follow such a path of deception. Wilbur M. Smith offers this timely comment:

There is one theme that underlies all the work of Satan and of Antichrist, and that is *deception*. . . . Even Eve acknowledged that Satan had deceived her, Genesis 3:13. The Apostle reaffirmed it in I Timothy 2:14. Deception is referred to in our Lord's great prophetic discourse four times in Matthew 24, verses 4 and 5 and 11 and 24. The false prophet in Revelation 13, 14, 19, 20 is characterized by this activity of deception. To me one of the most terrible statements in all the Bible is in Revelation 12:9 where we read *Satan . . . deceiveth the whole world.*[18]

2. Continuing Wars

"You will hear of wars and rumors of wars [*commotions*, Luke 21:9]. See that you are not troubled [*terrified*, Luke 21:9]; for all these things must come to pass, but the end is not yet [*the end will not come immediately*, Luke 21:9]. For nation will rise against nation, and kingdom against kingdom" (Matthew 24:6–7). Wars have continued throughout the Church age, intensifying gradually until the whole earth will have been engulfed in their flames.

Papini makes this interesting commentary about the time immediately following the crucifixion:

> When Jesus was killed, the "peace" of Augustus still existed, but very soon nations rise against nations and kingdoms against kingdoms. Under Nero the Britons rebel and massacre the Romans, the Parthians revolt and force the legions to pass under the yoke; Armenia and Syria murmur against foreign government; Gaul rises with Julius Vindex.
>
> In 69, insurrection breaks out in the north, with the Batavians led by Claudius Civilus; and in Palestine the insurrection of the Jews is fomented by the Zealots, who claim that the Romans and all the heathen should be driven out in order that God might return to triumph with His own people. In less than two years Italy is invaded twice, Rome taken twice, two emperors kill themselves; two are killed.
>
> . . . For forty years the country [Palestine] had had no peace, not even the peace of defeat and slavery. Under the Roman procurators the disorders knew no truce; the flames of the revolt flared ever more boldly. The holy place, during the great rebellion, had

become a refuge for assassins; and the Zealots took possession of the Temple.[19]

3. Natural Disasters

"There will be famines, pestilences [*troubles,* Mark 13:8], and [*great,* Luke 21:11] earthquakes in various places. All these are the beginning of sorrows" (Matthew 24:7–8). Caused by a series of poor crops, famine came even to Rome in the time of Claudius. Pestilence followed under the reign of Nero. Earthquakes in A.D. 61 and 62 occurred in Asia, Achaia and Macedonia, and the Italian cities of Naples, Nocera and Pompeii were shaken in 63. Thus earthquakes prepared the way for the destruction of Jerusalem in A.D. 70. But that was not yet to be the end (Matthew 24:6; Mark 13:7).

Earthquakes have continued throughout history, and the impression of Jesus' teaching is that they will increase in number as we approach the end of the Church age. The use of *in various places* (*kata topous,* "throughout places") indicates that wars, earthquakes and other destructions will be scattered worldwide.

Notice this interesting progression: In the 1700s there were eight recorded earthquakes that left sizable devastations. During the 1800s the number of earthquakes worldwide registering over 7.0 on the Richter scale averaged 10.5. The average number of earthquakes registering over 7.0 through the 1990s was 17.66. Luke speaks of "great" earthquakes (21:11). The book of Revelation predicts four end-time earthquakes that will deliver catastrophic damage: Revelation 6:12, 14; 8:5; 11:13; and the final, ultimate earthquake described in 16:18.[20]

4. Celestial Signs

"There will be fearful sights and great signs from heaven" (Luke 21:11). Along with disasters on earth, Luke records that there will be "terrible sights (*phobetron*) and signs in the sky."[21] In his famous Pentecost sermon, Peter describes the Holy Spirit outpouring, then quotes the prophet Joel: "I will show wonders in heaven above and signs in the earth beneath: blood and fire and vapor of smoke" (Acts 2:19).[22]

5. *Heavy Persecutions*

"Then [*Before all these things,* Luke 21:12] they will deliver you up to tribulation [*councils,* Mark 13:9; *synagogues and prisons,* Luke 21:12] and kill you, and you will be hated by all nations for My name's sake" (Matthew 24:9). I. Howard Marshall offers some good insights on the Olivet Discourse as presented in Luke, the account that says more on the subject of persecution. "In the preceding section," he writes, "the disciples were warned against the danger of being misled; now they are warned against the danger of succumbing to persecution."

In Luke 21:12–17 three types of persecution are mentioned: first, the danger of being arrested and tried in the courts; second, betrayal by one's closest relatives; and third, the general hatred of all men.[23] Mark's gospel uses the verb *paradidonai,* "to hand over," at the beginning of three verses (13:9, 11, 12) that emphasize persecution.

The harsh treatment of the Church has persisted throughout history, and overcoming Christians have continued to be persecuted and martyred every year since the founding of the Church. *The New Foxe's Book of Martyrs* tells their stories from A.D. 37 to 1997 and shares an astounding discovery: "More Christians were martyred in this century alone than in all the past centuries combined." Recent investigations indicate 160,000 martyrs each year.[24] Yet we are the Church triumphant!

6. *Lawless Apostasy*

"Then many will be offended, will betray one another, and will hate one another. Then many false prophets will rise up and deceive many. And because lawlessness will abound, the love of many will grow cold" (Matthew 24:10–12). From this milieu of deception, lawlessness and lack of love, an evil world system will develop that will spawn the diabolical leader of the last days known as the Antichrist, or "lawless one" (2 Thessalonians 2:8).

The "mystery of lawlessness" is already at work, but we still await the arrival of Antichrist, the master of deception. The best information on this subject is found in 2 Thessalonians 2 and Revelation 13. This subject will be addressed in chapter 9 when we discuss Paul's letters to the Thessalonians.

7. *Enduring Triumph*

"But he who endures to the end shall be saved" (Matthew 24:13). This section of the discourse finds its highest fulfillment, in my estimation, as an overview of the whole Church age. When Jesus urged His followers to endure "to the end," He meant first that each disciple must persevere to the end of natural life in serving Christ in his or her assigned time and generation. In a more general sense, Jesus meant that His people must overcome, generation after generation, to the end or consummation of the total era, when He would return.

In this sense *the end* is the consummation of the Church age and the beginning of the millennial age to come.[25] In verse 9 "hated by all nations" on account of Jesus' name indicates more than a localized activity or narrow window of time. All these events did begin locally, but eventually became global.

Some feel that *the end* (or "the end of the age") refers to the end of the Jewish age, which is considered to be A.D. 70, when Jerusalem was destroyed. But nothing in Scripture warrants the assertion that a new dispensation began at that time. Actually the Jewish age ended at the cross, which is why Jesus made His dramatic statement in Matthew 23:38 (fulfilling Jeremiah 22:5): "Your house is left to you desolate."

When Christ died on the cross, He cried out, "It is finished!" (John 19:30). As He expired, the veil in the Temple was rent in two (Matthew 27:51; Mark 15:38; Luke 23:45), and a new way opened to God for everyone who believes (Hebrews 10:20). The death, burial, resurrection and ascension of Jesus Christ marked the end of the Jewish age and the beginning of the new covenant.

The destruction of city and Temple were merely the natural calamity and aftermath precipitated by the rejection and crucifixion of Jesus. They were also the dramatic fulfillment of Jesus' remarkable prophecy.

8. Worldwide Proclamation

"This gospel of the kingdom will be preached in all the world as a witness to all the nations, and then the end will come" (Matthew 24:14). This frequently quoted verse (repeated in abbreviated form in Mark 13:10) is considered by many, including myself, one of the key signs of Jesus' coming. Some stress that this has already been fulfilled during the time of the early Church (based on Acts 2:5; Romans 1:8; Colossians 1:5–6, 23).[26]

It does appear that the world of the apostolic Church was reached with the proclamation of the Gospel. The Good News went far and wide! Paul's ministry in Ephesus, for example, "continued for two years, so that all who dwelt in Asia heard the word of the Lord Jesus, both Jews and Greeks" (Acts 19:10). As another example, consider southern India, in those days more than 4,500 difficult travel miles from Jerusalem. Yet the apostle Thomas carried the message there in the first century and planted the Christian Church that still exists today. The early Church took seriously Jesus' commission to "be witnesses to Me in Jerusalem, and in all Judea and Samaria, and *to the end of the earth*" (Acts 1:8, emphasis added).

At the present time, however, there are nations and people groups yet to be reached. And in every generation the global proliferation of population, the continuing establishment of new nations and the discovery of hidden people groups have necessitated the harvest call for laborers and the spreading of the Good News of Jesus Christ (Matthew 9:37–38; Luke 9:2; John 4:35). The Great Commission of Matthew 28:19–20 remains to be fully carried out, since it refers to both the establishment of disciples in all the nations and the proclamation of the Gospel. This does not mean that all people will be saved; rather it speaks of a universal witness that gives all people the opportunity to receive Christ.

The Great Commission and Matthew 24:14, Mark 13:10 and Acts 1:8 are all bonded together in spirit. An urgent task remains to be done before the end. As George Ladd fervently states:

> Here is the motive of our mission: the final victory awaits the completion of our task. "And then the end will come." There is no

other verse in the Word of God which says, "And then the end will come." When is Christ coming again? When the Church has finished its task. When will This Age end? When the world has been evangelized. "What will be the sign of your coming and the close of the age?" (Matt. 24:3). "This gospel of the kingdom will be preached throughout the whole world as a testimony to all nations; and then, AND THEN, the end will come." When? *Then;* when the Church has fulfilled its divinely appointed mission.[27]

The following statistics give us an idea of where we stand in terms of world evangelization:

According to the Lausanne Statistics Task Force, which was where the International Evangelism Convention of 1992 was held with Billy Graham, in 1500 AD there were 5 million Christians among a population of 344 million people. That equates to 1 out of every 70 people on the planet were Christians. By 1900 the ratio changed to 1 out of 25. In 1989 the ratio was 500 million Christians to a world population of 3.5 billion, or 1 in every 7. The latest count shows it is now 1 in every 6.[28]

A. B. Simpson was interviewed in the late 1800s by a journalist who asked him, "Do you know when Jesus will return?"

"Yes," he replied, "and I will tell you if you write exactly what I say, including references, and nothing more."

The journalist agreed.

Simpson said, "Write down Matthew 24:14: 'And this gospel of the kingdom shall be preached in all the world for a witness unto all nations; and then shall the end come.'"

The journalist wrote those words. Then, looking up expectantly, he asked, "What else, sir?"

Simpson replied, "Nothing else."[29]

9. Miraculous Testimony

"Whatever is given you in that hour, speak that; for it is not you who speak, but the Holy Spirit" (Mark 13:11). Usually neglected by commentators, this ninth "birth pang" is of great significance. The personal presence of the Holy Spirit to aid persecuted saints provides encouragement for the most trying of circumstances. Jesus cautioned His followers not to worry about preparing statements when brought before religious and secular magistrates and courts; no rehearsals would be necessary! Dynamic, appropriate words would be given by the Holy Spirit in the moment of need.

Peter and John were the first apostles to experience this amazing phenomenon. Acts 4:5–21 tells how these empowered men defied the austere Jewish Sanhedrin with their bold assertions. Later, in Acts 7, Stephen brought a masterful, extemporaneous, Spirit-inspired message to that same Sanhedrin—and was rewarded by being made the first martyr of the Christian era.

Throughout Church history the witness of the Spirit has come through dedicated men and women. Pressed and threatened, Martin Luther, the German monk, raised his voice in prophetic expression on April 18, 1521, at the Diet at Worms. His courageous stand changed the course of history, and his closing words have rung down through the Church age ever since: "Here I stand. I can not do otherwise. God help me! Amen."[30] God used Luther's words to launch the Reformation—according to historian Philip Schaff, "the greatest event in history."[31]

In modern times some of the best illustrations of Church growth and persecution come from places like Pakistan, Sudan and China, where Christians confront brutal treatment. The testimonies of hardship amid suffering and the inspirational words of the Holy Spirit given to answer the tormentors are beyond the comprehension of comfortable Westerners.[32]

Overview

All nine birth pangs gradually increase in intensity and severity until the time of delivery ("the end"). Although occurring to a lesser degree before the destruction of the Temple, they will reach worldwide proportions before the end of the age. The birthing process can be a long and arduous process, but great joy and relief are experienced when the child is born. Many of us have learned that birth pangs are not easy to deal with, but they are vital for delivery—and they are woven into the very fabric of creation. Every generation must experience them or die out.

Why Would God Destroy Jerusalem?

In the next chapter we will discuss the destruction of Jerusalem and the awful devastation of the people.

Eight Scriptures explain the termination of God's relationship with Israel, and why Jerusalem was forsaken and a new covenant (that of Jesus Christ) inaugurated that would include all peoples.

1. Left Desolate

Jesus said, "See! Your house is left to you desolate" (Matthew 23:38; "abandoned and empty," GNB). This is, I believe, both a dramatic quotation and (as I mentioned earlier) a fulfillment of Jeremiah 22:5 (also note 12:7): "'If you will not hear these words, I swear by Myself,' says the LORD, 'that this house shall become a desolation.'" Jesus was referring to the abandonment of Jerusalem by God.

We have seen that the Jewish age closed with this statement by Jesus. When He died on the cross, a new era opened in which anyone, Jew or Gentile, could be saved through faith. A carnal, nationalistic religion was exchanged for a spiritual, international fellowship in the Body of Christ. The people of God now comprise those of every ethnic group who love and serve the Lord Jesus Christ.

Luke 13:35 carries a parallel thought and adds: "You shall not see Me until the time comes when you say, 'Blessed is He who comes in the name of the LORD!'" It seems that the Jewish people's ability to see Him, and that of the Gentiles as well, depends on their willingness to acknowledge His messiahship.

2. Parable of the Vineyard Owner

This unusual story, found in Matthew 21:33–45 and Mark 12:1–11, tells of a landowner who planted a vineyard. Then, leasing it to some vinedressers, he went to a far country. Periodically he sent his servants, and finally his son, to collect the benefits. The vinedressers beat, stoned and killed the servants, and even the landowner's son. The owner finally came and destroyed his enemies and leased the vineyard to others who would respect his wishes.

The spiritual object of the parable is this: "The kingdom of God will be taken from you and given to *a nation bearing the fruits of it*" (Matthew 21:43, emphasis added). Matthew notes that the chief priests and Pharisees perceived that Jesus was speaking against them (verse 45). Thus the Kingdom passed from the Jews (as a nation and religion) to a nation (the Church with both Jewish and Gentile believers) who will respect it.

3. The Wineskins

Jesus made it clear, as recorded in Matthew 9:17, Mark 2:22 and Luke 5:37–38, that the old, stiff, dried-out wineskins of outdated, formalized religion could not contain the fresh wine of the Spirit. New wine, He said, would require new wineskins. The evolving people of God, led by the active Holy Spirit, could no longer be kept in a religious system of unbelief. God's salvation was to be made available to those in every nation who would believe in Jesus as Messiah. The Church thus became God's agent of change for bringing the nations to Himself. Natural Israel, meanwhile, will continue in her state of unbelief until she turns to Jesus as her Messiah.

4. Parable of a Fig Tree

Jesus told a parable, found in Luke 13:6–9, that applied directly to His ministry to Israel. The owner of a fig tree had checked out its fruitfulness for three years in a row. He was greatly disappointed, for apparently the tree, not an immature one, was fit to bear fruit and did not. Why keep such a barren tree? Why allow it to waste ground that could be put to fruitful use, and even exhaust the ground by taking nourishment from it? The owner's vineyard keeper intervened, however, asking for one more year of personal attention, concluding by saying, "If it bears fruit, well. But if not, after that you can cut it down."

The fruitless fig tree represented Israel, which had been exposed to three years of Christ's ministry. The owner of the tree is the Father; Christ is the keeper of His vineyard. The extra year covers the remainder of Jesus' earthly ministry and His post-resurrection ministry. Israel as a nation did not respond, so the fruitless fig was finally finished.

5. Cursing the Fig Tree

A strange episode—an enacted parable—took place on one of the closing days of Jesus' public ministry, which bears directly on the destruction of the Temple. We read in Matthew 21:18–22 and Mark 11:12–14, 20–24 that Jesus cursed a fruitless fig tree and it withered away. The leafy tree had testified hypocritically to all passing by that there were figs to be had, but Jesus found none.

Cursing the tree seems cruel to some modern commentators, who call the action a "miracle of destruction." Jesus actually did no more than any concerned farmer would do. A farmer would chop the tree down; Jesus simply withdrew its life. The episode was intended as a living parable of the coming desolation of the Jewish Temple, which hypocritically flashed its golden plates in the sun but lacked true righteousness and holiness within.

After cursing the fig tree, Jesus entered the Temple and, finding it fruitless as well, purged it (probably with a handmade whip) to cleanse it of its trafficking. Jesus said to the tree, "Let no one eat fruit from you ever again." He said to the Jews, "Your house is left to you desolate."

Why curse the tree for being fruitless when, as Mark says, "it was not the season for figs"? Toward the end of March the leaves begin to appear and then cover the tree in about a week. At the same time, and sometimes before, quite a crop of small knobs appears—not the real figs, but a kind of forerunner. About the size of green almonds, these knobs are eaten by the local people when hungry. F. F. Bruce says, "These precursors of the true fig are called *taqsh* in Palestinian Arabic. Their appearance is a harbinger of the fully formed appearance of the true fig some six weeks later. So, as Mark says, the time for figs had not yet come. But if the leaves appear without any *taqsh,* that is a sign that there will be no figs. Since Jesus found 'nothing but leaves'—leaves without any *taqsh*—he knew that 'it was an absolutely hopeless, fruitless fig tree', and said as much."[33]

The same reasonable judgment was rendered on the Temple and religion of the Jews. Both Temple and fig tree had a beautiful outward show of life, but no fruit beneath the leaves.

6. Time of Visitation

We read in Luke 19:41–44 that as Jesus drew near to Jerusalem, He began to weep. "If you had known . . . the things that make for your peace! But now they are hidden from your eyes" (verse 42). He foretold how the Romans would first enclose the city, then devastate it and kill the people. All because "you did not know the time of your visitation" (verse 44). They missed the advent of their Messiah because they did not recognize Him for who He was. As a city and nation they rejected Him—to dire consequences.

7. The Torn Veil

When Jesus died on the cross, the heavy veil guarding the entrance into the most holy sanctuary was miraculously split in two by the power of God. This drastic action, told in Matthew 27:51, Mark 15:38 and Luke 23:45, showed that the old Levitical system was now superseded by a new covenant, and that the barrier between God and man was now destroyed. Hebrews 10:19–20 says we have "boldness to enter the Holiest by the blood of Jesus, by a new and living way which He consecrated for us, through the veil, that is, His flesh. . . ." Hebrews 6:19–20 says, "This hope we have as an anchor of the soul, both sure and steadfast, and which enters the Presence behind the veil, where the forerunner has entered for us, even Jesus."

8. The Fruit of Unbelief

In Romans 11 Paul taught that the Jews were like unfruitful branches on an olive tree that were broken off because of their unbelief in Jesus Christ. The Gentiles, in spite of their status as wild olive branches, were grafted into the tree of God because they did believe in Jesus Christ. This living, fruitful olive tree represents the true people of God in our day. Some of the branches are Jewish, some are wild Gentile graft-ins, but all have a common denominator: an active faith in Jesus Christ.

Paul prayed for his people's salvation (Romans 10:1) and emphasized that "they also, if they do not continue in unbelief, will be grafted in, for God is able to graft them in again" (Romans 11:23). Paul also mentioned that "hardening in part has happened to Israel until the fullness of the Gentiles has come in" (Romans 11:25).

God in His mercy works in every nation, and every individual in a given nation. He has a great love for natural Israel, but she now must come to God in faith through Jesus Christ, just as every other people must do. Thank God, many Jewish people are accepting Christ in our day, and when they do they are grafted into the great tree of God, becoming members of the Body of Christ. This trend is on the increase!

In the next chapter we will discuss the two great topics covered in the latter part of the Olivet Discourse: the destruction of Jerusalem and the glorious Second Coming of Christ.

SEVEN

JUDGMENT AND GLORY

Overwhelmed by Jesus' description of the coming nine "birth pangs," the disciples sat before their Master startled and wide-eyed. *What could come next?* Pausing for effect, Jesus began to answer in detail their concerns about Jerusalem and the end of the age.

The Beloved City Will Be Destroyed

This new section of the Olivet Discourse (found in Matthew 24:15–22; Mark 13:14–20; Luke 21:20–24) dramatically describes the destruction of Jerusalem and the Temple.

Here are the various synoptic opening words:

- Matthew 24:15–16: "Therefore when you see the 'abomination of desolation,' spoken of by Daniel the prophet, standing in the holy place" (whoever reads, let him understand), "then let those who are in Judea flee to the mountains."
- Mark 13:14: "When you see the 'abomination of desolation,' spoken of by Daniel the prophet, standing where it ought

not" (let the reader understand), "then let those who are in Judea flee to the mountains."

- Luke 21:20–21: "When you see Jerusalem surrounded by armies, then know that its desolation is near. Then let those in Judea flee."

Bible commentators do not question that this section refers to Jerusalem. But there is a striking difference of opinion on *when* that destruction will occur. Almost all the Hebrew prophets threatened judgment against Jerusalem (for example, Micah 3:12; Jeremiah 26:6, 18). Destroyed previously by the Babylonians, with the people carried away captive, the city repeated its rebellion against God. The ultimatum of doom was inevitable. It would be the visible manifestation of what Jesus had said earlier of their spiritual life: "Your house is left to you desolate" (Matthew 23:38). The unfruitful fig tree was cursed . . . and would die.

Jesus substantiated His prediction of the destruction of Jerusalem (mentioned in all three synoptics) by referring to the "abomination of desolation" mentioned by the prophet Daniel:

> "After the sixty-two weeks Messiah shall be cut off [Jesus crucified], but not for Himself [He died for us!]; and the people of the prince [Titus] who is to come shall destroy the city and the sanctuary. The end of it shall be with a flood, and till the end of the war desolations are determined.
>
> "Then he [consider that this is the Messiah, not the Antichrist] shall confirm a covenant with many for one week [that is, seven years]; but in the middle of the week [after three and a half years] he shall bring an end to sacrifice and offering [by His death on the cross].[1] And on the wing of abominations shall be one [Titus] who makes desolate, even until the consummation, which is determined, is poured out on the desolate."[2]
>
> Daniel 9:26–27

This "abomination of desolation" (or "the desolating sacrilege") appears three times in Daniel (9:26–27; 11:31; 12:11). The first place, the above reference, clearly refers to Jesus the Messiah, His crucifixion and the desolation that would follow. The second reference (and possibly the third as well) had already taken place before Jesus' day: "They shall defile the sanctuary fortress; then they shall take away the daily sacrifices, and place there the abomination of desolation" (11:31). This text is purely historical, referring to the defilement of the Temple under the reign of Antiochus Epiphanes in the second century B.C. At that time Jerusalem was conquered and the Jewish sacrifices ended. The Temple was defiled by the sacrifice of a swine on the altar and the setting up of a statue of Zeus in the Holy Place.

This seems an obvious meaning, yet some feel that Daniel 11:31 refers to the time of the last-days Tribulation. John F. MacArthur, for instance, says it "must have referred to a yet-future, greater reality than the blasphemy of Antiochus, which initially seemed to be its fulfillment. . . . Jesus' entire reply is an extended answer to the more important question about the signs of His coming and the end of the age."[3]

Fortunately Luke gave a straightforward explanation of the "abomination of desolation."[4] He did not use that expression mentioned in Matthew and Mark, but stated in terms understandable to the Gentile mind what Jesus actually meant: "When you see Jerusalem surrounded by armies, then know that its desolation is near" (Luke 21:20).[5] The Roman army did devastate the city and the Temple in A.D. 70. Their acts of atrocity, cruelty and idolatry were undoubtedly what constituted the abomination. R. C. Sproul comments:

> Whether the *abominable sacrilege* refers to actual idolatry, or to the entrance of Roman imperial-eagle standards into the temple area, is immaterial. It was common practice then, and for long centuries before, to assert sovereignty over a nation by dethroning its gods and replacing them by those of the conqueror.[6]

This was indeed a time of great distress. Josephus asserts that 1,100,000 perished in the siege of Jerusalem and 97,000 were carried away captive.[7] Some would say this is an exaggeration, which may be true, but it does indicate a grievous time. In his *Wars of the Jews* Josephus describes the burning of the Temple and slaughter of the people:

> While the holy house was on fire, everything was plundered that came to hand, and ten thousand of those that were caught were slain. . . . Children, and old men, and profane persons, and priests, were all slain in the same manner. . . . . The flame was also carried a long way, and made an echo, together with the groans of those that were slain; and because this hill was high, and the works at the temple were very great, one would have thought that the whole city had been on fire. Nor can one imagine anything either greater or more terrible than this noise . . . a shout of the Roman legions, who were marching all together, and a sad clamour of the seditious who were now surrounded with fire and sword.[8]

Jesus had foretold such devastation to the Temple that not one stone would be left standing on another. It came literally to pass. The Roman soldiers dismantled the burned-out structure, prying apart the great stones as they frantically sought any gold that had melted into the cracks during the conflagration.

"There will be great tribulation," says Matthew 24:21, "such as has not been since the beginning of the world until this time, no, nor ever shall be." Luke states it realistically and graphically: "There will be great distress in the land and wrath upon this people" (21:23). This was a tribulation unique in history, with a divine objective never to be repeated.[9] This tribulation was directed to a nation—known for its racial, religious, national identity—with a divine objective clear to all.

I see no compelling reason to consider the passages in Daniel as referring to the great Tribulation of the last days, particularly since the synoptic context so clearly refers to the Jewish population at the time of the destruction of Jerusalem. Some suggest that "the destruction of Jerusalem, described in Luke 21, is a type of the Great Tribulation detailed in Matthew 24."[10]

The three uses of the word *tribulation* (Greek, *thlipsis*) in Matthew 24 speak of three times of occurrence:

- *Tribulation* is used of both the immediate future and the overall Church age (24:9).
- *Tribulation* describes the time of Jerusalem's devastation (24:21).

- *Tribulation* describes the time just prior to the Second Coming (24:29).

Luke 21 could illustrate a coming "last days" Tribulation, but it seems unnecessary to make his text—so clearly a parallel passage—refer to something very different from Matthew's account. While Matthew wrote for a Jewish audience, Luke obviously wrote for a Gentile audience (which is why most of us understand his statement more clearly).

In any event, what had seemed impossible to the disciples came literally, tragically, to pass.[11]

Awesome Happenings in the Last Days

The disciples had asked for "signs," discernible evidence that the end was at hand and that His return was imminent. Having finished His discussion on the destruction of the city, Jesus turned His attention to the end times. First He described the tragic religious deception that would pervade society; then He told of awesome cosmic signs in heaven and earth.

False Christs, False Prophets

This short block of thought, mentioned only by Matthew and Mark, warns of false Christs and false prophets whose diabolical mission will be to lead astray, especially to deceive about Christ's coming (Matthew 24:23–28; Mark 13:21–23). This type of deception will characterize the entire time of the Church's witness and presence in the earth. Wilbur Smith's comment is of particular interest:

> A false christ is different from a false prophet. And Christ predicted both of them. A false christ does not simply preach and teach and proclaim what is contrary to the revealed Word of God, but he actually sets himself up as the Messiah. There had been many of these, especially in Israel, from the days of Bar Cochba down to the 19th Century. I have a book in my library written by a Jewish

Rabbi on the 16 false messiahs. This is very, very significant. *Israel never had a false messiah until she crucified her first true Messiah.*[12]

(emphasis added)

The section describing false Christs is placed *after* the destruction of Jerusalem, yet it coincides with the opening birth pang (Matthew 24:4–5). Could this confirm the ongoing nature of the nine events that will persist to the end of the age?

Christ's coming, in this context, will be like a bolt of lightning that no one can miss (Matthew 24:27). Jesus declared that there will be nothing secretive about His return requiring the interpretation of some religious leader. This is verified by the reference in Matthew 24:28 to vultures (NIV) (*eagles*, NKJV)[13] gathering over a carcass.

But this prediction has been given an assortment of astonishing interpretations:

- The body is that of Christ, and the vultures His enemies (Moffatt).
- God's children gather to feed on Christ (Calvin and others).
- The eagles allude to the Roman military eagles on the standards carried by the army that swarmed over corrupt Jerusalem (Kik).
- The carcass is Israel, and the eagles Rome (Russell).
- The swiftness of the coming of the Son of Man is emphasized by the sudden appearance of vultures when the carrion appears (Manson).
- It will be as impossible for humanity not to see the coming of the Son of Man as it is for vultures to miss seeing carrion (Klostermann).

My conclusion, after realizing that the vulture illustration is one of fourteen illustrations all saying the same thing (#41–54 in "The Gospel Record," p. 60), is this: Jesus was emphasizing that His coming would happen quickly and be evident to all, just as we know an animal has died by the sudden arrival of circling vultures.[14]

Cosmic Signs in Heaven and Earth

Matthew 24:29–31 provides further teaching on the coming of the Son of Man (supplemented by Mark 13:24–27 and Luke 21:25–28). Jesus makes an astounding prediction of cosmic signs, then proceeds to offer a brief but most complete statement on His Second Coming. Luke's account also proceeds directly to the cosmic signs in heaven and on earth, emphasizing that the signs "spell panic for the rest of mankind, [but] they are the signal for the disciples to take fresh heart, for the coming of the Son of man will bring them redemption."[15]

> "Immediately after the tribulation of those days [*In those days, after that tribulation,* Mark 13:24] the sun will be darkened, and the moon will not give its light; the stars will fall from heaven [*the sky,* NASB], and the powers of the heavens will be shaken. [Luke 21:25–26 adds, *There will be . . . on the earth distress of nations, with perplexity, the sea and the waves roaring; men's hearts failing them from fear and the expectation of those things which are coming on the earth.*] Then the sign of the Son of Man will appear in heaven, and then all the tribes of the earth will mourn, and they will see the Son of Man coming on [*in,* Mark 13:26] the clouds [*in a cloud,* Luke 21:27] of heaven with [*great,* Mark 13:26] power and great glory. And He will send His angels with a great sound of a trumpet, and they will gather together His elect from the four winds, from one end of heaven to the other" [*from the farthest part of earth to the farthest part of heaven,* Mark 13:27]. [Luke 21:28 adds, *Now when these things begin to happen, look up and lift up your heads, because your redemption draws near.*]
>
> Matthew 24:29–31

Matthew records that unusual signs in sun, moon and stars are to happen "immediately" after the "tribulation" of those days. Mark tempers the statement to say, "In those days, after that tribulation," and Luke says simply, "There will be signs."

This is the third time *tribulation* appears in Matthew's account, with a specific time associated with each occurrence. As it appears here, *immediately after* best suggests Tribulation at the conclusion of the Church age, just before Christ's coming. There is an obvious close to the paragraph dealing with the tribulation associated with Jerusalem's destruction (Matthew 24:22; Mark 13:20; Luke 21:24), followed by a short paragraph focusing on false Christs and false prophets.

Although the discourse is printed for us like a continuous, non-stop lecture, there probably were pauses and breaks in Jesus' presentation. Possibly the Lord paused at this point in His presentation, thereby adding to His disassociation of this mention of tribulation from the tribulation at the time of Jerusalem's destruction.

Sun, moon and stars. "The sun will be darkened, and the moon will not give its light; the stars will fall from heaven [*the sky*, NASB], and the powers of the heavens will be shaken" (Matthew 24:29). Earth's light sources will be violently affected. These events will demand and hold the frightened attention of the whole world. Considered symbolic by some, the signs mentioned by Jesus are best explained as literal, violent, earth-shaking happenings, beyond anything the present inhabitants of earth can imagine.[16] More discussion on this in chapter 12, "The Book of Revelation: The Final Triumph."

Imagine yourself seated among this informal group. Jesus is speaking directly to you, even looking into your eyes. He answers your questions in a careful yet fervent way. In this intimate setting Jesus explains the future as clearly as possible, not speaking in mysterious symbols. In such a setting why should He use imagery in His teaching?

As Moses was very clear when addressing Pharaoh about the ten awesome plagues, Jesus spoke clearly and directly to His disciples about Jerusalem's destruction and His own glorious return. Doesn't that suggest that we be careful not to brand Jesus' statements as symbolic imagery simply because we cannot imagine their literal fulfillment? These cosmic signs are yet future, and can be expected as a literal part of the last days before Jesus' glorious return on clouds with angels.

Most commentators agree that these astronomical signs have not yet happened—at least, nothing that has become common knowledge[17]—so their fulfillment must be future both to the time of Jerusalem's devastation and to the present time. The celestial signs and the coming of the Son of Man will not immediately follow "the abomination of desolation," but rather will follow the "distress of nations" (Luke 21:25), the Tribulation of the last days and all the tribulation that has preceded that time.

Distress on the earth. "And on the earth distress of nations, with perplexity, the sea and the waves roaring; men's hearts failing them from fear and the expectation of those things which are coming on the earth, for the powers of the heavens will be shaken" (Luke 21:25–26). Appearing only in Luke's account, these two verses clearly lift this portion of the discourse out of a localized Palestinian activity (the destruction of Jerusalem) to a global involvement of terrifying proportions. Jesus' description sounds like something from a scientific discussion on astral catastrophe.

While considering this text, I happened to view a TV documentary called "Three Minutes to Impact." Concerned scientists discussed the not-so-remote possibility that a large asteroid, such as the mountain in Australia called Ayer's Rock, one and a half miles in diameter,[18] could fall from the sky on the city of New York. It would be an extinction-level event—truly catastrophic. The massive skyscrapers—in fact, the whole city—would be instantly obliterated as the giant rock crashed into the ground, exploding the upper layers of the earth's crust. Blazing rocks would also fall like meteors on Washington, D.C., and even more distant cities like Chicago. Impact-generated waves of terrifying, mountainous proportions would race toward coastal cities along the Eastern seaboard and across the Atlantic. Global fires, floods, volcanic eruptions, earthquakes—all this to be capped by an ominous darkening atmosphere sealing off the light of sun, moon and stars. It would be the end of life as we know it. And experts say this is scientifically tenable.

The sign of the Son of Man. "Then the sign of the Son of Man will appear in heaven [*the sky,* NASB]" (Matthew 24:30). Various explanations have been offered concerning this sign, such as the moon turned to blood or the sign of the cross in the heavens. A literal, word-for-word translation from the Greek would be: "And then will appear the sign of *the Son of Man in heaven. . .*" (emphasis added).

But the appearance of *the Son of Man Himself in heaven* is the sign! Substitute *which is* for *of,* and the meaning becomes clear: "And then will appear the sign, *which is* the Son of Man in heaven."

All tribes will mourn. "All the tribes of the earth will mourn" (Matthew 24:30). When Jesus returns He will be visible to all the inhabitants of planet earth.[19] John declared: "He is coming with clouds, and every eye will see Him, even they who pierced Him. And *all the tribes of the earth will mourn* because of Him. Even so, Amen" (Revelation 1:7, emphasis added).

Coming with clouds. "They will see the Son of Man coming on the clouds of heaven [*in the clouds,* Mark 13:26; *in a cloud,* Luke 21:27]" (Matthew 24:30). Put all the thoughts together: He is coming in, on and with the clouds of heaven. We need not be concerned about which preposition is best; as Beasley-Murray points out, variations are "certainly due to stylistic considerations."[20] (Other references include Matthew 26:64; Mark 14:62; 1 Thessalonians 4:17.)

Clouds in the Bible represent the divine glory and presence of the Lord:

- Israel was led by a pillar of cloud (Exodus 13:21–22).
- When Moses' Tabernacle was dedicated, "the cloud covered the tabernacle of meeting, and the glory of the LORD filled the tabernacle" (Exodus 40:34).
- The glory of the Lord appeared in the cloud (Exodus 16:10).
- God told Moses, "I will appear in the cloud above the mercy seat" (Leviticus 16:2).
- At the dedication of Solomon's Temple, "the priests could not continue ministering because of the cloud; for the glory of the LORD filled the house of God" (2 Chronicles 5:14).
- On the Mount of Transfiguration "a bright cloud overshadowed them; and suddenly a voice came out of the cloud, saying, 'This is My beloved Son, in whom I am well pleased. Hear Him!'" (Matthew 17:5).
- Jesus was taken up in a cloud, and the heavenly messengers said He would return in like manner (Acts 1:9–11).
- Jesus will come again in clouds of glory (Mark 13:26; 14:62).
- John saw "another mighty angel (possibly the Lord Jesus?) coming down from heaven, clothed with a cloud. And a rain-

bow was on his head, his face was like the sun, and his feet like pillars of fire" (Revelation 10:1).

- Jesus is seen seated on a white cloud: "I looked, and behold, a white cloud, and on the cloud sat One like the Son of Man, having on His head a golden crown, and in His hand a sharp sickle" (Revelation 14:14).
- The saints themselves are called "a cloud of witnesses" (Hebrews 12:1).

Clouds also represent the Lord coming to deliver His people and judge His enemies (Isaiah 19:1; Nahum 1:3). Literal clouds will be associated with Jesus' coming, but an awesome, special presence of God will transform this natural phenomenon into a spectacular display of divine holiness. While His people rejoice in His appearing, the people of earth "are pictured as in terror and confusion before the overwhelming might of the Lord of Hosts when he steps forth into the world to act in judgment and salvation."[21] Those clouds will be a sight to behold—majestic, mighty, terrifying.

With great power and great glory. "They will see the Son of Man coming . . . with power and great glory" (Matthew 24:30; Luke 21:27), or, "with great power and glory" (Mark 13:26). See the discussion of glory in chapter 5 in the section "On the Road to Jerusalem."

The sending and gathering. "He will send His angels . . . and they will gather together His elect from the four winds, from one end of heaven to the other" (Matthew 24:31). ". . . From the farthest part of earth to the farthest part of heaven" (Mark 13:27). Jesus will come with all His holy angels (Matthew 16:27; 25:31; Mark 8:38; Luke 9:26). Recall our discussion about angels in the section in chapter 5 entitled "Bethany Beyond the Jordan."

The angels are sent forth with the great trumpet call described below. They go to the farthest reaches of earth and heaven to gather the elect. Resurrection life will unite the spirits and glorified bodies of those who died in Christ. The angels will sweep those revived saints, along with the living, transformed saints, up to meet the Lord in the air.

An intriguing thought by Johnston M. Cheney on this verse opens new possibilities: "Could this regathering 'from one end of the heavens to the other' refer to man's invading space? If so, the supernatural character of this One [i.e., Jesus] is again emphasized [i.e., the fulfillment of His prophecy], for such a possibility was scientific foolishness until the present generation."[22] Can you imagine a believer in Christ who has died and is buried on the moon (or beyond) responding to the resurrection call of Christ and then being ushered into Christ's presence by angels?

Jesus told a parable in His third discourse in Matthew about the mystery of the Kingdom, which grabbed the interest of His disciples. After the multitude had been sent away and the Twelve had entered a house, they asked Him excitedly to interpret the parable of the wheat and tares. As the story goes, a farmer had sowed good seed in his field, but an enemy had come by night and sowed tares. As the crop matured, the tares became apparent. But the farmer allowed both to grow together until the harvest, at which time the reapers would gather the wheat for storage and the tares for burning. The puzzled disciples asked for the interpretation.

Jesus said this pictured "the end of the age" (Matthew 13:39): "The Son of Man will send out His angels, and they will gather out of His kingdom all things that offend, and those who practice lawlessness. . . . The angels will come forth, separate the wicked from among the just, and cast them into the furnace of fire" (Matthew 13:41, 49–50). How this will happen we do not know, but it will apparently be part of the Second Coming.

With a great trumpet. "He will send His angels with a great sound of a trumpet" (Matthew 24:31). A miraculous trumpet call summoned Israel to receive the Ten Commandments. God had the people consecrate themselves to prepare for meeting with Him. "When the trumpet [sounded] long" (Exodus 19:13), they were to approach the mountain. On the third day "there were thunderings and lightnings, and a thick cloud on the mountain" (verse 16). The entire mountain shook violently, as the Lord descended upon it in fire. "The sound of the trumpet was very loud, so that all the people who were in the camp trembled" (verse 16).

Of all instruments, the trumpet has the most piercing sound and the longest range; this is why it is used to describe the sound from heaven. Exodus 20:18 specifies the trumpet as one of the miraculous phenomena of that day. Apparently its call was not the sounding of a ram's horn or a musical instrument made by man. The piercing sound was of divine origin! This is borne out by the fearful trembling of the people when they heard the trumpet call become "louder and louder" (verse 19).

Later God instructed Moses to make two silver trumpets. These were used for summoning the congregation, signaling the camps to move, summoning the leaders, sounding an alarm, going to war and offering burnt offerings and peace offerings (Numbers 10:1–10). Also, Israel had a special day each year called "a memorial of blowing of trumpets" (Leviticus 23:24). Trumpets have always been part of God's program.

When Israel marched around the walls of Jericho, seven priests carried seven trumpets of rams' horns before the Ark. On the seventh day they marched around the walls seven times, after which the priests sounded a long blast on their horns. This was the signal for the people to shout. And the walls came tumbling down (Joshua 6:4–5, 15–16)!

Christ will also descend from heaven with a shout and with a trumpet sound (1 Thessalonians 4:16)!

Only once did Jesus mention the sounding of a trumpet at His coming, and that is in our immediate text. The apostle Paul mentions a trumpet twice. First: "We shall all be changed—in a moment, in the twinkling of an eye, at the last trumpet. For the trumpet will sound, and the dead will be raised incorruptible, and we shall be changed" (1 Corinthians 15:51–52). Paul's second reference: "The Lord Himself will descend from heaven with a shout, with the voice of an archangel, and with the trumpet of God. And the dead in Christ shall rise first" (1 Thessalonians 4:16).

"The last trumpet" mentioned above could possibly refer to Revelation 10:7: "In the days of the sounding of the seventh angel [the last to sound], when he is about to sound, the mystery of God would be finished, as He declared to His servants the prophets." Or "the last trumpet" could refer to Revelation 11:15: "Then the seventh angel sounded: And there were loud voices in heaven, saying, 'The kingdoms of this world have become the kingdoms of our Lord and of His Christ, and He shall reign forever and ever!'"

John records in Revelation 1:10 that he heard "a loud voice, as of a trumpet." Turning he beheld the Son of Man. Later John heard the voice of the Lord again "like a trumpet speaking with me, saying, 'Come up here. . . .' Immediately I was in the Spirit" (Revelation 4:1–2).

A trumpet summoned the people of Israel to Mount Sinai, and the divine trumpet will summon the Church to meet Christ in the air.

The Secret Time of His Glorious Return

Matthew 24:34, 36 records two important statements by Jesus. In them He encapsulates the essence of His two main answers in the discourse:

- The *specific* signs and time of Jerusalem's destruction (within the disciples' lifetimes)
- The *unspecified* time of Christ's return and the end of the age (in the indefinite future)

We saw in chapter 5 (when we discussed the controversial verse 34) that the generation (Greek, *genea*[23]) alive at the time of Jesus' discourse would see all the nine sign events and the destruction of Jerusalem: ". . . This generation will by no means pass away till all these things take place." *All these things* refers to the happenings before the city's destruction. Approximately forty years remained between the time Jesus spoke those words and the time that the Romans under the crown prince Titus actually destroyed the Temple.

Each synoptic's description of the city's destruction stands in stark contrast to Mark's description of "the Son of Man coming in the clouds with great power and glory" (13:26). This is surely more than just a "highly figurative description of the divine judgment . . . enacted in the Roman siege and destruction of Jerusalem."[24] Why spiritualize the glorious Second Coming? Such an approach only neutralizes Jesus' dynamic intent. Strict preterists like J. Stuart Russell stress that the two events (the city's destruction and Second Coming) are merely different aspects of the same great event.[25] Russell does give cogent arguments for the city's destruction as a fulfillment of Jesus' words, but I do not find his assumption that the glorious coming of Christ finds fulfillment in that sad event a reasonable or credible explanation—or, more importantly, one that is in accord with the more than four hundred New Testament references on the Second Coming. I agree with I. Howard Marshall that "the two sets of events are chronologically separate."[26]

Matthew 24:36 and Mark 13:32 leave the timing of Jesus' *parousia* unspecified. No one can tell the exact time of His coming:

- "Of that day and hour no one knows" (Matthew 24:36).
- "You do not know what hour your Lord is coming" (24:42).
- "For the Son of Man is coming at an hour you do not expect Him" (24:44).
- "The master of that servant will come on a day when he is not looking for him and at an hour that he is not aware of" (24:50).
- "You know neither the day nor the hour in which the Son of Man is coming" (25:13).

The signs of Jerusalem's destruction, Jesus explained, would be like the budding of a fig tree as summer approached. These descriptions (Matthew 24:15–28; Mark 13:14–23; Luke 21:20–24) literally did come to pass within a generation's time.

Jesus explained the *unspecified* time of His Second Coming, in contrast, by using the story of Noah. He illustrated its unexpectedness and suddenness by describing two workmen in the field and two women grinding on their handmills. One of the men and one of the women were judged ("taken away" like the people in Noah's time) and the other two were "left" (remaining secure and acceptable to the Lord).

Only Luke includes Jesus' strong exhortation for us not to be careless and unconcerned about spiritual things, for *every* inhabitant of earth will experience judgment:

> "Take heed to yourselves, lest your hearts be weighed down with carousing, drunkenness, and cares of this life, and that Day come on you unexpectedly. For it will come as a snare on all those who dwell on the face of the whole earth. Watch therefore, and pray always that you may be counted worthy to escape all these things that will come to pass, and to stand before the Son of Man."
>
> Luke 21:34–36

Let us guard ourselves, stay alert and be fervent in prayer.

A Modern-Day Parable

Jesus closed His Olivet Discourse with five challenging parables about spiritual watchfulness (which we looked at, among others, in chapter 4). He gave more attention to vigilance than to the description of His *parousia*. We Christians are not to sleep spiritually like the worldly people who will be caught in a snare of judgment. ". . . 'Watch' means *to be spiritually awake* in contrast to the world which is slumbering in the sleep of sin."[27]

This watchfulness equates with Isaiah's use of the word *wait*: "Those who wait on the LORD shall renew their strength; they shall mount up with wings like eagles, they shall run and not be weary, they shall walk and not faint" (Isaiah 40:31). John E. Hartley, in the *Theological Wordbook of the Old Testament,* explains the Hebrew meaning of the word *watch*:

> The root means to wait or to look for with eager expectation. . . . Waiting with steadfast endurance is a great expression of faith. It means enduring patiently in confident hope that God will decisively act for the salvation of his people. . . . Those who wait in true faith are renewed in strength so that they can continue to serve the Lord while looking for his saving work.[28]

I have discovered in my preaching that modern people do not always relate well to the parables of Jesus. Most of us, especially Westerners, relate better to space exploration, electronics or contemporary living. The ancient stories have meaning but not relevancy, because they are not where most of us live. Let me construct a modern parable, then, adapting Jesus' principles, in order to illustrate His exhortation about watchfulness.

A man borrows a million dollars to acquire a McDonald's hamburger franchise. These are not easy to get, but they usually bring a high financial yield for the investment. The new owner is proud of his acquisition and works hard to make the franchise produce. Long hours, hard work and diligence begin to pay off. After a year, with things running well, he decides to branch out into other business interests. One of his biggest concerns is his replacement as manager of the local operation.

Finally he thinks he has found the right person. The prospective manager is put through a grueling course of management study and on-the-job training. The young man learns what the franchise owner and company expect of him. He knows that to fail either would be a disaster. His deportment in managing the store is excellent. As the new manager he will do well.

Now the owner takes an extended leave of absence. This he can now do, for his manager is well qualified and has demonstrated remarkable ability. There will be phone calls and progress reports, of course, since the owner will be away for some months, pursuing other business interests, but he has confidence in his new manager. The operation must remain in prime condition and continue to return a good profit. They part in mutual satisfaction.

From what the owner can tell, the young manager does well. His diligence and hard work seem to be paying off. The phone calls seem encouraging and the written reports indicate business is holding steady. What the owner does not realize, however, is that the manager is getting physically tired and emotionally drained. The constant strain of supplying workers who can do the job for minimal pay is beginning to get to him. It is a profitable but relentless business.

One mid-morning four or five months later, the owner returns to town, drives to the restaurant and parks. His eyes take in the clutter around the building, the scraggly landscaping and broken-down children's equipment in the play area. The newest advertising banners from the company are not posted in the windows; in fact, promotions several months old are still on display. He pushes open the door, only to find it blocked by a bucket and mop. Napkins and wrappers litter the floor. Where is the manager? When he orders a Big Mac, the young worker behind the counter mutters, without meeting his eyes, that they are out of Big Macs. The order-takers are unfriendly and disheveled; some are in partial uniform.

The owner sits down in the cleanest booth he can find and prepares to sample his substitute order. In what condition will he find the kitchen and restrooms? As he observes the scene before him—and samples his cold burger—a car drives up and parks in a convenient customer spot. The replacement manager, carrying his tie and his hair askew, ambles into the establishment and yells at some of the help. They yell back. Then he spots the owner in the nearby booth. His face blanches as burning eyes pierce into his own.

What has happened to his attitude?

At first he operated the business as though the owner were still in town, but after three or four months, with no sign of his return, his vigilance began to slip. *Why should I work so hard,* he groused, *when that guy is just collecting the benefits of my labor?* So he began to sleep late, arrive at the restaurant late and allow his attitude to grow lax. Soon the entire operation showed signs of deterioration.

But now the day of reckoning had arrived. He would never find out that the owner carried a new contract in his pocket for him to manage two stores. Even the present job would be taken from him. The young man had forfeited a promising career through negligence.

Note Luke 12:42–46 (MESSAGE):

> The Master said, "Let me ask you: Who is the dependable manager, full of common sense, that the master puts in charge of his staff to feed them well and on time? He is a blessed man if when the master shows up he's doing his job. But if he says to him-

> self, 'The master is certainly taking his time,' begins maltreating the servants and maids, throws parties for his friends, and gets drunk, the master will walk in when he least expects it, give him the thrashing of his life, and put him back in the kitchen peeling potatoes."

If you are like me, you have been discouraged by your inability to keep the Second Coming of Christ constantly in mind. Even in your best moments you do not remember specifically that He is coming back. In the light of Jesus' strong statements connected with the parables of the Olivet Discourse, you might even start feeling condemnation.

My discovery is this, based on the closing five parables: It is not so much that you continually remind yourself of Christ's appearance, as that you are faithful for the task at hand. You simply know He will come soon, and you diligently pursue the will of God and your personal assignment. Then, when He comes, you are ready. For although you have not been thinking constantly about His return, you have done those things that the Master required. He will not ask if you thought constantly of His coming; He will simply require an accounting of your assignment.

May hope make you responsible and patiently vigilant in your duties!

The amazing climax of the discourse is a sixteen-verse statement concerning the judgment that will occur when the Son of Man comes. The Lord Jesus Christ will sit on His glorious throne and separate the nations before Him as a shepherd separates the sheep from the goats. The sheep will be those who have recognized Jesus in the hungry, the thirsty, the stranger, the naked, the sick and the imprisoned.

Jesus will say to these spiritually sensitive and compassionate ones: "Assuredly, I say to you, inasmuch as you did it to one of the least of these My brethren, you did it to Me" (Matthew 25:40).

Then, to the "goats" who showed no compassion, the King will utter this scathing denunciation: "Depart from Me, you cursed, into the everlasting fire prepared for the devil and his angels" (verse 41).

Waiting Forwardly

A fascinating story is told in Luke 2. An elderly, godly man named Simeon, who lived in Jerusalem, waited for "the Consolation of Israel" (verse 25). The Holy Spirit had revealed to him that he would not die until "he had seen the Lord's Christ" (verse 26). This prompted a remarkable sharpening of his perception of people. He did not know what the Christ would look like. Would he be tall, short, dark, bearded? The NLT says Simeon was "constantly expecting the Messiah" (verse 25). His life became a search for a person about whom he had no clue!

The NKJV says that Simeon waited, but there is a deeper meaning. This word has a basic meaning of "look." Max Lucado shares this insight:

> Of all the forms of *look*, the one which best captures what it means to "look for the coming" is the term used to describe the action of Simeon: *prosdechomai. Dechomai* meaning "to wait." *Pros* meaning "forward." Combine them and you have the graphic picture of one "waiting forwardly." The grammar is poor, but the image is great. Simeon was waiting; not demanding, not hurrying, he was waiting.[29]

One day the Spirit prompted Simeon to go to the Temple. There he came on Joseph and Mary holding the month-old Jesus. Simeon's life of expectation and faithfulness now found glorious fulfillment. He who had waited forwardly for so long now looked directly upon His Messiah!

I know a little of his feeling. Because I am a traveling minister, I frequently arrive in airports without knowing who will pick me up. I never worry about it; I know someone will be there and that I will recognize him or her. A sign, a puzzled look—I will know. But I must watch with expectancy.

The next chapter will present eleven thoughts about the Second Coming mentioned in the book of Acts. Luke's record of the early Church shows that Christ's return was a dynamic part of their belief system. In fact, the very first reference in Acts (given in the first chapter) is one of the most challenging and often-quoted verses on the subject.

EIGHT

WHAT ACTS SAYS ABOUT THE SECOND COMING

One of the most important books in the New Testament, the Acts of the Apostles, gives us historical material about the early Church found nowhere else in the New Testament. We see the Church in her glorious beginnings. Did that Church believe in Christ's return?

The following eleven concepts found in the Acts record are some of the strongest statements to be found on the subject. Clearly it was an apostolic doctrine. In only sixteen verses we find eleven fascinating ideas.

The Acts Record
Everything Luke Wanted the Church to Know About Jesus' Glorious Return

1. **Jesus Christ is coming again in the same manner in which He left**	Acts 1:11
2.—the same Jesus raised from the dead,	Acts 1:11
3.—in the same physical body.	Acts 1:11
4. **This will be the coming of the great and notable day of the Lord,**	Acts 2:20

5. preceded by a darkened sun and a moon turned into blood. — Acts 2:20
6. **Presently Jesus must remain in heaven until all things are fulfilled,** — Acts 3:20–21
7. and God makes Christ's enemies His footstool. — Acts 2:35
8. **His coming will climax refreshment and restoration, and initiate the regeneration.** — Acts3:20–21
9. **Jesus will return as the Judge of the living and the dead.** — Acts 10:42; 17:31; 24:25
10. **The resurrection of the dead is the hope of God's people, and this will happen at His return.** — Acts 23:6; 24:15, 21; 26:6–8; 28:20
11. **We must, through many tribulations, enter the Kingdom of God.** — Acts 14:22

Coming Again in the Same Manner

> When He had spoken these things, while they watched, He was taken up, and a cloud received Him out of their sight. And while they looked steadfastly toward heaven as He went up, behold, two men stood by them in white apparel, who also said, "Men of Galilee, why do you stand gazing up into heaven? This same Jesus, who was taken up from you into heaven, *will so come in like manner* as you saw Him go into heaven."
>
> Acts 1:9–11 (emphasis added)

What a spectacular sight! Having given farewell remarks to the disciples, Jesus lifted pierced hands to bless them (Luke 24:50) . . . and His body began to rise from the earth!

Unfortunately their last moments with Christ were marred by their misguided Jewish hopes. They still looked for a temporal, visible kingdom: "Lord, will You at this time restore the kingdom to Israel?" (Acts 1:6). Jesus brushed aside their question and instead gave them a mission statement: "You shall receive power when the Holy Spirit has come upon you; and you shall be witnesses to Me in Jerusalem, and in all Judea and Samaria, and to the end of the earth" (verse 8).

Fulfilling this mission to the uttermost parts of the earth would *precede* His glorious visible return. As G. Campbell Morgan said, "He gathered the whole earth into His declaration of purpose."[1]

Parting words now finished, lift-off began. Luke recorded that He was "carried up" (Luke 24:51) as though drawn by heavenly magnetism. A cloud of divine glory[2] enveloped the rising figure, and then, like the fiery chariot of Elijah, bore Him beyond mortal sight, ushering Him triumphantly into the very presence of the Ancient of Days.

Earlier Daniel the prophet describes this scene in a prophetic vision:

> "I was watching in the night visions, and behold, One like the Son of Man, coming with the clouds of heaven! He came to the Ancient of Days, and they brought Him near before Him. Then to Him was given dominion and glory and a kingdom, that all peoples, nations, and languages should serve Him. His dominion is an everlasting dominion, which shall not pass away, and His kingdom the one which shall not be destroyed."[3]
>
> Daniel 7:13–14

Earthly ministry completed, Jesus made bold entrance to heaven, where He assumed the throne of David. It was at this point that the messianic Kingdom of God was inaugurated in spiritual power. Jesus' enthronement was not to wait for His future return to earth. Mark says, "After the Lord had spoken to them, He was received up into heaven, and sat down at the right hand of God" (Mark 16:19). Paul explains that God "raised Him from the dead and seated Him at His right hand in the heavenly places. . . . And He put all things under His feet, and gave Him to be head over all things to the church" (Ephesians 1:20–22; see also Colossians 3:1).

Meanwhile the disciples gazed upward in mute astonishment,[4] transfixed by the amazing sight of their rabbi soaring unassisted into the sky. As the Son of God vanished from view, two men attired in white suddenly appeared.[5] These heavenly messengers gave *the* definitive statement about Christ's return: He "will so come in like manner as you saw Him go into heaven" (Acts 1:11). *In like manner* means literally "the same idea twice" and, according to Robertson, indicates an emphatic repetition.[6] That is, *the fact and manner of the Second Coming are described by what the disciples had just seen*. The meaning here is that Jesus will return in a real, visible, bodily form. To interpret His return as spiritual or mystical would be a radical and violent departure from Scripture's clear meaning.

In like manner refers to several points:

- Jesus went up as a person, not a spirit; He will return as the same Person the disciples knew.
- He ascended in His physical, resurrected body; He will return in that same body.
- He went up in clouds; He will descend in clouds.
- He went up to heaven unopposed; He will return as King of kings and Lord of lords.
- He rose upward in defiance of gravity; He will come back unassisted by gravity.
- His departure was accompanied by the appearance of heavenly messengers; He will return with saints and angels.
- He left making a statement of great authority; He will return with a declaration!
- The disciples looked when He was taken up; the Church will be looking when He returns.

There will also be some differences:

- Only His followers viewed His ascension; all mankind will see His return.
- He departed alone, with little visual splendor; He will return with greatest glory and power with His angels.
- The departing Jesus gave a charge; the returning Jesus will demand an accounting.

- He ascended without public fanfare; His return will cause the greatest terror among the ungodly and the greatest joy among His own.

The Great Day of the Lord

Seventeen variations of the term *day* are used in the New Testament to describe that time when Christ comes and brings judgment to the world and reckoning to His people. The following expressions refer to the actual event itself and to associated happenings immediately before and after. This includes the thousand-year millennial period of messianic reign on the earth. As Peter says in an unusual confirmation: "With the Lord one day is as a thousand years, and a thousand years as one day" (2 Peter 3:8; see also Psalm 90:4). His quote indicates that "one day equals a thousand years" was a concept common in Jewish thinking.

Peter's quotation of part of Joel's famous prophecy (Acts 2:17–18) relates the outpouring of God's Spirit to the Day of Pentecost. Verses 19–20 refer to the Second Coming and to the physical signs that introduce that coming:

> "I will show wonders in heaven above and signs in the earth beneath: blood and fire and vapor of smoke. The sun shall be turned into darkness, and the moon into blood, before the coming of *the great and notable day of the Lord*."
>
> (emphasis added)

This reference to signs in the sun and moon corresponds to Jesus' statement in the Olivet Discourse (Matthew 24:29; Mark 13:24; Luke 21:25) and John's description in Revelation 6:12. These unusual celestial happenings are precursors of Christ's coming, heralds of the Day of the Lord.

The following seventeen "day" statements (of which just two are from Acts) all refer to the same time at the end, but each makes a specific emphasis, such as judgment and wrath, rewards, fellowship, resurrection, redemption, visitation or completion. From time to time God has chosen to intervene in history to judge godless peoples and vindicate His name. The following expressions refer to God's final act in human history—that great day when He brings the righteous to their reward, and those who have rejected Him to judgment.[7] A new era is introduced—that of the Kingdom of God in unrestrained glory, splendor and power.

1. **"The day of the Lord":** 1 Thessalonians 5:2; 2 Thessalonians 2:2; 2 Peter 3:10. Acts 2:20: *"The sun shall be turned into darkness, and the moon into blood, before the coming of the great and notable day of the Lord."*
2. **"The day":** Matthew 25:13; Luke 17:30; Romans 2:16; 13:12; 1 Corinthians 1:8; 3:13; 1 Thessalonians 5:5, 8; Hebrews 10:25. (Note "this Day," 1 Thessalonians 5:4.) Romans 2:16: . . . *In the day when God will judge the secrets of men by Jesus Christ, according to my gospel.*
3. **"That day":** Matthew 7:22; 24:36; Mark 13:32; Luke 21:34; 2 Thessalonians 2:3; 2 Timothy 4:8. Luke 21:34: *"Take heed . . . lest . . . that Day come on you unexpectedly."*
4. **"In that day":** Matthew 7:22; Luke 10:12; 2 Timothy 1:18. 2 Thessalonians 1:10: *When He comes, in that Day, to be glorified in His saints. . . .*
5. **"On that day":** 2 Timothy 4:8: . . . *The crown of righteousness, which the Lord, the righteous Judge, will give to me on that Day, and not to me only but also to all who have loved His appearing.*
6. **"Until that day":** Mark 14:25; 2 Timothy 1:12. Matthew 26:29: *". . . Until that day when I drink it new with you in My Father's kingdom."*
7. **"Last day":** John 11:24; 12:48. John 6:39–40, 44, 54: *". . . I will raise him up at the last day."*
8. **"The day of our Lord Jesus Christ":** 1 Corinthians 1:8: . . . *That you may be blameless in the day of our Lord Jesus Christ.*
9. **"The day of Christ":** Philippians 1:10; 2:16. 2 Thessalonians 2:2: . . . *Not to be soon shaken in mind or troubled, either by spirit or by word or by letter, as if from us, as though the day of Christ had come.*

10. **"Day of the Lord Jesus":** 2 Corinthians 1:14. 1 Corinthians 5:5: . . . *That his spirit may be saved in the day of the Lord Jesus.*
11. **"Day of Jesus Christ":** Philippians 1:6: . . . *He who has begun a good work in you will complete it until the day of Jesus Christ.*
12. **"In His day":** Luke 17:24: *". . . Also the Son of Man will be like the lightning in His day."*
13. **"The day of wrath":** Romans 2:5; Revelation 6:17. Romans 2:5: . . . *You are treasuring up for yourself wrath in the day of wrath and revelation of the righteous judgment of God.*
14. **"Day of judgment":** Matthew 10:15; 11:22, 24; 12:36; Mark 6:11; Acts 17:31; Romans 2:16; 2 Peter 2:9; 1 John 4:17; Jude 6. 2 Peter 3:7: *The heavens and the earth . . . are reserved for fire until the day of judgment and perdition of ungodly men.*
15. **"Day of redemption":** Ephesians 4:30: . . . *Sealed for the day of redemption.*
16. **"Day of visitation":** 1 Peter 2:12: . . . *They may, by your good works which they observe, glorify God in the day of visitation.*
17. **"Great day of God":** Revelation 16:14. 2 Peter 3:12: *Looking for and hastening the coming of the day of God. . . .*

Jesus Must Remain in Heaven

We have already discussed how Jesus was taken up, or received, into heaven. He was then given a special appointment or assignment from the Father until the *parousia*. Awaiting the time to return, Jesus now functions in heaven as:

- *Our heavenly High Priest,* hearing our confession and blotting out sin (Hebrews 4:14–16; 7:24–25).
- *The mediator between God and mankind,* interceding on our behalf (1 Timothy 2:5; Hebrews 8:6; 9:15).
- The *occupant of the messianic throne of David,* governing the world (Revelation 3:21).
- *Head of the Church,* sending times of refreshment (Ephesians 1:22).

Peter understood by the Holy Spirit that his Master's absence was necessary and required. Jesus was retained or held back (in a sense, "held captive" in heaven) until all things were fulfilled. Jesus must remain in heaven until the decreed time of the Second Coming.[8]

I talked in my opening chapter about the sand in the hourglass draining from the top bulb to the bottom. We might think about each granule representing a prophecy or historical event ordained by God to be fulfilled before Christ can and will come. The Great Commission alone has initiated an immense number of activities throughout the nations of the world that are destined for fulfillment before He returns.[9] *We live in the time of fulfillment!*

Times of Refreshing, Restoration and Regeneration

Peter preached his second sermon at the Temple following the Day of Pentecost. In it he offered a strong exhortation to his listeners:

> "Repent therefore and be converted, that your sins may be blotted out, so that *times* [Greek, *kairos*] *of refreshing* may come from the presence of the Lord, and that He may send Jesus Christ, who was preached to you [*appointed for you,* NASB] before, whom heaven must receive [*retain,* Williams] until the *times* [Greek, *chronos*] *of restoration* of all things, which God has spoken by the mouth of all His holy prophets since the world began."
>
> Acts 3:19–21 (emphasis added)

We noted in chapters 2 and 3 that spanning the time between the first and second advents of Jesus Christ is the era of Gospel proclamation, sometimes called the Church age. During this period, in response to the Church's seeking of God, the Lord sends "times of refreshing"—that is, seasons of spiritual renewal and revival. Along with these periodic blessings, the restoration and fulfillment of the divine program travel on parallel tracks. Both refreshment and restoration will climax gloriously together in the Second Coming of Christ.

Refreshing

"Refreshing" *(anapsuxeos)* has the idea of fresh air suddenly relieving a hot, stifling atmosphere. The Greek word appears only here in the New Testament. Robertson suggests the meaning "to cool again or refresh" and uses, as an example, how Onesiphorus "often refreshed" Paul in his harsh imprisonment (2 Timothy 1:16).[10] *The Amplified Bible* says "that times of refreshing—of recovering from the effects of heat, of reviving with fresh air—may come from the presence of the Lord" (Acts 3:19).

Times of refreshing. "Times" is the translation of *kairos,* a Greek time-word that calls attention to certain special features during a period or season.[11] The word denotes "quite generally a particular time."[12] Peter refers here to those special times during the Church age when outpourings of the Spirit refresh God's people. Kittel's *Theological Dictionary* describes *kairos* as commonly meaning a "'decisive point' . . . often with a stress on the fact that it is divinely ordained," such as when "Jerusalem does not recognize the unique *kairos* when Jesus comes to save it (Luke 19:44)." *Kairos* times can mean points of time, or "specific points in the development of God's plan."[13] These times of refreshing are extremely important to the Church.

From the presence of the Lord. Literally, "the face" (*prosopou*). The *Twentieth Century New Testament* renders this as "direct from the Lord himself." The phrase also occurs in Acts 5:41; 7:45; 2 Thessalonians 1:9. In this text it refers to the refreshment that comes from the bright and smiling presence of God.

That He may send Jesus Christ. The Father sent the Son the first time (John 3:17; 7:28–29; 17:18), and now Peter states that the Father will send Him again, although the exact time of that return is not known (Matthew 24:36). Jesus will come as the authorized envoy or representative of the Father who sent Him.[14]

Restoration

The context of Peter's second sermon is impressive. A lame beggar more than forty years old, known by all of Jerusalem because he sat daily at the Temple gate begging, was dramatically healed.

Now he stood with the apostles, not begging but giving praise to God! In his message Peter did what Jesus had often done; he used a miraculous sign to establish and illustrate a spiritual truth.[15] One of the themes of Peter's message was *restoration*—and what better visual aid than a lame man returned to perfect health standing right beside the preacher!

The term *restoration* is reminiscent of the two signs given Moses to persuade Pharaoh: first, changing a rod into a serpent and then restoring it; and second, pulling a leprous hand from his bosom, putting it back into his bosom, and then bringing it forth again in a perfectly restored condition.

The Greek word translated "restoration" (*apokatastaseos*[16]) has been used in the papyri and inscriptions in regard to the repair of temples; the repair of public roads; the restoration of estates to rightful owners; and the balancing of accounts. It is also used as a technical medical term denoting the complete restoration of health, or the restoration to its place of a dislocated joint. Josephus used the word to describe return from captivity, and Philo, the restitution of inheritances in the year of Jubilee.

Peter used the term to describe divine restoration. *The Jerusalem Bible, New English Bible* and Phillips' *New Testament in Modern English* render it "universal restoration." *Today's English Version* words it "all things to be made new." *The Message* says, "For the time being he must remain out of sight in heaven until everything is restored to order again just the way God, through the preaching of his holy prophets of old, said it would be."

Times in the Greek text of this verse is *chronos,* a word that contrasts with the *kairos* we discussed earlier. It is significant that the two words were used together by Jesus just before His ascent into heaven: "It is not for you to know *times* [*chronos*] or *seasons* [*kairos*] which the Father has put in His own authority" (Acts 1:7, emphasis added).

The two terms can overlap in meaning and even serve as synonyms, but usually *chronos* is a larger, more inclusive term. In this case it refers to all Church history, including today. *Kairos,* in contrast, refers to those points of time in Church history when God sends renewal for shorter periods.

Peter used *chronos* in Acts 3 to describe a time (just then inaugurated) of the restoration of all things spoken of by the prophets.[17] The focus of Peter's attention was not carnal ordinances or nationalistic restoration or a material Temple. He did not speak of restoring the devil and his angels or hardened, unrepentant sinners. Peter realized that God's great purposes of restoration are to be fulfilled in and through the new Israel of God, the Church, composed of Jews and Gentiles, the people of God from all nations! This period of restoration is the Church age, climaxing at the Second Coming of Christ. During this era there will be periodic showers of the Holy Spirit. Like Peter, we today can also claim our own time in history as "these days" (Acts 3:24).

Regeneration

"The regeneration" is mentioned by Jesus in Matthew 19:28: "Assuredly I say to you, that in *the regeneration,* when the Son of Man sits on the throne of His glory, you who have followed Me will also sit on twelve thrones, judging the twelve tribes of Israel" (emphasis added). But although "the regeneration" is not mentioned in Acts, commentators often associate it with "the times of restoration of all things" (Acts 3:21).

In my more complete explanation in chapter 5, I mentioned that *regeneration* is the translation of the Greek word *palingenesia* (*palin,* again; *genesis,* birth), which is used only twice in the Greek New Testament. The meaning here is the "renewal" of all things.[18] It refers in particular to a time of Kingdom renewal and high-level spiritual refreshing.

The Kingdom of God, as Jesus taught it, is not only spiritual, but literal as well. The whole earth will be filled with God's glory and Christ's reign. *The regeneration* refers to the consummation of the spiritual Kingdom of God in a literal, glorious Kingdom of God on earth—one that is free of impurity and unrestricted in righteous influence. Jesus will sit on His glorious throne. The apostles will be seated on thrones, too. When will this take place? According to Matthew 19:28:

- "When I, the Son of Man, sit upon my glorious throne in the Kingdom" (NLT).
- "In the new world" (RSV).
- "In the world that is to be" (NEB).
- "At the renewal of all things" (NIV).

Does this regeneration or restoration involve the Jewish people? Israel is included, along with the more than two hundred registered nations, and large numbers of people groups. All the ethnic peoples of the world are included in God's great program. In Matthew 25:32 all nations, including Israel, will come before Christ's throne for judgment, and no group of people will receive preferential treatment. Commendation and condemnation will be meted out to nations, but will actually focus particularly on individuals. The apostles on thrones will act as assessors of how the Gospel was received and righteousness promoted. Their ministry will judge in particular the twelve tribes of Israel. The overcoming martyrs will, by their very presence, bring reward and condemnation to both God's people and the ungodly.

As I mentioned earlier, Matthew 25:31 pinpoints the *time* of His throne: "When the Son of Man *comes* in His glory, and all the holy angels with Him, *then* He will sit on the throne of His glory" (emphasis added). The Second Coming initiates the literal throne and the time of judgment. This time of accounting is also the occurrence of the first resurrection, "the resurrection of the just" (Luke 14:14).

This clearly verifies Jesus' knowledge of the Millennium described in Revelation 20. Although Jesus did not mention a specific thousand-year period, His description of thrones and ruling in Matthew 19:28 and resurrection in Luke 20:34–36 does describe the Millennium as John declared it. Jesus also tied together the resurrection, judgment, fellowship with His people and eternal life, connecting these happenings with the age to come (Matthew 13:39–40, 49; Luke 18:30; 20:35; 22:16, 18). Mark 10:30 could be considered parallel to Matthew 19:28, thereby indicating that the regeneration equals the age to come equals the Millennium.

Jesus taught that the Kingdom of God was spiritually at hand, but He foretold a time when the Kingdom would literally come, and He and His followers would enjoy fellowship together (Luke 22:18). Jesus did not use the Latin word *millennium* (a term more familiar to us), but He did use *regeneration* and *the age to come* (terminology more familiar and less confusing to His Jewish listeners). This answers the question "Did Jesus ever talk about the Millennium?" The answer is yes, but He used different terms to describe it.

Eight Re *Words*

Christ will faithfully discharge His heavenly duties until the end of the Gospel age, which will also be the consummation of the times of refreshing and restoration discussed above. The following diagram utilizes eight words that fit the theme of our main text, Acts 3:19–21: *His coming will climax refreshment and restoration, and initiate the regeneration.*

All the words begin with *re,* which means "again" or "anew," and have particular application to this Gospel era.

The Eight *Re* Words

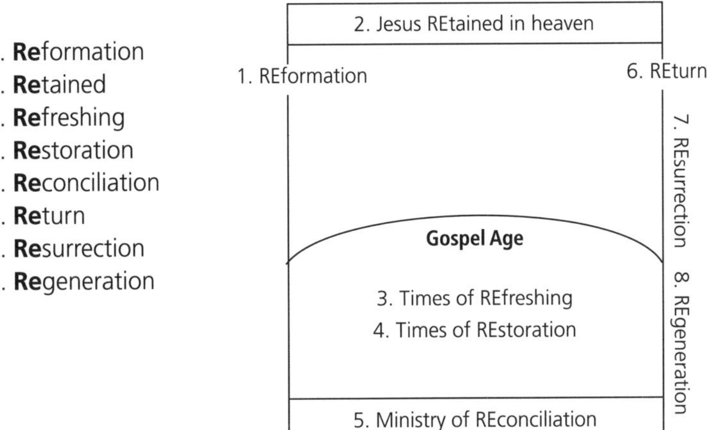

Notice in the diagram how the eight *re* words relate to the Second Coming:

1. *Reformation* (Hebrews 7:12; 9:10–11): Christ fulfilled the Old Testament era, replacing it with the salvation of the new covenant.
2. *Retained* (Acts 3:21): Jesus must remain in heaven until all things spoken by the prophets are fulfilled.
3. *Refreshing* (Acts 3:19): Periodic times of spiritual renewal are sent by Christ to the Church.
4. *Restoration* (Acts 3:21): All biblical prophecy will find accomplishment and fulfillment during this period.
5. *Reconciliation* (2 Corinthians 5:19): Unsaved mankind can be reconciled to God through the work and message of Christ during the Church age.
6. *Return* (Acts 3:20): Christ will be sent a second time by the Father.
7. *Resurrection* (Luke 20:35): The righteous dead will be raised at Christ's coming.
8. *Regeneration* (Matthew 19:28): The renewal of the earth and a new order as the messianic reign of Christ takes place—the jubilee concept realized in full potential.

Judge of the Living and Dead

Jesus will return as the Judge of the living and the dead. Three verses in Acts bear this out (emphasis added):

Peter to Cornelius' household: "And He [Christ] commanded us to preach to the people, and to testify that it is He who was ordained by God to be *Judge of the living and the dead*" (Acts 10:42).

Paul at Athens: "Because He has appointed *a day on which He will judge the world* in righteousness by the Man whom He has ordained. He has given assurance of this to all by raising Him from the dead" (Acts 17:31).

Paul before Felix the governor: As he [Paul] reasoned about righteousness, self-control, and *the judgment to come*, Felix was afraid (Acts 24:25).

There is no question but that everyone, Christian and non-Christian alike, will stand before the great Judge of all the earth. In chapter 10 we will discuss the Judgment Seat of Christ (Romans 14:10; 2 Corinthians 5:10). A challenging question remains before us: Is there only one Judgment that will involve all people, saints and sinners, at the Second Coming? Or will there be two sessions of judgment, one before the Millennium for the righteous and one afterward for the ungodly?

The number of Scriptures linking the Second Coming and judgment cannot be ignored. The amillennialists and postmillennialists generally prefer the first approach and the millennialists the latter. The question of whether or not Christians will be judged is of considerable interest to most of us, and we will discuss this important subject in ensuing chapters, blending the two approaches.

I would like to say now, however, that any judgment will not be a prolonged, drawn-out affair involving the six billion people now alive, along with all the dead. Everyone will not stand at attention before God's throne while each and every person is slowly reviewed and interrogated in minute detail about his or her life. Nor will the apostles on their thrones be deliberating the pros and cons of people's lives. Their presence, representing the apostolic truths of the new covenant, will be sufficient to elicit a true, uncritical awareness of divine justice in every person.

I am convinced that there is built into the human brain the computer-like ability to bring up information instantly from the past. For example, I just clicked *word count* on my computer. I decided I would start counting myself, just to see how long it took the computer to bring up the information. Before I even said *one*, my computer registered that so far I had used 5,048 words in this chapter. Each word, when typed, is immediately programmed into the computer's memory.

In a similar way our deeds are also registered within our beings the moment they take place. The "books" that are opened at the Judgment will not consist of handwritten parchments. As we stand before the Lord, each of us will have an instant awareness of the value of everything we have ever done. No one will question the divine judgment issued or the apostolic assessment, for all will be overwhelmed with the integrity and holiness of the mighty God, who can do no wrong. Some will be saved and some will be lost. No one will be *sent* to heaven or hell; God will regard the dignity of every human being by honoring his or her choice.[19] Our eternal futures are unquestionably determined by our choices.

Resurrection Is Our Hope

The apostle Paul constantly affirmed that the hope of God's people lies in the resurrection of the dead, which for the righteous will occur at the Second Coming. Before conversion Saul belonged to the sect of the Pharisees, who believed in resurrection and were always at odds with the Sadducees, the other main Jewish body, who did not believe in such supernaturalism. Saul's dramatic conversion occurred when he personally encountered the resurrected Jesus (Acts 9:5), and from that time on he proclaimed that Christ had overcome death and that there would be a resurrection of both the just and the unjust.[20] Immediately this became a cardinal doctrine with Paul.

In the closing chapters of Acts, Paul, the prisoner of Rome, defended his Gospel message and personal innocence before a series of Jewish and Roman authorities. Since he had appealed to Caesar, Paul probably testified before Nero himself. When offering his defense before Ananias, the high priest, and Felix, the governor, Paul declared: "I have hope in God, which [my accusers] themselves also accept, that there will be a resurrection of the dead, both of the just and the unjust. . . . 'Concerning the resurrection of the dead I am being judged by you this day'" (Acts 24:15, 21). According to F. F. Bruce, Paul "simply insists that the only valid charge that can be brought against him is a theological one, and one in which all who believe in the resurrection should share."[21]

Paul insisted that the hope of national Israel stands or falls on the doctrine of the resurrection of the dead. That final resurrection is affirmed by the resurrection of Jesus the Messiah: "Christ is risen from the dead, and has become the firstfruits of those who have fallen asleep" (1 Corinthians 15:20). Paul in his epistles clearly identified this resurrection of the just with the Second Coming of Christ. That is why the *parousia* is called by Paul "the blessed hope" (Titus 2:13).

Tribulation, Gateway to the Kingdom

The early Church knew about suffering. For the average person it was not an easy time to live anyway, but when one was viciously and unjustly attacked for living according to Christ's teachings, it became almost unbearable. The persecution and suffering of the early Christians is legendary. In fact, such a lifestyle became so common for the Christian that Paul could say in Acts 14:22, "We must through many tribulations enter the kingdom of God." It seemed like a basic principle. Paul told Timothy, "All who desire to live godly in Christ Jesus will suffer persecution" (2 Timothy 3:12).

This is not an easy doctrine for today's Western Christian to accept; affluence takes a terrible toll on dedication and spirituality. The pleasures of life have an insidious way of dulling our spiritual sensitivities. Yet even in our own time there is terrible persecution and martyrdom in many places of the world—with this consideration: When persecution comes, God places a special grace on His people. Not only can they endure, but they can even sing while being burned at the stake!

Paul testified, "I take pleasure in infirmities, in reproaches, in needs, in persecutions, in distresses, for Christ's sake. For when I am weak, then I am strong" (2 Corinthians 12:10). Peter contrasted our present sufferings with Christ's Second Coming: "Beloved, do not think it strange concerning the fiery trial which is to try you, as though some strange thing happened to you; but rejoice to the extent that you partake of Christ's sufferings, that when His glory is revealed, you may also be glad with exceeding joy. If you are reproached for the name of Christ, blessed are you, for the Spirit of glory and of God rests upon you. On their part He is blasphemed, but on your part He is glorified" (1 Peter 4:12–14).

My copy of *The Zondervan Topical Bible* devotes six double-column pages to verses on the subject of persecution. It seems that the

Hebrew prophets, the apostles, the early Church and Jesus Himself stress a theme throughout the Bible that cannot be ignored.

In 1 and 2 Thessalonians Paul makes some of his strongest and clearest statements on the Second Coming. Some of these statements were made previously by Jesus, but fifteen are found nowhere else in the New Testament. They will be our focus in the next chapter. Also in chapter 9 we face the one verse that is the foundation for the Rapture theory. Can it be proven?

NINE

ASSURANCE FOR THE MYSTIFIED THESSALONIANS

Paul's two letters to the church at Thessalonica are commonly regarded as the first written epistles of the New Testament. Their key theme: the glorious coming of Jesus Christ. Paul must have taught on this subject in the church during his brief stay there (Acts 17:2; Philippians 4:16; 1 Thessalonians 2:9; 2 Thessalonians 3:8), but in his absence certain troubling doubts had arisen in the minds of his dear disciples. Some Christians had died, and their friends wondered what the status of the departed would be at the Second Coming.

Paul emphasized that those who have already died in Christ would be at no disadvantage, but would certainly take part in the great resurrection of the righteous at Christ's return. By putting this essential teaching in writing, the apostle could preserve the information as well as circulate it among the other churches. He wanted the issue settled, so he made every effort to clarify the matter.

His comments in 1 and 2 Thessalonians constitute about seven percent of the total New Testament verses on the Second Coming, and about 25 percent of the total number of essential ideas in the

New Testament related to Christ's return. I have marked with an asterisk fourteen points in these two epistles not found elsewhere in the New Testament after their entry in the following narrative.

The Thessalonian Record

Everything Paul Wanted the Thessalonians to Know About Jesus' Glorious Return

1. **The second coming of Jesus Christ, God's Son** (the same Jesus raised from the dead),	1 Thessalonians 1:10
2. has not yet taken place,*	2 Thessalonians 2:2
3. but when it does it will be a total surprise to the world,	1 Thessalonians 5:2–8
4. yet expected by the Church.	1 Thessalonians 1:10; 5:4
5. **The Lord Jesus Christ—the Lord Himself—**	1 Thessalonians 2:19; 3:13; 4:16; 2 Thessalonians 2:1
6. will be revealed descending from heaven	1 Thessalonians 1:10; 4:16; 2 Thessalonians 1:7
7. with power and glory	2 Thessalonians 1:9
8. with all His saints	1 Thessalonians 3:13; 4:14
9. and mighty angels	2 Thessalonians 1:7
10. in the clouds.	1 Thessalonians 4:17
11. **He will come with a shout,**	1 Thessalonians 4:16
12. the voice of an archangel,*	1 Thessalonians 4:16
13. and the trumpet of God.	1 Thessalonians 4:16
14. **The day of Christ (that Day) will not happen until after the apostasy (falling away) begins and the man of lawlessness (sin) is revealed.***	2 Thessalonians 2:1–3
15. The Lord will come, in that Day.	2 Thessalonians 1:10
16. The day of the Lord comes as a thief in the night to the ungodly, but not to the saints.	1 Thessalonians 5:2–8
17. **His appearance will be in flaming fire***	2 Thessalonians 1:7–8

18. which judges the unbelievers and disobedient — 2 Thessalonians 1:8–9
19. and slays the man of lawlessness with the breath of His mouth and bright appearance,* — 2 Thessalonians 2:8
20. bringing sudden destruction with no escape.* — 1 Thessalonians 5:3
21. **When He comes, the bodies of any deceased Christians will be raised from the dead first—** — 1 Thessalonians 4:15–16; 5:10
22. their bodies rejoined to their living spirits* — 1 Thessalonians 3:13; 4:14
23. —and after that resurrection the saints still alive on the earth will be caught up to meet the Lord and the other saints in the air* — 1 Thessalonians 4:15, 17; 2 Thessalonians 2:1
24. and the clouds. — 1 Thessalonians 4:17
25. This will involve God's elect people from everywhere. — 1 Thessalonians 3:13
26. So we will always (permanently) be with the Lord and live together with Him.* — 1 Thessalonians 4:17; 5:10
27. **The saints who have walked in this life with blameless hearts of holiness** — 1 Thessalonians 3:13; 5:23
28. will all gather together in His presence, — 1 Thessalonians 2:19; 3:13; 2 Thessalonians 2:1
29. and the Lord will be glorified in His saints, — 2 Thessalonians 1:10; 2:14
30. and be marveled at among all who believe.* — 2 Thessalonians 1:10
31. We will find final relief from earth's afflictions, — 2 Thessalonians 1:7
32. and be granted complete and final salvation,* — 1 Thessalonians 5:9
33. being established blameless in holiness before God.* — 1 Thessalonians 3:13

34. **The believers' participation in this event will be Paul's greatest joy.***	1 Thessalonians 2:19
35. **Use these words—a doctrine given to us by God—**	1 Thessalonians 4:15
36. to comfort one another and cause you to be alert, sober and firm.	1 Thessalonians 4:18; 5:6; 2 Thessalonians 1:10
37. **Waiting patiently, soberly and expectantly for Him,**	1 Thessalonians 1:10; 5:5–8; 2 Thessalonians 3:5
38. be at peace and believe our testimony,*	2 Thessalonians 1:10
39. for He will bring it to pass.	1 Thessalonians 5:24

* Thought found nowhere else in the New Testament

Comments on the Narrative

Paul's comments in 1 and 2 Thessalonians on the Second Coming are some of the strongest, clearest, most complete statements in the New Testament. The fact that the very first letters of Paul address this subject is too great to be overlooked: Christ's return was considered a fundamental doctrine. Note, too, that the first letter to the Thessalonians has a statement about Christ's coming at the end of each chapter.

We have already addressed in previous chapters some of the concepts in the above narrative, so I will not elaborate on them again. The second and third sections (#5–10 and #11–13) confirm that the apostles continued to teach what Jesus had already taught.

Let's begin with an important point. As you look over the Scriptures I have included in the numbered "records" (and also in Appendix B, where all 453 New Testament verses are used), I hope you will agree that these references refer to only *one* Second Coming. Various Bible interpreters would feel compelled to eliminate some of my verses from the Thessalonian list. Some would say that certain of those verses apply to the Rapture and others to the Second Coming. Other commentators would say that certain verses apply to God's coming in judgment on Jerusalem, and the rest to the Second Coming. What an assortment of conflicting ideas!

Some believe that the resurrection text of 1 Thessalonians 4:14–17 refers to a "Rapture" of the saints occurring *before* the Tribulation and *before* the glorious Second Coming. *This, however, is not evident in Paul's basic statement.* Paul speaks to the Thessalonians of only one Second Coming, as he does in his other epistles.

First Thessalonians 4:14–17 clearly refers to the Second Coming. It is the Rapture in the sense that living and dead saints are "caught up" *together* to meet the Lord in the air. But in order to see this as describing a Rapture prior to the Second Coming, one must posit a two-phase coming of Jesus—one before the Tribulation and one after. Such an interpretation is based on the belief that the Church will not go through the Tribulation.[1]

There is no hint, however—in Thessalonians, the Olivet Discourse, the other epistles or the book of Revelation—that this is the case. The Rapture of the Church before the Tribulation is simply not taught in the New Testament; it is an assumption. Paul writes both Thessalonian epistles (and the other epistles as well) with only one coming in mind.

Bible scholar Bob Gundry is one who strongly refutes a pretribulation Rapture. "Now if Jesus really was going to come back before the tribulation," he writes, "for the purpose of taking Christians out of the world, you'd sure expect the New Testament to say so. . . . Absolutely nowhere in the New Testament do we read such a statement or anything resembling it."[2]

A contrasting approach is given by Pastor John MacArthur, a well-known scholar who advocates the dispensational premillennial position. He says: "Scripture suggests that the Second Coming occurs in two stages—first the Rapture, when He comes *for* the saints and they are caught up to meet Him in the air (1 Thess. 4:14–17), and second, His return to earth, when He comes *with* His saints (Jude 14) to execute judgment against His enemies."[3]

My own reading of the Thessalonian epistles confirms Paul's effort to set forth an understandable teaching on Christ's *one* advent. To attempt to apply any of those references to a special Rapture before the Second Coming is, to me, a distortion of Paul's simple, uncomplicated presentation. If he meant for this understanding to be part of the Church's belief system, he would have said so clearly. Nor would such an important teaching have been ignored by Jesus and His apostles.

In this chapter we will give special consideration to four portions of the Thessalonian epistles:

1. The great resurrection
2. The day of the Lord
3. The vengeance of God
4. The Antichrist

1. The Great Resurrection

> If we believe that Jesus died and rose again, even so God will bring with Him those who sleep in Jesus. For this we say to you by the word of the Lord, that we who are alive and remain until the coming of the Lord will by no means precede those who are asleep. For the Lord Himself will descend from heaven with a shout, with the voice of an archangel, and with the trumpet of God. And the dead in Christ will rise first. Then we who are alive and remain shall be caught up together with them in the clouds to meet the Lord in the air. And thus we shall always be with the Lord.
>
> 1 Thessalonians 4:14–17

Those who sleep in Jesus. Verse 14 refers to those people who have died (Matthew 27:52; John 11:11–14; Acts 7:60; 1 Corinthians 15:6, 18) and whose spirits have gone to be with the Lord. The term *sleep* does not imply "soul sleep"—some intermediate state of unconsciousness in which there is no after-death awareness. The soul of the Christian who has died is awake in the eternal world of Christ, but the body is asleep (or unaware) in the earth where he or she has been left physically (Luke 16:19–31; 23:43; 2 Corinthians 5:8; Philippians 1:21–23; Revelation 7:15–17).

At the Second Coming God will bring with Jesus "those who are asleep" (1 Thessalonians 4:15)—that is, the spirits of the departed saints—who will then be reunited with their resurrected bodies. Paul says that "whether we wake or sleep, we should live together with Him" (5:10).

Paul's statement was meant to reassure his friends (and us) that whether a person is alive in Christ or has died in Christ, he or she will obtain ultimate salvation that will include the redemption of his or her body through the resurrection.

We who are alive and remain. Verse 15 is dealing with two groups—the already departed and the survivors. Both groups are believers. The already departed are those who have physically died in Christ but who are spiritually alive and active with Jesus. The survivors are those still alive on earth when Christ comes. When Paul says, "*We* who are alive and remain," he does not mean that he himself expects to be alive; rather, he speaks as one *presently* alive on behalf of all those who will be alive at that time. (We addressed this question in chapter 2.) Paul's statement is not a theological concept but a literary device.

We do not know exactly what question was bothering the Thessalonians, but it related to whether those still living on earth at the time of the Second Coming would have an advantage over those who had already died. Would there be any Rapture at all for the dead saints? Would their bodies simply remain buried? Would those who had already died experience a lesser degree of glory? Paul dismissed these fears, assuring them that both the departed dead and the living survivors will share equally in the resurrection (although not in the rewards—more on that in chapter 10). In fact, the departed will go on *ahead* of those who are still alive.

The Lord Himself will descend. There is no question but that verse 16 refers to Christ Jesus (see #5 in "The Thessalonian Record"). He returns as total victor, mighty conqueror, champion of righteousness, the Lord of glory! He will descend from heaven in the fullness of the power of almighty God. This is merely the climax of His victorious march through the centuries. He has conquered, He is presently conquering and, in this text, He returns as conqueror. He is King of kings and Lord of lords! He will not return to convert but to judge, rule and fellowship with His people.

With a shout. The moment of Jesus' coming will be known by all. All things will be fulfilled, and heaven will no longer hold Him back. He comes for His people, His bride!

The *shout* of verse 16 can be translated "a shouted command" (*keleusma*), a term that originally referred to "the order which an officer shouts to his troops, a hunter to his dogs, a charioteer to his horses, or a ship-master to his rowers."[4] This leader, however, will be the Lord Christ, Master of all things, declaring life to His people throughout the earth.

The dead in Christ will rise. As Jesus speaks, the souls of the redeemed who are in heaven are quickly joined to their former physical bodies, which have been instantly and gloriously renovated and resurrected by the power of the Holy Spirit. The dead in Christ rise first. As Jesus said, "The dead will hear the voice of the Son of God; and those who hear will live" (John 5:25).

Recall an earlier time that Jesus cried with a loud voice: "Lazarus, come forth!" (John 11:43), and a solitary man, still wrapped in graveclothes, emerged from a stinking tomb. Actually, Lazarus' raising from the dead was a revivification, a return to natural mortal life on earth as he had known it, a *physical* resurrection. Lazarus later died again, and his body now awaits the great resurrection of the righteous.

The same type of resurrection occurred for many saints who had died in Jerusalem. They were raised from the dead as temporary witnesses to Jesus' resurrection (Matthew 27:52–53).

Now, in verse 16, the shout of the Son of God explodes like thunder across the sleeping cemeteries of the world. Those who died in Christ hear heaven's wake-up call and emerge from their graves with newly reconstructed, resurrected, glorified bodies. The famous text of 1 Corinthians 15:51–53 describes the scene:

> Behold, I tell you a mystery: We shall not all sleep, but we shall all be changed—in a moment, in the twinkling of an eye, at the last trumpet. For the trumpet will sound, and the dead will be raised incorruptible, and we shall be changed. For this corruptible must put on incorruption, and this mortal must put on immortality.

Christ Himself, by the power of His Spirit, will reach personally into every place of mortal, bodily decay, and bring the flesh and bones of each of His saints into eternal wholeness and vitality. Jesus Christ "will transform our lowly body that it may be conformed to His glorious body, according to the working by which He is able even to subdue all things to Himself" (Philippians 3:21). Our bodies will be like our Lord's resurrection body—physically recognizable but no longer constrained by natural laws such as gravity. Ladd posits that "this is not a body made out of spirit or constituted of spirit; it is a [physical] body completely infused by the power and quickened by the life of the Holy Spirit, a body perfectly designed for the enjoyment of eternal life."[5]

The resurrection of dead saints is a powerful demonstration of Christ's intense love for each and every one of His followers. Death can no longer hold back the physical remains of the Christians' bodies; the power and intensity of Jesus' love will draw together the redeemed souls and the now-glorified bodies of every individual whom God has joined to Him. The bodies of the believers will be redeemed!

A "house" of indestructible, incorruptible, eternal resurrection life will now clothe the flesh and bone that have been raised from the dead by the power of the Lord's resurrection. Our wish has been granted! "For in this we groan, earnestly desiring to be clothed with our habitation which is from heaven" (2 Corinthians 5:2); our desire is "the redemption of our body" (Romans 8:23).

The miraculous transformation of saints will occur at the Second Coming of Christ, after the Tribulation and at the beginning of His Millennial reign. The ungodly dead will be raised at a later time to face the final Judgment (see the discussion of resurrection in chapter 12).

We who are alive. Christ's commanding word will join the voice of an archangel and the trump of God. At the sound of the trumpet the physical survivors on earth, many of them exhausted from Tribulation and massive persecution but nevertheless triumphant, will be glorified by the Spirit of God, their physical bodies changed by resurrection power in the blink of an eye. These living survivors—the "we who are alive" of verse 17—will be clothed with the same kind of glorified, immortalized bodies as their resurrected brothers and sisters. Together they will be energized by the quickening power of Jesus' own life: "He who raised Christ from the dead will also give life to your mortal bodies through His Spirit who dwells in you" (Romans 8:11).

Caught up together. The awesome sights and sounds of resurrection will pervade the universe. The bodies of God's people who have died will be raised. Living survivors will be changed. Thus both the living and the dead in Christ will be bodily transformed. And then all these glorified ones will be caught up *simultaneously* in the clouds (verse 17) to meet the Lord. What an awesome sight! The grandest host ever assembled, the great army of the Lord, will rise to meet the Lord in the air.

It will be a grand jubilee reunion of formerly dead and newly changed living believers with the Lord and with each other. Vincent's *Word Studies* says it will happen "by a swift, resistless, divine energy."[6] Kittel's *Theological Dictionary* says it will be an expression of "the mighty operation of God."[7] Well said! And from that point we shall *always* be with the Lord. Paul described it in 2 Corinthians 4:14: "Knowing that He who raised up the Lord Jesus will also raise us up with Jesus, and will present us with you."

Paul described the transformation of the departed dead and the living survivors *who are in Christ.* But what about the ungodly? There is no discussion of the resurrection of the ungodly dead or any transformation of the ungodly living. Paul indicates that the ungodly living *will be dying—not being resurrected.* God will repay "in flaming fire taking vengeance on those who do not know God, and on those who do not obey the gospel of our Lord Jesus Christ. These shall be punished with everlasting destruction from the presence of the Lord and from the glory of His power, when He comes, in that Day" (2 Thessalonians 1:8–10). The ungodly will await their resurrection *after* the Millennium, when they will stand condemned before God's great white throne.

Caught up is the expression that gave birth to the popular religious word *rapture*. It is the translation of *harpazo* in the Greek text and *rapio* in the Latin Bible. Both words mean "to catch away," but it was the Latin word that caught on. Our English word *rapture,* though it does not appear in the Bible and is based on the

Latin, is regularly used in Christian circles to describe the instant translation of Christ's followers from the earth to meet Him in the air.

Since *harpazo* is used thirteen times in the New Testament, we are supplied with various interesting applications of the word. My *Greek-English Concordance*[8] lists these appearances under six headings: *catch up, take by force, catch away, pluck, catch* and *pull*. Here are some of the references with my descriptions:

A wolf *catching* a sheep (John 10:12)

Jesus perceiving that the crowd was about to come and *take Him by force* (John 6:15)

The Romans *forcefully removing* Paul from the Jewish mob (Acts 23:10)

The devil *snatching away* the seed sown in a human heart (Matthew 13:19)

Jesus' assurance that no one can *snatch us out of* the hand of Jesus and God (John 10:28–29)

Christians *pulling* the ungodly *out of* the fire (Jude 23)

The Spirit *catching* Philip *away* to Azotus (Acts 8:39–40)

Paul *caught up* into paradise (2 Corinthians 12:2, 4)

The male Child that was *caught up* to God and His throne (Revelation 12:5)

The above references illustrate suddenness, seizure, force, rapidity, violence and removal from a situation. The *Interlinear Greek-English New Testament* says that we "shall be seized in clouds to a meeting of the Lord in air." The dangerous, destructive aspects of the above illustrations do not apply to the Rapture; rather, it is the suddenness and power involved that are related. Perhaps the best illustration is that of one of the least-discussed miracles in the New Testament—when God suddenly *transported* Philip's physical body from a desert location to the city of Azotus (Acts 8:39–40).

To meet the Lord. *To meet* (verse 17) was apparently an expression used in connection with "the official welcome of a newly arrived dignitary."[9] Imagine the angels of God going forth to gather this great company of redeemed, resurrected ones and usher them upward to meet the Lord of glory (Matthew 24:31). All the angels with all the saints!

2. The Day of the Lord

> Concerning the times and the seasons, brethren, you have no need that I should write to you. For you yourselves know perfectly that the day of the Lord so comes as a thief in the night. For when they say, "Peace and safety!" then sudden destruction comes upon them, as labor pains upon a pregnant woman. And they shall not escape. But you, brethren, are not in darkness, so that this Day should overtake you as a thief. You are all sons of light and sons of the day. We are not of the night nor of darkness. Therefore let us not sleep, as others do, but let us watch and be sober. For those who sleep, sleep at night, and those who get drunk are drunk at night. But let us who are of the day be sober, putting on the breastplate of faith and love, and as a helmet the hope of salvation. For God did not appoint us to wrath, but to obtain salvation through our Lord Jesus Christ.
>
> 1 Thessalonians 5:1–9

In chapter 8, "What Acts Says about the Second Coming," I listed seventeen New Testament phrases (with references) associated with this momentous event. They may contain different points of emphasis or shades of meaning, but the Day of the Lord (as I have stated earlier) is *one* great happening with closely associated phases of that event. Eleven verses from eight books, for instance, tell us that it is a day of judgment. It is also, however, a day of redemption and a day of visitation. Whether it is called "the day," "that day," "last day," "His day" or "Day of God," the same occurrence and period of time are meant.[10]

Seven occurrences of *day* appear in Thessalonians (emphasis added), all of which (like all the other references) refer to the same event—the Second Coming of Christ:

- *The day of the Lord* so comes as a thief in the night (1 Thessalonians 5:2).
- But you, brethren, are not in darkness, so that *this Day* should overtake you as a thief (1 Thessalonians 5:4).
- You are all sons of light and sons of *the day* (1 Thessalonians 5:5).
- But let us who are of *the day* be sober (1 Thessalonians 5:8).
- When He comes, in *that Day*, to be glorified in His saints . . . (2 Thessalonians 1:10).
- [Don't be] troubled . . . as though *the day of Christ* had come (2 Thessalonians 2:2).
- *That Day* will not come unless the falling away comes first, and the man of sin is revealed (2 Thessalonians 2:3).

If we had only 1 Thessalonians 5 as a reference, we might not pose so many questions. But we also have 1 Thessalonians 4 and 2 Thessalonians 1 and 2, and these, according to some commentators, raise serious problems for the overall interpretation.

Postmillennialists generally would *not* apply any of the above seven "day" references to the Second Coming. Keith A. Mathison, for instance, an articulate spokesman for this position, feels that "all of the chapters [in the Thessalonian epistles] except 1 Thessalonians 4 refer to the coming of Christ for judgment in A.D. 70."[11] By this view there are two comings of Christ to accommodate the various references:

1. A first-century fulfillment in A.D. 70 when the destruction of Jerusalem represented divine judgment, hence "a day of the Lord." First Thessalonians 5 and 2 Thessalonians 2 refer to this time.
2. First Thessalonians 4 refers to our bodily resurrection at the Second Coming of Christ.

It seems to me, on the other hand, that 1 Thessalonians 5 is simply a continuation of Paul's discussion of the Second Coming in the previous chapter. There is no evidence to indicate that he is changing the subject, that (in Mathison's words) he is "answering two separate questions in 1 Thessalonians 4:13–18 and 5:1–8."[12] One must come to this text with strong preconceptions to connect this teaching with the judgments associated with the destruction of Jerusalem in A.D. 70, but some of my godly friends do indeed see it that way.

I see it, rather, that Paul's four uses of *day* in 1 Thessalonians 5:2, 4–5 and 8 all refer to the Second Coming. The first two references echo references elsewhere that speak of the unexpected suddenness of Christ's appearance. Paul quickly states, however, that Christians "are not in darkness, so that this Day should overtake you as a thief" (verse 4). Twice then Paul refers to believers as "of the day" (verses 5 and 8)—that is, children of the resurrection and the light of God's Kingdom. Verse 10 clearly ties this section in with the Second Coming: "Whether we wake or sleep, we should live together with Him."

We will discuss the last three references to *day* from the above bulleted list, all three from 2 Thessalonians, in the next two sections.

3. The Vengeance of God

> [God will] give you who are troubled rest with us when the Lord Jesus is revealed from heaven with His mighty angels, in flaming fire taking vengeance on those who do not know God, and on those who do not obey the gospel of our Lord Jesus Christ. These shall be punished with everlasting *destruction* from the presence of the Lord and from the glory of His power, when He comes, in that Day, to be glorified in His saints and to be admired among all those who believe, because our testimony among you was believed.
>
> 2 Thessalonians 1:7–10 (emphasis added)

Revealed from heaven. To those who are afflicted (not just "troubled"), Paul extends the warm invitation to "rest with us" at the revelation of the Lord Jesus from heaven. The word *rest* hardly touches the deep meaning suggested here. The battle will be over, the war won and we will go home with our Lord.

Also in verse 7 Paul uses the word *revelation* (*apokalypsis*, meaning "to uncover, unveil, disclose") in several ways. Here it describes the glorious disclosure or manifestation of the Lord Jesus at His Second Coming. First Corinthians 1:7 says we are "eagerly waiting for the revelation [*apokalypsis*] of our Lord Jesus Christ." Doesn't the phrase *revealed from heaven with His mighty angels* sound like the description Jesus used in Matthew 24:30–31? "They will see the Son of Man coming on the clouds of heaven with power and great glory. And He will send His angels." Luke 17:30 adds, "It will be in the day when the Son of Man is revealed."

In flaming fire. With verse 8 a new dimension is introduced to our enlarging picture of the Second Coming—fiery judgment. William Hendriksen, in the *New Testament Commentary,* says that "the phrase 'in flaming fire' indicates the Lord's holiness manifested in judgment (cf. Ex. 3:2; 19:16–20; Is. 29:6; 66:15, 16; Ps. 50:3; 97:3)."[13] Isaiah 66:15–16 captures this meaning:

> The LORD will come with fire and with His chariots, like a whirlwind, to render His anger with fury, and His rebuke with flames of fire. For by fire and by His sword the LORD will judge all flesh.

Peter reveals that the universe will be purged by fire (2 Peter 3:7, 11–12), and Paul uses an interesting application of fire in 1 Corinthians 3:10–15. We might picture a town in which fire breaks out and sweeps through the narrow streets. Buildings made of brick and stone would be unharmed, while flimsy, inflammable shacks would be lost. Paul concludes: "The Day will declare it, because it will be revealed by fire; and the fire will test each one's work, of what sort it is. If anyone's work which he has built on it endures, he will receive a reward. If anyone's work is burned, he will suffer loss" (verses 13–15).

Taking vengeance. Some wonder if the picture of fiery vengeance (verse 8) is not merely a *symbol* of judgment, rather than a literal prediction. I think we have all wondered this at some time. Yet there remains the haunting fear that the reality will be even more terrible—or more glorious—than the symbol used. I think we should stick with Paul's description of the revelation of Jesus Christ. He will come from heaven with the angels of His power and in flaming fire.

Punished. An awesome punishment (verse 9) will be meted out to those "who do not know God, and on those who do not obey the gospel of our Lord Jesus Christ" (verse 8). It does seem that this warning flows out of verse 6, which emphasizes that the Lord will "repay . . . those who [have troubled]" or been cruel to the Church.

The consequences are beyond our comprehension: eternal punishment or banishment from the presence of God, His power and glory and His loving favor.[14] This is not annihilation or being done away with; rather, it is living eternally apart from Christ, His love and His people.

When He comes. Jesus Christ will come "in that Day, to be glorified in His saints and to be admired among all those who believe" (verse 10). The severity of punishment for those who refused is more than matched by the loving favor bestowed on those who believed. Their greatest aspiration is realized—to have Christ fully glorified in their lives. We will experience splendid glorification as we enter the resurrection state, but above and beyond that is the spiritual fulfillment of Christ's own nature finding complete satisfaction in our lives.

This section in 2 Thessalonians 1 shows that the Lord Jesus will be revealed from heaven—first, to be glorified in the saints, and second, to render vengeance to the disobedient.

4. The Antichrist

> Let no one deceive you by any means; for that Day will not come unless the falling away comes first, and the man of sin is revealed, the son of perdition, who opposes and exalts himself above all that is called God or that is worshiped, so that he sits as God in the temple of God, showing himself that he is God. . . . And then the lawless one will be revealed, whom the Lord will consume with the breath of His mouth and destroy with the brightness of His coming.
>
> 2 Thessalonians 2:3–4, 8

The coming . . . our gathering. This opening verse of 2 Thessalonians 2 clearly refers to the Second Coming: "The coming of our

Lord Jesus Christ and our gathering together to Him." We will gather or congregate to Him! Only 1 Thessalonians 4:17 uses the expression *caught up*, but the thought of "gathering together to Him" is another way of describing the same experience.

As though the day of Christ had come. The Day of Christ has *not* come, as verse 2 makes clear, and they were not to be upset or troubled. In modern English Paul would probably say it as it is put in the NLT: "Please don't be so easily shaken and troubled by those who say that the day of the Lord has already begun. . . . Don't be fooled by what they say."

I have already mentioned that some believers feel these passages refer to the time of Jerusalem's destruction in A.D. 70. This interpretation of the Second Coming would have us believe (at least as far as these verses are concerned) that Christ has already come. Exactly what Paul warned us about! The use of *the Day of Christ* clearly identifies this as the Second Coming.

Will not come unless. This passage clearly states that "that Day" (the Second Coming) will *not* come unless there first comes a great falling away or apostasy *(apostasia)*[15] and the man of sin or lawlessness *(anomias)*[16] is revealed (verse 3). Who is this man? When will he arrive? Is he alive now? Will he be an actual man? We all wonder about these questions, and the answers are not yet definitive enough for adequate discussion. We do know that the "mystery of lawlessness" (verse 7) is already at work and that there are many antichrists (1 John 2:18). Some have identified the coming Antichrist with the Roman emperors, especially Nero. In more recent times, a number of others have been suggested, such as Napoleon, the Roman Papacy, Benito Mussolini, Adolf Hitler, Ronald Reagan and Saddam Hussein. As long as powerful rulers rise up, some will apply the title of Antichrist to them.

What Paul speaks of here, however, is beyond the Roman emperors or recent ambitious national leaders. This last days personage represents the full intent and fury of God's ancient enemy, the devil. Sincere followers of Christ will discern this impostor when he arrives, but many, unfortunately, will be deceived and worship him. There are no clear answers now for nervous Christians, only the admonition to seek the Lord and walk with Him carefully. It will be awesome to see the last days unfold before us.

He who now restrains. This paragraph by Arthur H. Lewis gives insight regarding verse 7:

> There is an explicit declaration of the restraint placed upon the evil forces of this age in Paul's second letter to the Thessalonians. Although lawlessness is working in the world, the full force of wickedness is not allowed because "he who now restrains it will do so until he is out of the way" (II Thess. 2:7). It is reasonable to believe that it is the divine power of the Holy Spirit at work in the hearts of all men which effectively limits their potential to do wrong.[17]

Consume . . . and destroy. This lawless one will perish in the brightness of Christ's coming, consumed with the breath of His mouth (verse 8). The glorious fire of the Lord's presence will bring final vengeance on this agent of Satan. The NEB translation refers to "that wicked man whom the Lord Jesus will destroy with the breath of his mouth, and annihilate by the radiance of his coming." Williams comments: "So overwhelmingly bright and radiant will be the appearance of Christ that, like fire, it will consume and even annihilate this final concentration of evil."[18]

Additional Thoughts from Revelation

The above text, along with Revelation 13, are the two main sources for believing in an Antichrist of the last days. Notice the similarity in evil expression in 2 Thessalonians 2 and Revelation 13. "The man of lawlessness" is described like the beast. Deception characterizes both; both claim deity and demand worship; both perform lying signs and wonders; both will suffer judgment at the Second Coming of Christ.

There is no actual Scripture that calls a specific man the Antichrist. And, surprisingly, nothing in the teaching of Jesus describes such a personality.

The apostle John makes three important comments:

- "Little children, it is the last hour; and as you have heard that the Antichrist [note: *the* is not in the Greek text] is coming, even now many antichrists have come, by which we know that it is the last hour. . . . Who is a liar but he who denies that Jesus is the Christ? He is antichrist who denies the Father and the Son" (1 John 2:18, 22).

- "Every spirit that does not confess that Jesus Christ has come in the flesh is not of God. And this is the spirit of the Antichrist, which you have heard was coming, and is now already in the world" (1 John 4:3).
- "Many deceivers have gone out into the world who do not confess Jesus Christ as coming in the flesh. This is a deceiver and an antichrist" (2 John 7).

The book of Revelation presents in visionary form the climax of the colossal antagonism between God and Satan that has existed since the beginning. The devil, in mockery and evil counterfeit of God's holy nature, manifests himself as a monstrous trinity:

1. Father: The dragon—the devil himself (Revelation 12:9, 13, 17)
2. Son: The beast from the sea—the Antichrist (Revelation 13:1–10)
3. Spirit: The beast from the earth—the false prophet that glorifies the first beast (Revelation 13:11–18)

The "beast rising up out of the sea" (13:1) is reminiscent of Daniel's vision (Daniel 7), in which he saw four beasts coming up out of the sea. The beasts represented a succession of four worldly empires; the sea symbolized humanity and its social agitation. Tyrannies generally arise out of disturbed and stormy social and political conditions, and that is the situation described in Revelation 13. The beast has characteristics like the dragon, and draws his power and great authority from the dragon. Ladd comments: "The beast, like Paul's man of lawlessness (II Thess. 2:9), is not merely the concentration of political and military power; it is the embodiment of satanic evil, drawing its power and authority from the dragon."[19]

The beast, by deception and subjugation, will seek to gain the loyalties of all humankind, drawing them away from the worship of the true God. Worldwide authority will be granted the beast temporarily by God. Wilbur Smith summarizes: "The first beast . . . is against God. He is satanically energized. He is supreme in military matters. He possesses world-wide power and persecutes the saints of the earth."[20]

The beast from the earth arises out of the social stability created by the first beast. He is twice called "the false prophet" (Revelation 16:13; 20:10). Acting as a spokesperson for the first beast and performing lying signs and wonders, he deceives the whole earth, diverting everyone's worship to an improvised image of the beast.

In the end Christ and His people triumph over the unholy three. Cast into the lake of fire, the devil, the Antichrist and the false prophet will be tormented forever and ever (Revelation 20:10).

Tribulation Emphasis

Both 1 and 2 Thessalonians contain strong statements about the enduring persecution and tribulation that will happen to believers:

- You became followers . . . having received the word *in much affliction* (1 Thessalonians 1:6).
- You also *suffered the same things* from your own countrymen, just as they [the churches in Judea] did from the Judeans (1 Thessalonians 2:14).
- No one should be shaken by these *afflictions*; for you yourselves know that we are appointed to this (1 Thessalonians 3:3).
- [We boast of] your patience and faith in *all your persecutions and tribulations* that you endure . . . that you may be counted worthy of the kingdom of God, for which you also suffer (2 Thessalonians 1:4–5).

Paul seemed to assume that rough treatment by the world is standard operating procedure for dedicated Christians. If he were to step into a time tunnel and project himself into our day, he would be amazed at how many Christians talk of escaping tribulation! The Church is triumphant, and has always overcome the advances of the enemy and the persecution of the ignorant. Paul knew of the suffering of the Thessalonians, but gave them commendation and encouragement to press on, for the glorious end would be worth it all!

Although the apostle had much to say to the Thessalonians, he was not finished with the subject. In his other epistles Paul sent teaching to the churches at Rome, Galatia, Philippi, Corinth and Ephesus. He also made mention of the Second Coming to Timothy and Titus, his two younger understudy apostles. The next chapter will cover this additional information.

TEN

HERE COMES THE JUDGE

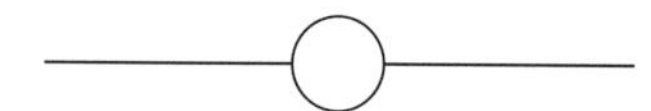

Yes, the great Judge of heaven and earth is headed our way! The Lord, the Creator of all things, will soon come to reclaim for Himself a humanity and creation that have gone astray. His glory and power will break forth in such a total work of redemption that His people and His creation will forever be freed of the effects of sin and corruption. It will be glorious indeed!

But there is a downside. This same God of glory is a God of uncompromising justice. This means that in addition to complete redemption, He will also take appropriate action toward those who stubbornly resisted His will and purpose—and appropriate reward for those who faithfully followed in the ways of their God.

Now we approach an intriguing subject—that of judgment, rewards and punishment. To get there we will consider the 34 points about the Second Coming made in Paul's other ten letters. Although most of the teaching does not repeat what Jesus taught, it does amplify, clarify and elaborate on some of His ideas. Paul, by the way, was very consistent in his teaching wherever he went.

By glancing at Appendix B on p. 220, you can easily see that some of the Pauline letters have only a few verses referencing the Second Coming—for instance, 2 Corinthians (8), Galatians (1), Ephesians (4), Colossians (3). In contrast several have a large number—Romans (22), 1 Corinthians (23), Philippians (10). The pastoral epistles have a few verses each, but they are some of the strongest, clearest statements in the New Testament: 1 Timothy (3), 2 Timothy (6) and Titus (3).

One thin reference in Galatians need not concern us. In that letter Paul focused on the debate between faith and circumcision. His six chapters are tightly structured and carefully worded with that theme in mind; to include more would be a distraction in an argument on another subject. This is true of some of the other epistles as well.

Once again I have arranged the 34 key thoughts—gleaned this time from Paul's letters other than to the Thessalonians—into a single narrative account. Note that fifteen points are unique to these epistles and are marked with an asterisk. After the narrative, we will discuss two important concepts: the transformation of the creation and the judgment at the end.

The Record of the Pauline Epistles
Everything Paul Wanted the Church to Know About Jesus' Glorious Return

1. **We are to look for the glorious appearing of the great God and Savior Jesus Christ,**	Titus 2:11–13
2. for this is our blessed hope,	Romans 8:24–25; Galatians 5:5; 1 Timothy 1:1; Titus 2:13
3. and it is at hand—so we should live accordingly.	Romans 13:11–12; Philippians 4:5
4. We fully expect/eagerly anticipate Christ's coming from heaven.	1 Corinthians 1:7; Philippians 3:20; Titus 2:13
5. **He comes at the sounding of the last trumpet.***	1 Corinthians 15:52
6. **His coming will declare the absolute authority of Christ as supreme Ruler, King and Lord of all the universe,**	1 Timothy 6:14–15
7. and we shall reign with Him.	2 Timothy 2:12

8. **At that time those who died in Christ will be resurrected,** — 1 Corinthians 6:14; 15:22–23; 2 Corinthians 4:14
9. and He will change our physical bodies by the powerful working of His Spirit.* — 1 Corinthians 15:42–44, 51–53; 2 Corinthians 5:1–5; Philippians 3:10–11, 14, 21; Colossians 3:4
10. This change will happen as fast as the blink of an eye.* — 1 Corinthians 15:52
11. This will be the adoption, the redemption of our bodies. — Romans 8:23–25; Ephesians 1:14
12. The transformation of the creation will occur at this time. — Romans 8:21
13. **He will come on "that day,"*** — 2 Timothy 1:12, 18; 4:8
14. —"the day," — Romans 2:16; 13:12; 1 Corinthians 3:13; 2 Corinthians 1:14
15. —"in the day of wrath," — Romans 2:5
16. —"the day of our Lord Jesus Christ," — 1 Corinthians 1:8; 5:5; 2 Corinthians 1:14; Philippians 1:6, 10; 2:16
17. —"the day of redemption."* — Ephesians 4:30
18. **The living and dead will be judged at His appearing.** — Romans 2:16; Ephesians 6:8; Colossians 3:24–25; 2 Timothy 4:1
19. When He comes He will bring to light things hidden in darkness as well as the counsels of hearts.* — 1 Corinthians 4:5
20. We will stand before His Judgment Seat and receive our reward,* — Romans 14:10–12; 1 Corinthians 3:8; 2 Corinthians 5:10
21. and crowns of righteousness will be given to all who love His appearing. — 2 Timothy 4:8
22. **His glory will be revealed in us,** — Romans 8:18–19; Ephesians 5:27
23. and we believers shall appear with Him in glory,* — Colossians 3:4
24. and find relief from earth's afflictions. — Romans 8:18
25. All partial (incomplete) things will be done away.* — 1 Corinthians 13:10

26. There will be a remnant of believing Israel saved. — Romans 9:27–28; 11:15, 25–26
27. **It is important to keep God's commandment with blameless hearts of holiness until Christ comes.*** — 1 Timothy 6:14
28. As often as we partake of Communion, we remind ourselves of Christ's death until He comes.* — 1 Corinthians 11:26
29. The Church is to participate in spiritual gifts until Christ's coming.* — 1 Corinthians 1:7
30. Christ will confirm/sustain His people until the end, that we may be blameless at the Second Coming.* — 1 Corinthians 1:8
31. He will keep what I have committed to Him until that Day.* — 2 Timothy 1:12; 4:18
32. And in that day we will boast of each other.* — 2 Corinthians 1:14
33. The Church will judge the world and angels. — 1 Corinthians 6:2–3
34. **The poignant prayer of the apostle Paul: "O Lord, come!"** — 1 Corinthians 16:22

* Thought found nowhere else in the New Testament

Transformation of the Creation

> For the earnest expectation of *the creation eagerly waits* for the revealing [disclosure] of the sons of God. For the creation was subjected to futility, not willingly, but because of Him [i.e., God] who subjected it in hope; because *the creation itself also will be delivered from the bondage of corruption* into the glorious liberty of the children of God [the freedom that springs from the glory of the children of God]. For we know that *the whole creation groans and labors with birth pangs* together until now.
>
> Romans 8:19–22 (emphasis added)

The NLT for verse 21 reads: "All creation anticipates the day when it will join God's children in glorious freedom from death and decay." The creation needs deliverance and transformation for the same reason that our bodies need glorification and resurrection. And F. F. Bruce has rightly said that "just as humanity at present falls short of the glory of God, so creation as a whole cannot attend the full end for which it was brought into being. *Like humanity, creation must be redeemed because, like humanity, creation has been subject to a fall"* (emphasis added).[1]

God's full redemption of man will be completed in the resurrection of the righteous dead. This is what Paul calls "the revealing of the sons of God" (verse 19). He refers to the first resurrection when our bodies will be changed by the Spirit of God into glorified bodies: "The trumpet will sound, and the dead will be raised incorruptible, and we shall be changed. For this corruptible must put on incorruption, and this mortal must put on immortality" (1 Corinthians 15:52–53). John says: "Beloved, now we are children of God; and it has not yet been revealed what we shall be, but we know that when He is revealed, we shall be like Him, for we shall see Him as He is" (1 John 3:2).

The creation eagerly awaits this happening, for it signals the time when the creation itself will be delivered, or set free, from "the bondage of corruption" (Romans 8:21) that has been placed on the earth because of sin. Adam, the first man, brought himself, his race and all of nature under a divine curse because of his sin and rebellion. Christ, through His life, death and resurrection, has broken the curse of sin and inaugurated the plan that will ultimately redeem and glorify both His people and planet earth.

G. Campbell Morgan wrote: "For His coming, not only the Church, but the whole creation, waits. Today the sons of God, as such, are unknown, or despised and persecuted; but when the Master comes, they will be revealed with Him—and it is for this consummation that the earth is waiting. . . . Creation is to be freed from its groaning and travailing in pain; the blight upon nature will be removed, and a perfect manifestation of its beauty will take the place of all it now suffers in company with fallen humanity."[2]

The word *creation* in this context refers to the totality of created things, except humanity. C. K. Barrett, in his translation, calls it "the whole created world."[3] The earth, nature and creatures were plunged into "the bondage of corruption" through Adam's sin. This resulted in thorns and weeds, volcanic eruptions and tidal waves, droughts and floods, the law of decay and the state of frailty and degradation and competition and death. This compulsory bondage was allowed by God, for it provided a way for humankind and creation ultimately to be free of sin, death and rebellion.

God's faith for this project becomes our hope. Mankind, like the creation, groans (see, for example, 2 Corinthians 5:2) and anxiously awaits the consummation of this age and the inauguration of the age to come. But the deliverance of the material creation cannot come until the saints of God have been glorified—and this will happen at the Second Coming of Christ.

Verse 21 says, further, that "the creation itself also will be delivered from the bondage of corruption into *the glorious liberty* of the children of God" (emphasis added). A better translation than *the glorious liberty* would be "the freedom which springs from the glory" (Barrett).[4] In other words, *glory* is not meant to be just descriptive of the kind of liberty; rather, *the glory of the children of God* is an independent concept that stands in contrast to corruption. It is the glory of God that will break forth at the resurrection and Second Coming, and it will break the powers that cause our bondage and corruption. The human body "is sown in corruption, it is raised in incorruption. It is sown in dishonor, it is raised in glory. It is sown in weakness, it is raised in power. It is sown a natural body, it is raised a spiritual body" (1 Corinthians 15:42–44).

The redemption of the creation coincides with the redemption of the human body. This is by divine design, for it is man's body that links him with the material world. Adam was caretaker of the creation, and when he fell, the creation automatically fell, too. Christ came with a redemption that canceled the results of the Fall—not only for man, but also for the creation under man's supervision. For now, as Paul says in our text, creation can only wait, hope and groan. And although we have the Spirit helping us, we, too, can only wait, hope and groan as we anxiously await the coming transformation. When the people of God are completely set free from earthly bondage, all creation will also be set free.

Christ spoke of the renewing of the world in Matthew 19:28. Our English translations use "regeneration" for the Greek word *palingenesia*. A good translation would be "rebirth." The earth will be transformed and entrusted to a completely redeemed humanity. This lifts the significance of a literal Millennium to a new level (see Appendix D on p. 242).

In the next chapter we will discuss 2 Peter 3. The violent, cataclysmic change described there is a graphic picture of what will literally happen to bring about the cleansing of the earth from sin's bondage. F. F. Bruce makes this appropriate comment (emphasis added):

> These words of Paul point not to the annihilation of the present material universe on the day of revelation, to be replaced by a universe entirely new, *but to the transformation of the present universe so that it will fulfil the purpose for which God created it.* Here again we hear the echo of an Old Testament hope—the creation of "new heavens and a new earth in which righteousness dwells" (2 Pet. 3:13, quoting Is. 65:17; 66:22; cf. Rev. 21:1).[5]

We Will All Stand Before God

Perhaps the biggest surprise in the biblical teaching on the Second Coming is how consistently the topics of accountability and judgment are affirmed. Jesus and the six New Testament writers stress that *saints* (those who believe in Jesus Christ and have accepted His salvation) will be judged according to their works of mercy and grace, while *sinners* (the ungodly who have rejected Christ) will be judged by their rejection of God's salvation through Christ, as well as by their works.

Anyone who reads the New Testament soon realizes that *everyone* is to stand before God and be judged on the basis of individual works. It is not so clear, however, just when those judgments will take place.

Selective reading of the Scriptures might suggest that both saints and sinners will be judged together at the same time. I propose that harmonizing all the references brings to light that there will be *two* times of judgment: first, that of Christians, when Christ comes; and second, the Final Judgment, when everyone, saint and sinner alike, stands before God. The initial judging of Christians is called the Judgment Seat of Christ. The final judging of all is called the Great White Throne Judgment.

Let's look at the two final scenes of judgment.

The Judgment Seat of Christ

To appear before the Judgment Seat of Christ is a wonderful privilege for God's people. The purpose is not to determine whether you are assigned to heaven or hell during eternity. Your future with Christ was assured when you repented of your sins, called on God to forgive you and accepted Christ as your personal Lord and Savior. Rather, this judgment will be an assessment of your works and spiritual activity. Christ wishes to reward bountifully those who have served Him faithfully, and all will be given full, true realization of the value of their earthly testimony for Christ.

Every believer has a destiny *with* Christ (2 Corinthians 5:8), and each of us is individually accountable *to* Christ. Your attendance at the Judgment Seat of Christ is not by choice; it will happen automatically. "This involves not merely an 'appearance' in the court of heaven (cf. Romans 14:10) but the divine illumination of what has been hidden by darkness and divine exposure of secret aims and motives. The person thus scrutinized will then receive an equitable and full recompense ('what is due him')."[6]

> We must all appear before the judgment seat of Christ, that each one may receive the things done in the body, according to what he has done, whether good or bad.
>
> 2 Corinthians 5:10

> We shall all stand before the judgment seat of Christ.
>
> Romans 14:10

The Actual Seat

Paul was well acquainted with the *bema* or judicial bench used as a legal judgment seat. He testified to Festus, who was sitting on the judgment seat in Caesarea, "I stand at Caesar's judgment seat, where I ought to be judged" (Acts 25:10). We also read that angry Jews in Corinth "brought [Paul] to the judgment seat" (Acts 18:12; see also Matthew 27:19; John 19:13).

The place itself was unimpressive. The word *bema* referred to a judicial bench or seat where the magistrate was seated; the plaintiff stood before him. In Paul's time it referred to "a raised place mounted by steps; a platform . . . used of the official seat of a judge."[7] *Bema* gradually came to be used for a tribune acting as an attorney, two of which were provided in the law courts of Greece, one for the accuser and one for the defendant. *Bema* was also applied to the tribunal of a Roman magistrate or ruler.

Paul undoubtedly had the above legal picture in mind, but he was also aware that originally the word *bema*, besides being a judgment seat, referred to the simple but highly honored award throne used at the Olympic Games. The umpire of the Games sat on the *bema* judging the contestants. He crowned the winners of events with wreaths of laurel. Herod built such a structure "in the theatre at Caesarea, and from which he used to view the games and make speeches to the people."[8]

"Everyone who competes for the prize," Paul wrote in 1 Corinthians 9:25, "is temperate in all things. Now they [the Olympians] do it to obtain a perishable crown, but we [Christians] for an imperishable crown."

There will not be a literal *bema* with millions upon millions of people waiting in line to be judged. Paul used a human illustration to present a spiritual truth. In a moment of time it will happen. Christ will return and His followers will be changed and caught up to meet Him. No literal *bema* will appear; the servants of God will instantly find themselves clothed in white and wearing crowns of glory. The *bema* illustration that helps our present comprehension will be forgotten in the sudden explosion of God's love and grace upon His people. At the same time the living ungodly will be smitten and die, their souls joining all the rest of the ungodly dead.

Thus the Judgment Seat of Christ is more of an award throne for believers, but at the same time it will automatically and suddenly act as a preliminary judicial bench for unbelievers, putting them in confinement until their appearance before the Great White Throne a thousand years later.

Rewards

Christians are to adopt the same Olympian mentality in our Christian service as the Greek champions who underwent grueling training in order to bask in that moment of glory when the victors' wreaths were placed upon their heads—and to reap the great rewards when they returned home.

The truth is, a great deal of the teaching in the New Testament concerns the rewarding of the servants of Jesus Christ. Here is a listing:

Great reward in heaven (Matthew 5:12)
Open reward for secret ministry (Matthew 6:4)
A prophet's reward (Matthew 10:41)
Reward according to works (Matthew 16:27)
"Due" or honest reward (Luke 23:41)
Reward reckoned not of works (Romans 4:4)
The reward of our inheritance (Colossians 3:24)
Reward matched to our labor (1 Timothy 5:18)
Just reward (Hebrews 2:2)
Full reward (2 John 8)

What about crowns? Here are five from Scripture:

1. *The victor's crown:* The victory of fulfilling our Christian purpose (1 Corinthians 9:24–27; Philippians 3:12–14; Hebrews 12:1–2; 1 Peter 1:13)
2. *The soulwinner's crown:* The fruitfulness of winning others to Christ (Proverbs 11:30; Philippians 4:1; 1 Thessalonians 2:19–20; James 5:20)

3. *The crown of righteousness:* The motive of devotion to Jesus' coming (Philippians 4:5; 2 Timothy 4:5–8; 1 John 3:3)
4. *The crown of life:* The believer's endurance and acceptance of trials (John 16:33; James 1:2–3, 12)
5. *The shepherd's crown:* The faithfulness of caring for the Church (John 21:15–18; 1 Peter 5:1–4)[9]

Loss to a believer will be the realization of squandered potential and wasted opportunities. The Scriptures speak of "the potential of lost reward (Mark 9:41) and of being deceived out of our reward (Colossians 2:18)."[10]

A Spotless Appearance

This might seem distressing, as though we could appear before the Lord with a sense of deficiency or shame over our failed efforts. There is no doubting the sincerity with which we are challenged and warned by Paul and the other writers to work diligently in our service for Christ. Yet they also give the impression that the Judgment Seat of Christ is a wonderful experience in which we can actually appear perfect before Him.

Picture it this way. Each Christian stands before God, and the works and efforts of that person are heaped in a pile at his or her feet. Jesus comes with a burning torch of truth, igniting each one's pile. Soon all fruitless and foolish efforts, like perishable goods, are reduced to ashes. Those actions of eternal value, like imperishable goods, shine with eternal endurance. Even if all is burned up, the Christian who has been a true believer will still be saved for eternity. His position may not be as glorious as that of his fellows, but the eternal joy of the Lord will be his portion. First Corinthians 3:13–15 states that "each one's work will become clear; for the Day will declare it, because it will be revealed by fire; and the fire will test each one's work, of what sort it is. If anyone's work which he has built on it endures, he will receive a reward. If anyone's work is burned, he will suffer loss; but he himself will be saved, yet so as through fire."

Peter says, "Therefore, beloved, looking forward to these things, be diligent to be found by Him in peace, *without spot and blameless*" (2 Peter 3:14, emphasis added). Paul says we should be "eagerly waiting for the revelation of our Lord Jesus Christ, who will also confirm you to the end, *that you may be blameless in the day of our Lord Jesus Christ*" (1 Corinthians 1:7–8, emphasis added). John admonishes us to "abide in Him, that when He appears, we may have confidence *and not be ashamed before Him* at His coming" (1 John 2:28, emphasis added). Such references do stress the importance of our personal dedication.

The reason we can be spotless, blameless, confident and unashamed when He appears is that we have truly repented, accepted Christ, been born again and are living to the best of our ability to the glory of God; thus we become "unjudgeable" (by His grace!) before God. The blood of Christ has cleansed us from sin (1 John 1:7–9), the Holy Spirit has renewed us (Titus 3:5) and God's Word has imparted to us saving faith (Romans 10:9–10, 17). We are saved from both the power and the consequences of sin. Jesus called this kind of living "abiding" in Him (John 15:4).

We Christians will be instantly glad, then, that we are not judged for our confessed sins; and at the same time we will realize, without remorse, that our reward for serving God is exactly what it ought to be.

The Great White Throne Judgment

Revelation 20:11–15 describes the final judgment before the Great White Throne. There is a difference between the Judgment Seat of Christ and the Great White Throne. W. C. G. Proctor, in an article in *The New Bible Commentary*, makes this distinction clear:

> The Greek word [*bema*] means "award throne" and was used of the Olympic Games. The "judgment throne of God" in Rev. XX.11 is a different word. The idea of awards for the faithful is clearly taught by our Lord . . . and also in the New Testament writings generally. The word *appear* (2 Cor. V:10), too, suggests an appearance for awards, not for judgment. The word is more accurately

> translated as "made manifest". . . . The Greek word translated *receive* (10) is a word with a variety of meanings, one being to "supply", to "carry off", to "gain". The sense thus would be that Christians, working for Christ, may accomplish some things that are *good,* but some that are *bad* (lit. "worthless"). Of what kind they are will be revealed when "we are made manifest before the judgment seat of Christ".[11]

In stark contrast to the warm reception that the Second Coming brings to God's people, the ungodly shall, *at the same time,* be physically destroyed and spiritually consigned to the abode of the unrighteous dead (commonly called hell, hades, Gehenna or the bottomless pit). Paul describes "flaming fire taking vengeance on those who do not know God, and on those who do not obey the gospel of our Lord Jesus Christ. These shall be punished with everlasting destruction from the presence of the Lord and from the glory of His power, when He comes, in that Day, to be glorified in His saints" (2 Thessalonians 1:8–9).

After Christ returns and bestows awards from His Judgment Seat, He and His people will live and reign for a thousand years on the new earth. At the end of that time, Satan (who has been bound in the bottomless pit along with all ungodly ones) will be loosed, along with the host of the ungodly, and they will make one last (hopelessly feeble) attempt to destroy the work of God.

God's final judgment on Satan and the ungodly will take place in a moment of time, each person's conscience knowing instantly the rightness of divine justice. *This will be a judgment of destination for every individual.* The throne of God is seen in resplendent white, to emphasize the righteousness and justice dispensed to all mankind. The ungodly will in that day suddenly realize the marvelous grace of God as they view the redeemed of the Lord, standing in white, shining garments, their crowns blazing with glory. Thus in that day the saved and the unsaved will each receive the divine judgment that will determine their destinies.

Let me emphasize here that to stand uncondemned in that Day, our names must be written in God's Book of Life—the record of all those who have believed on the Lord Jesus Christ. Sins we have committed will not just go away with the passing of time.

They must be handled biblically. Sin needs to be confessed, forgiveness released and appropriate biblical restitution made, if Scripture calls for it. Be in that righteous number: Determine to live for Christ!

When this happens, you and I can say, like Paul, in the fullest sense of the word: "There is therefore now no condemnation to those who are in Christ Jesus" (Romans 8:1).

The next chapter raises a most interesting question: Can we speed up the Second Coming? Peter's answer may surprise you! Also, Peter's discussion of the earth's transformation sounds like something from modern science fiction. Could these things actually happen?

ELEVEN

OUR WORLD WILL BURST INTO FLAME

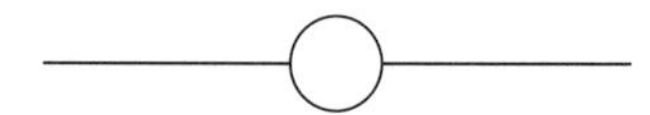

Once, long ago, the earth and its inhabitants perished by water. A flood beyond human comprehension, sent by God, snuffed out all life forms except the ones that occupied the barge-like ship captained by the patriarch Noah. A sheet of water covered the land, submerging even the mountains. When the terrible ordeal was over, God promised He would never again destroy the world with water.

He did decide, however, that the wickedness and perversion of the last days will be so pervasive that He will destroy the earth and its inhabitants by fire. This great conflagration will be ignited by the blazing glory of Jesus' return. As in Noah's day, all will perish except the righteous remnant who obey God's Word. These holy ones will be caught up into the skies to meet the Lord, even as the earth and its atmosphere burst into flame.

This is one of two significant concepts presented by the apostle Peter and discussed in this chapter. We now come to our fifth narrative account, based on the general epistles. James, Peter, John, Jude and the author of Hebrews present us with an impressive array of 31 ideas, five of which are unique to the general epistles. (Once again, in the narrative account below, these are marked with an asterisk.) We are assured that the doctrine of

Christ's return is an established truth, not some imaginative concoction or "clever fable."

As you read these words, I urge you to consider that before you is a summary of everything revealed in this section of the New Testament about the Second Coming of Jesus. These narratives represent a tremendous compendium of information that took untold hours to collect and organize. May they provide you with ideas that inspire your dedication to Christ and His return!

The Record of the General Epistles

Everything the Other Writers Wanted the Church to Know About Jesus' Glorious Return

1. **This doctrine is not made up from clever fables.**	Hebrews 6:2; 2 Peter 1:16
2. **Christ will appear a second time without sin unto salvation.***	Hebrews 9:28; 1 Peter 1:5
3. He will appear as our Chief Shepherd,	1 Peter 5:4
4. for those who look for Him.	Hebrews 9:28; 2 Peter 3:12
5. His glory will be revealed,	1 Peter 4:13
6. and we shall be like Him, for we shall see Him as He is.	1 John 3:2
7. We will be given unfading crowns of glory	James 1:12; 1 Peter 5:4
8. and great peace,	1 Peter 1:13
9. and we will be glad with exceeding joy that we once suffered with Him and underwent trials.	James 5:8; 1 Peter 1:7, 13; 4:13
10. **His coming is at hand.***	James 5:9; 1 Peter 4:7; 1 John 2:18
11. He comes with ten thousands of His saints,	Jude 14
12. as a judge	James 5:9
13. to execute judgment on all.	1 Peter 4:5; Jude 15
14. **His coming will be, to the unbelievers, like a thief at night**	2 Peter 3:10
15. since they believe the scoffers.	2 Peter 3:3–4

16. **Christ is patiently waiting for the right time to come so He will get the full harvest (not willing for anyone to perish).*** 2 Peter 3:9
17. We, too, must be patient, Hebrews 10:36–38; James 5:7–8
18. looking for and hastening His coming.* 2 Peter 3:12
19. **The Second Coming will be the day of visitation,** 1 Peter 2:12
20. —the Day, Hebrews 10:25
21. —the day of judgment, 2 Peter 2:9; 3:7; Jude 6
22. —the day of the Lord, 2 Peter 3:10
23. —the day of God. 2 Peter 3:12
24. **An immediate reaction in nature will occur: The heavens will pass away, being on fire,*** Hebrews 12:26–27; 2 Peter 3:10, 12
25. and the elements will melt and be dissolved by fire 2 Peter 3:7, 10, 12
26. and the works in it will be burned up. 2 Peter 3:10
27. **Therefore, let us be bold in conduct and godliness,** 2 Peter 3:11
28. being diligent to be found by Him in peace, without spot and blameless, 2 Peter 3:14
29. establishing our hearts, James 5:8
30. being sober and hoping to the end. 1 Peter 1:13
31. Abide in Him so that you may have confidence and not be ashamed. 1 John 2:28

* Thought found nowhere else in the New Testament

We Must Speed the Lord's Coming

A fascinating verse is tucked into point #18 in the above narrative:

> Since all these things will be dissolved, what manner of persons ought you to be in holy conduct and godliness, looking for and *hastening the coming of the day of God. . .* ?
>
> 2 Peter 3:11–12 (emphasis added)

The phrase *hastening the coming of the day of God* is both interesting and significant. Can we actually hasten the coming of that day? Simon Kistemaker, professor at Reformed Theological Seminary, calls this "a startling statement indeed. Peter is saying that we have a vital part in shortening the time set for the coming of God's day."[1] Two translations, says Kistemaker, are possible—*speed its coming,* which is active, and *long for,* which is reflexive. He feels that "the cumulative evidence from Scripture, intertestamental literature, and Jewish sources supports the first translation, 'and speed its coming.'"[2]

Biederwolf favors "hastening" in the sense of "hurry[ing] on . . . accelerating the advent of that day by our holy lives and our labors for the advancement of the Gospel."[3] Similarly the NLT urges us, in regard to the day of God, to "hurry it along." This appears to be a sound—and challenging!—interpretation.

The Earth Will Be Transformed

Now we look at one of the most awesome and graphic descriptions in Scripture of what will happen to the heavens, "the elements" and the earth at the consummation of human history. Professor Ladd reminds us that "the coming of Christ . . . includes the transformation of the entire physical order."[4] The last chapter of 2 Peter, a unique and powerful expression of the Second Coming of Christ, actually describes the destruction of the world as we now know it:

> *The day of the Lord* will come as a thief in the night, in which the heavens will pass away with a great noise, and the elements will melt with fervent heat; both the earth and the works that are in it will be burned up. Therefore, since all these things will be dissolved, what manner of persons ought you to be in holy conduct and godliness, looking for and hastening the coming of *the day of God,* because of which the heavens will be dissolved being on fire, and the elements will melt with fervent heat? Nevertheless we, according to His promise, look for new heavens and a new earth in which righteousness dwells.
>
> 2 Peter 3:10–13 (emphasis added)

I am convinced that Peter's awesome description of earth's meltdown and transformation goes hand in hand with Paul's description of the redemption of the literal creation (Romans 8:19–21, which we discussed in the last chapter). Paul gives the underlying reason for the earth's deliverance, while Peter describes *how* this cataclysmic change will take place. Just as man will undergo final glorification in the resurrection, so the earth must undergo final cleansing and transformation when faced with the awesome splendor of Christ's return.

Scoffers will come in the last days. Before giving the strong statement quoted above, which describes the world perishing by fire, Peter derides the scoffers who challenge the promise of Christ's coming (2 Peter 3:3–4). He reminds us that it was by the command of God ("the word of God") that the heavens and earth were originally created (verse 5). By that same word the original creation "perished" in the flood of Noah's time (verse 6). It was not annihilated, but it lost form and substance as a world; it was reduced to another form and state. And now, still under the decree of God's word, the present heavens and earth will be preserved until the day of judgment and purging by fire (verse 7).

Peter also points out that God does not operate under our time constraints—"with the Lord one day is as a thousand years" (verse 8)—and He is much more patient and longsuffering than we realize, "not willing that any should perish" (verse 9).

The heavens will pass away with a great noise. This means the atmospheric heavens will disappear with a great roar (verse 10). "Roar" seems to be a good translation of *roizedon*, which Robertson describes as "whizzing sound of rapid motion through the air like the flight of a bird, thunder, fierce flame."[5] Some feel that *a great noise* refers to the crash of the falling heavens or the roar of flames. The *Amplified* calls it "a thunderous crash." Biederwolf suggests, "The better translation is 'a rushing sound.'"[6] Kistemaker feels that this description by Peter is "as John describes the events of the last day: 'The sky receded like a scroll, rolling up' (Revelation 6:14; see Isa. 34:4). As the sky passes away, a crackling sound as of roaring flames will be heard."[7]

The elements will melt with fervent heat. The term *elements* in verse 10 (*stoicheia*) refers to the component parts of which a system of things is composed.[8] Some say the elements to be destroyed by fire are the heavenly bodies—sun, moon and stars. Others believe these will be the elements of earth, water and air. (Ancient peoples believed that the physical universe was composed of four elements: air, water, fire and earth.) Modern chemistry students study an atomic listing of more than one hundred chemical elements.

Possibly *elements* refers to the atomic structure of matter on the earth and objects in the atmospheric heavens—in other words, the material elements of the universe. Whatever they are, these elements, components or ingredients that are the constituent parts of the system of creation will be dissolved.

The Greek word for *dissolved* (verse 11) is the future passive of *luo*, a word meaning simply "to loose." There will be a loosening, a dissolving, a melting because of a fervent heat that defies imagination. The elements will literally be "scorched up."

Verse 12 tells us that the elements will "melt with fervent heat." Although some commentators hesitate to press a literal meaning, I see no problem in accepting the liquefaction of the earth's crust. We have all become familiar, through the medium of television, with the fiery lava flow of melted rock that issues from a live volcano. Peter's description merely takes what we have seen and magnifies it to a global dimension. This text does not decidedly state (as Biederwolf has pointed out) that the world is to be dissolved into nothing.[9] We still have the question before us of whether Peter meant annihilation or transformation. I believe he meant transformation. Let me explain why.

The earth and the works that are in it will be burned up. The "works" of verse 10, as distinct from "the elements," refer to the productions of God, man and nature. The fine cities we have built, the great architectural wonders, the stupendous scientific achievements, the artistic accomplishments of the ages—all of this will be of no consequence in that day.

Most versions use the translation "burned up" (verse 10), but there is uncertainty about this text because of the variant readings in the Greek manuscripts. Some say the earth "shall be found," while other ancient manuscripts say "discovered." What will happen to the earth? Notice the variety of translations:

- *Today's English Version*: "The earth with everything in it will vanish."
- *Twentieth Century New Testament:* ". . . will be disclosed."
- *Contemporary English Version:* ". . . will be seen for what they are."
- *Phillips:* ". . . will disappear."
- *Rotherham* and *Interlinear (Marshall):* ". . . will be discovered."
- *New International Version* and *New English Bible:* ". . . will be laid bare."

I like the NIV and NEB translation "will be laid bare." Kistemaker calls this "the most difficult and oldest Greek reading," suggesting that it is probably the original reading. It certainly fits the context. He says that "because the day of the Lord is seen as the judgment day, the verb *will be laid bare* most likely means that 'the earth and all man's works will appear before God's judgment seat.'"[10]

New heavens and a new earth. As we keep the above adjusted text reading in mind, verse 13 does *not* convey the impression of total annihilation, but the idea of change or transformation. My contention, then, is that the earth will undergo violent change at the glorious coming of Christ, and that a transformed earth, cleansed by fire of all imperfection, will be the new earth to be inhabited by the saints during the Millennium and the ages to come. I agree with this statement by Henry Alford made many years ago: "The flood did not annihilate the earth, but changed it; and as the new earth was the consequence of the flood, so the final new heavens and earth shall be of the fire."[11]

To Him be the glory both now and forever. "Forever" in verse 18 (*eis hemeran aionos*) can mean "unto the day of eternity" (Robertson).[12] Biederwolf calls this "'the day which shall dawn at the end of time and itself know no end'. The word 'eternity' is literally 'aeon', and the expression literally translated means, 'unto the day of the aeon', and is found only here."[13] My contention is that because the Millennium is the age (or eon) to come, Peter is declaring glory to our Lord and Savior Jesus Christ both now, to and into the thousand-year day of the Lord. On that transformed earth righteousness will make its home (Isaiah 65:17ff; 66:22; Revelation 21:1).

After the saints are fully redeemed and the earth is made completely new, the people of God will live and reign with Christ on the new earth and fulfill God's original intention for people *and* creation. (See Appendix D, in which we will draw together the teachings of Jesus, Paul, Peter and John in discussing Christ's millennial reign on a redeemed earth.)

The battle of the ages, between God and Satan, reaches its climax in our next chapter. We have finally come to the last section of the New Testament, rightfully called "The Revelation of Jesus Christ." There is not time for an in-depth study of all the mysterious subjects mentioned there, but six fascinating subtopics will interest you. You will particularly want to consider God's three-stage plan to do away with the devil! The subject of the Millennium is presented in Appendix D, since the information is sufficient for a chapter of its own.

TWELVE

THE BOOK OF REVELATION: THE FINAL TRIUMPH

John the apostle closes the canon of Scripture with the most prophetic and apocalyptic book of the New Testament. This mysterious *Revelation of Jesus Christ* has brought hope and expectancy to every generation, especially those suffering persecution. When tested by doubts and fears, Christians have turned to the end of the Bible again and again to read how everything turns out. Some of the descriptions boggle our minds, yet we sense in this unusual book the throbbing passion and urgency of God. And in it we find the final triumph of good over evil.

Read through the following narrative account with joy and childlike expectation; then we will discuss six important thoughts presented in this last book of the Bible.

The Record of the Revelation
Everything John Wanted the Church to Know About Jesus' Glorious Return

1. **Christ will come,** Revelation 1:4, 7–8; 4:8; 11:17
2. descending from heaven, Revelation 19:11

3. with clouds, — Revelation 1:7; 14:14–20
4. and every eye shall see Him, — Revelation 1:7
5. including those who pierced (crucified) Him.* — Revelation 1:7
6. All tribes of the earth shall wail (or mourn) because of Him. — Revelation 1:7
7. **He will come as the conquering King of kings and Lord of lords.** — Revelation 14:14–20; 17:14; 19:11–16
8. He will be accompanied by the armies (angels and saints) of heaven. — Revelation 19:14
9. It will be a day of wrath, and — Revelation 6:16–17; 14:14–20
10. the time of the judging of the dead. — Revelation 11:17–18; 20:11–14
11. The Lord will gather the harvest of the earth. — Revelation 14:14
12. In the days of the sounding of the seventh angel, the mystery of God will be finished, and* — Revelation 10:7; 11:15
13. Christ's reign will be initiated.* — Revelation 11:15
14. **When He comes, He will reward each person appropriately for his or her work.** — Revelation 21:7–8; 22:12
15. **Christ's coming will occur after cosmic signs in sun, moon and stars.** — Revelation 6:12–13
16. **It will be the time of the first resurrection.** — Revelation 20:5–6
17. **Five times Jesus said, "I am coming quickly" (soon).** — Revelation 2:16; 3:11; 22:7, 12, 20
18. Twice we are told that He will come unexpectedly "like a thief" —so we must stay alert! — Revelation 3:3; 16:15
19. **Three of the seven churches of Asia Minor were challenged spiritually to bring correction in the light of His coming.** — Revelation 2:25; 3:3, 11
20. We must wake up and repent of permitting false teachings.* — Revelation 3:3
21. Hold fast to your faith (what you have), for fear of losing your crown. — Revelation 2:25; 3:11

22. Heed the prophetic words of this book.* Revelation 22:7
23. **The Bible closes with the heartfelt prayer of John the apostle: "Amen. Even so, come, Lord Jesus!"*** Revelation 22:20

* Thought found nowhere else in the New Testament

Descriptions of His Coming

Revelation begins and ends with the Second Coming: "He is coming" (Revelation 1:7) and "Come, Lord Jesus!" (22:20). This final book of the Bible is the apocalypse, or "unveiling," of Jesus Christ.

He who is to come. Four times in Revelation this awesome description of God and Christ is used: "He who is and who was and who is to come" (1:4, 8; 4:8; 11:17). This is the testimony of the great "I AM" of Old and New Testaments whose presence dominates past, present and future (Exodus 3:14; John 8:58). *Who is to come* bears special significance for Christ's Second Coming.

All will see Him. Jesus will come with clouds and be seen by all, including by those who pierced Him (Revelation 1:7). Recall John 19:37 (quoting Zechariah 12:10): "They shall look on Him whom they pierced." There will be great mourning in all tribes of the earth by those who rejected Him!

The great day of His wrath. The book of Revelation seems to follow a linear progression of events: seven churches, seven seals, seven trumpets, seven bowls. In Revelation 6:16–17 worldly men cry out to the mountains and rocks, "Fall on us and hide us from the face of Him who sits on the throne and from the wrath of the Lamb! For the great day of His wrath has come, and who is able to stand?" The sixth seal of God's Book has just been broken open, releasing terrifying signs in the heavens.

Then the last or seventh seal is opened (8:1). Seven trumpet-sounding angels proceed in turn to release wrath on the earth. Apparently the Lord will return when the wrath is culminated and the seventh angel sounds (10:7; 11:15–18).

The time has come for you to reap. The graphic description of Jesus reaping the harvest of the earth (14:14–20) undoubtedly refers to the Second Coming.

As a thief. Revelation 16:15 is suddenly dropped into the middle of a very tense chapter. Christ will come as a thief to the world in the sense that He will be unexpected. The Church is admonished, however, to watch, to be diligent in spiritual things and to be ready.

Riding a white horse. Then Jesus Christ, the Word of God, leads the armies of heaven against the nations of the world (19:11–16).

Satan's Three-Stage Demise

The most apparent theme in Revelation is that of the total and final triumph of God over His archenemy, Satan. The following diagram will help explain the divine three-phase plan to defeat the devil:

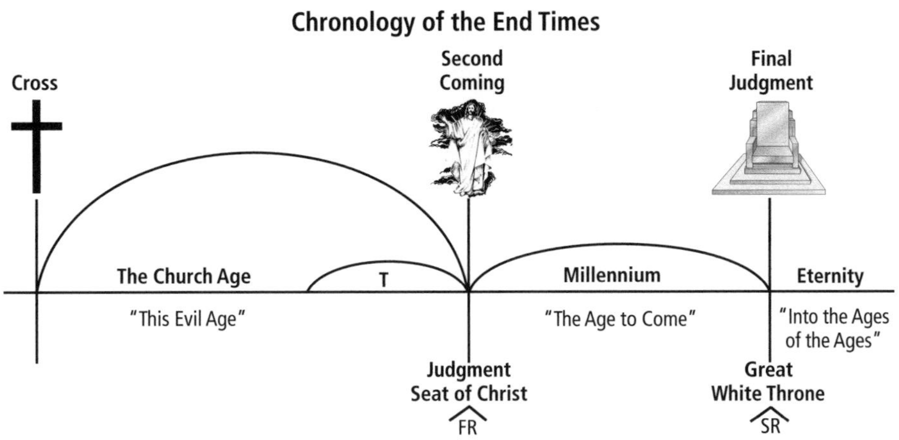

Three Stages for Three Enemies

Sin	1. Cross	2. Second Coming	3. Final Judgment
Devil	1. Cross	2. Abyss	3. Lake of fire
Death	1. Jesus' resurrection	2. 1st resurrection	3. 2nd resurrection

Notations: FR=First Resurrection; SR=Second Resurrection; T=Tribulation

Notice at the bottom of this chart the three enemies mentioned: sin, the devil and death. The KJV uses the word *destroy* to describe Christ's victory over all three. The Greek word *katargeo* means "to nullify or break the power of, to defeat, to put out of action." The NASB says "to render powerless." Notice that each enemy is dealt a severe blow of judgment (and further curtailment and containment) at each of the following three stages.

1. The Death, Burial and Resurrection of Jesus Christ

When Jesus died for us and shed His precious blood, He made atonement for sin. Thus sin, like death and Satan, has been defeated. Hebrews 9:26 teaches that Christ "put away sin by the sacrifice of Himself." Romans 6:6 points out "that our old man was crucified with Him, that the body of sin might be done away with [*katargeo*], that we should no longer be slaves of sin." Jesus' blood now cleanses us from sin when we make confession to Him (1 John 1:8–9).

Christ has defeated Satan. That initial, decisive victory has already been accomplished! Hebrews 2:14–15 says that "He Himself likewise shared in the same [flesh and blood], that through death He might destroy [*katargeo*] him who had the power of death, that is, the devil, and release those who through fear of death were all their lifetime subject to bondage." The devil finds himself stripped of power to overcome the people of God who know their position in Christ.

Death is overcome, then, by the resurrection of the Son of God. Jesus is the firstfruits (1 Corinthians 15:23) of the whole Church, which will later also overcome death totally. Second Timothy 1:10 heralds "the appearing of our Savior Jesus Christ, who has abolished [again, *katargeo*] death and brought life and immortality to light through the gospel." And finally 1 Corinthians 15:25–26: "He must reign till He has put all enemies under His feet. The last enemy that will be destroyed [*katargeo*] is death."

2. The Second Coming of Christ Accompanied by the First Resurrection

The man of sin (the Antichrist) and all sinners are destroyed at the brightness of Christ's coming (2 Thessalonians 1:7–10; 2:8).

The Church, in stark contrast, appears blameless, trusting in the precious blood of Christ to cleanse her from all sin. Paul prayed, "May your whole spirit, soul, and body be preserved blameless at the coming of our Lord Jesus Christ" (1 Thessalonians 5:23).

The devil is cast into the abyss, the bottomless pit, and stripped of all influence and deceptive powers for a thousand years (Revelation 20:1–3). Death, the last enemy, is conquered by the Church. The dead in Christ are resurrected with glorified bodies, and the living saints are also transformed with glorified bodies by the power of God (1 Corinthians 15:51–53; 1 Thessalonians 4:16–17). Notice Paul's dramatic statement in 1 Corinthians 15:54: "When this corruptible has put on incorruption, and this mortal has put on immortality, then shall be brought to pass the saying that is written: *'Death is swallowed up in victory.'*"

3.The Final Judgment Accompanied by the Second Resurrection

Loosed momentarily (or resurrected) at the end of the Millennium, the ungodly join Satan in one final effort to destroy God and His program (Revelation 20:3, 7–10). Then sin, sinners, Satan, the beast, the false prophet, death and Hades are all rendered final judgment and consigned to the lake of fire.

Many sincere Christians (as we have noted) believe that this present time between the first and second comings of Christ is the period known as the Millennium. They also believe that the binding of Satan described in Revelation 20 is now in effect. Satan is presently bound so that he cannot deceive the nations.

Admittedly the Bible makes some very strong statements concerning our present victory over Satan. Add to the Scriptures given above Luke 10:19, Ephesians 2:6, Colossians 2:15 and 1 John 3:8. All these references indicate that Satan has been rendered powerless by the death, burial, resurrection and ascension of Christ to those who claim the authority of Christ given to them.

But does this mean Satan is out of operation? Paul speaks of resisting the devil (Ephesians 6:10–18). James tells us to "resist the devil and he will flee" (4:7). Peter exhorts us to "resist him, steadfast in the faith" (1 Peter 5:9). John records that the devil "who deceives the whole world" will be cast out of heaven (Revelation 12:9). This casting out will occur before the Millennium, and since it has not yet happened, we can hardly say that the devil is bound and unable to deceive people presently. I have preached in twenty foreign countries and can testify that Satan is actively deceiving people everywhere!

The apostle John also confirms this when he says, "The whole world lies under the sway of the wicked one" (1 John 5:19). Satan will take advantage of our gullibility, so we must not be ignorant of his deceptive strategies (2 Corinthians 2:11). This illusive enemy can transform himself into an angel of light (2 Corinthians 11:14). The devil-inspired beast of the last days, before the coming of Christ, will deceive people and cause them to receive the mark of the beast (Revelation 19:20). It is very difficult, in the light of the above Scriptures and the plain facts of society, to make the binding of Satan in Revelation 20 apply to his *inability* to deceive people.

Christians sometimes pray for more power to deal with the devil. Actually we already have the power of the Holy Spirit. What we need to do is use the authority Jesus Christ has provided. I like this statement by Pastor Sue Curran: "It is not our task to defeat Satan; Jesus has already done that. It is our task only to *enforce the victory of Calvary*. . . . We are not called to fight the devil; rather we are commissioned to *enforce the victory of Calvary*."[1]

My impression is that the description of Revelation 20 is so dramatically violent, with such literal events involved, that the picture John saw surely awaits fulfillment. Satan will be seized, bound with a chain and cast into the abyss; a lid will be shut, a lock secured and a seal set on his prison.

Remember that the first phase in God's three-phase plan to defeat the devil is the cross and resurrection, and that the second phase includes the devil's temporary demise. Only after the thousand years are fulfilled will the third phase occur and he be cast into the lake of fire, where he will remain eternally. Our enemy has been defeated by Christ, then, but we must enforce Christ's victory.

The situation reminds me of the continuing warfare in the South Seas islands after World War II. Japan had formally surrendered to the Allied forces, yet we heard about cases several years after the surrender in which Japanese soldiers in the jungles, who had not heard of the surrender, were still fighting the war! The victory was legitimate, but it had to be enforced through mopping-up operations.

This is the situation with our enemy. The following chart shows the course of Satan's defeat:

The Demise of Satan

Church Age	Millennium	End of Millennium	Eternity
Satan defeated	Satan bound	Satan loosed (temporarily)	Satan sentenced
Nations deceived	Earth freed	Righteous attacked by ungodly	Lake of fire

Why Two Resurrections? And Are They the Same Kind?

Every Christian believes that all the dead will be raised. But will they all be raised at once, or will there be two resurrections—one for the righteous and one for the unrighteous? Revelation 20:4–6 teaches that there will be two resurrections, and there is no compelling reason to believe that the two resurrections do not refer to the same kind of literal, bodily resurrection.

This may seem obvious, but the argument is given by some that the first resurrection occurs at our spiritual conversion, and the second when our dead bodies are raised.

This is like comparing apples and oranges. The first and second resurrections must be of the same nature. *Anastasis* signifies bodily resurrection. An old remark by Alford is often quoted on this subject, and I think it remains accurate: "If, in a passage where *two resurrections* are mentioned . . . the first resurrection may be understood to mean *spiritual* rising with Christ, while the second means *literal* rising from the grave, then there is an end of all significance in language, and the Scripture is wiped out as a definite testimony to anything."[2]

The godly and the ungodly will both be raised from the dead.[3]

- Paul said, "I have hope in God . . . that there will be a resurrection of the dead, both of the just and the unjust" (Acts 24:15).
- Jesus said, "The hour is coming in which all who are in the graves will hear [My] voice and come forth—those who have done good, to the resurrection of life, and those who have done evil, to the resurrection of condemnation" (John 5:28–29).
- John recorded, "Blessed and holy is he who has part in the first resurrection" (Revelation 20:6).

Revelation 20 tells us that a thousand years separate the two resurrections. Whereas Paul's discussions concentrate on the resurrection of the righteous, which will occur at the Second Coming, John is describing the destruction of the ungodly who are still alive. The two resurrections can be summarized like this:[4]

- *First resurrection*: that of the just (those who have done good—the blessed and the holy); those who are followers of Jesus Christ. Occurs at the Second Coming and brings these righteous ones into a state of eternal blessedness.
- *Second resurrection*: that of the unjust (those who have done evil—the unblessed and the unholy); those who have rejected Jesus Christ. Occurs at the end of the thousand years and brings these unrighteous ones into a state of eternal damnation.

The Great White Throne

As I understand it, and as we discussed in chapter 10, the judgment of God will come in two phases. The first part will take place at the Second Coming, in a moment of time, when the saints will be resurrected, glorified, welcomed and rewarded. This is our moment of appearing before the Judgment Seat of Christ. At the same moment the ungodly will be slain by the glory of Christ's appearance. Their souls will immediately join the souls of all who have perished throughout the ages. All these will be consigned to the abode of the wicked dead, which is called hell, Hades, the abyss or the bottomless pit. (Actually this is what happens now when an ungodly person dies.)

The second phase of God's judgment will come at the Great White Throne at the end of the thousand years. Christ and His people will have been reigning together on the cleansed planet earth. (The righteous will already have received their rewards at the Second Coming.)

The center of activity is the throne of God. It is described in Revelation 20:11 as "white," to proclaim the righteousness, integrity and justice of God. Although the color has not previously been given, I feel it is one and the same throne of God mentioned throughout Revelation.

As the saints in radiant white garments and shining crowns bask in the glory of God around the throne, the release is granted to Satan and the wicked dead. He and his followers issue forth like a black cloud out of the abyss, and the souls of the wicked are joined to their resurrected bodies. These incorrigibles have not learned their lesson. They are not penitent; rebellion still rages within them. Their very actions decree their fate: fire from the presence of God and consignment to the lake of fire.

This may seem like an oversimplification. It may also seem confusing. Why would God release the devil when He already has him locked up? But this sequence blends all the biblical sources together harmoniously.

Think of it like this. A bank robbery occurs, with innocent bystanders getting killed. The robbers are apprehended, hauled off to jail and denied bail. The proof of their guilt is clearly beyond doubt. They remain in jail for a month and then are led from their cells to be presented for indictment. In court they stage an uprising, resist the sheriff and deputies, and even attempt to kill the judge. They are subdued, brought to trial and given life sentences with no parole.

Satan and the wicked, like the guilty robbers, are first apprehended at the Second Coming and thrown into the escape-proof prison of the bottomless pit. At the end of their waiting period (the Millennium), they are momentarily released to come to court, but they attempt a major escape, combined with a physical assault on the people of God. Then the righteous Judge of creation renders the verdict *guilty*, which none can question. He sentences the wicked to the place of confinement—everlasting fire prepared for the devil and his angels (Matthew 25:46).[5]

He Comes Quickly

Five times in Revelation we are told, "Behold, I am coming quickly!" *Quickly* means that Christ's program, like the sand in the hourglass, is moving rapidly to conclusion, even though His arrival may yet be a great way off. It is essential, meanwhile, that we remain watchful—alert, ready and prepared. We are to base this watchfulness not on His immediate coming, but rather on *one that is inevitable.*

Worldly people may miss the distinction. Younger people are downright impatient with it. I can tell you, however, from my vantage point of seventy years, that time really does move swiftly. When Christ comes, all of us will affirm, "He really did come quickly!" Having been a Christian for 59 years, I can say that my life has passed too quickly, yet I yearn for Jesus' coming now more than ever. Listen to Hebrews 10:37, then: "For yet a little while, and He who is coming will come and will not tarry."

Preparation for His coming is so simple that anyone can get ready. Have you followed the prescribed course?

You must first of all repent of any personal rebellion and sin against God, asking Him in Jesus' name to forgive you and make you His child. Make an about-face in lifestyle (which is the meaning of *repent*), relinquish your own will and willingly submit to Jesus Christ.

By following this simple course of action, you automatically make Jesus both your Savior and your Lord. Some call it being saved or born again. Those are biblical terms that describe the initial steps of becoming a Christian, and they should be followed by water baptism and association with a good, spiritual church. Reading the Bible every day and praying should also become part of your new life. In short, you should, by the power of the Holy Spirit, start living for God in the way that the New Testament describes.

The presence of God will become real and meaningful in your life, and you will find that it becomes a delight to serve the Lord Jesus Christ. And the better you come to know Jesus, you will find yourself looking forward more and more to His coming.

Here are His promises to those who love and serve Him. Read them with the eyes of your heart:

> "Behold, I come quickly! Hold fast what you have, that no one may take your crown."
>
> Revelation 3:11

> "Behold, I am coming as a thief. Blessed is he who watches, and keeps his garments, lest he walk naked and they see his shame."
>
> Revelation 16:15

> "Behold, I am coming quickly! Blessed is he who keeps the words of the prophecy of this book."
>
> Revelation 22:7

> "And behold, I am coming quickly, and My reward is with Me, to give to every one according to his work."
>
> Revelation 22:12

> He who testifies to these things says, "Surely I am coming quickly."
>
> Revelation 22:20

May our response ever be, "Even so, come, Lord Jesus!"

THIRTEEN

AT LAST! PUTTING ALL THE PIECES TOGETHER

The children spilled the puzzle pieces out onto the table. Excitement ran high as they scrambled to find the segments that fit together, especially those with straight edges that would make up the sides. Certain parts that had similar coloration were grabbed up and grouped together. These complementary pieces speeded up the assembly at first; then things began to slow down to a time of serious, contemplative examination of each piece. At times a child would attempt to force together two incompatible segments. Parental assurance was given that all the parts of the puzzle were there, and that it was not necessary to force or pound the parts together. Also, no pieces would be left over. Slowly, marvelously, the pieces came together, and a beautiful picture emerged!

Now, finally, we come to the climax of our own puzzle. A biblical doctrine with 453 New Testament verses that produce 159 key ideas is a puzzle in its own right. As with natural puzzles, it helps to see a picture of the final product before you start. We have such a picture before us: the one glorious Second Coming of Christ, as He appears on clouds accompanied by angels and saints. Now you have been presented with my findings, and I hope you will agree that the pieces fit.

Six previous records, or narratives, have been given in past chapters that have brought together references and thoughts in the various sections of the New Testament. In this chapter the pieces of the puzzle are assembled in a manner that gives orderly, comprehensive meaning to the wonderful teaching of the Bible on the Second Coming of Christ.

The New Testament Record
Everything God Wants Us to Know About Jesus' Glorious Return

1. **The Second Coming—the return to earth—of the Lord Jesus Christ, God's Son, is a doctrine given by divine inspiration**	Acts 1:11; 1 Thessalonians 4:15; 5:2; Hebrews 6:2
2. (not made up from clever fables)	2 Peter 1:16
3. to impart comfort and hope, and cause you to be alert, sober and firm,	1 Thessalonians 4:18; 5:6; 2 Thessalonians 1:10; Titus 2:11–13
4. and to urge holy living upon the Church.	1 John 3:3; Revelation 22:7, 12
5. **The exact time (day or hour) of His coming is not known (although believers should know the times and seasons)**	Matthew 24:36, 42; 25:13; Mark 13:32–36; Luke 12:39–40
6. but we know that the Second Coming of Christ has not yet taken place.	2 Thessalonians 2:2
7. **We are to look for the glorious appearing of the great God and our Savior Jesus Christ,**	Titus 2:13; 2 Peter 1:16
8. for this is our blessed hope,	Romans 8:24–25; Galatians 5:5; 1 Timothy 1:1; Titus 2:13
9. and it is at hand, and He is expected to come very soon (quickly).	Philippians 4:5; James 5:9; 1 Peter 4:7; 1 John 2:18; Revelation 3:11; 22:7, 12, 20
10. Watch (be alert), therefore!	Matthew 24:42; Mark 13:35, 37; Romans 13:11–12

11. **Worldly people will scoff about such a thing happening,** 2 Peter 3:3–4
12. but it will be fully expected and eagerly awaited by the Church, Matthew 24:42; 1 Corinthians 1:7; Philippians 3:20; 1 Thessalonians 1:10; 5:4; Titus 2:13
13. which does understand the season or signs of the times (as a person recognizing the signs of summertime), Matthew 24:32; Luke 21:29–31
14. and which notes "when these things begin to happen." Luke 21:28
15. **His coming will be sudden, abrupt and startling—unexpected, not foreseen, not anticipated, not looked for by people of the world—as illustrated by the following 14 true-life situations. His coming will be like. . .** Luke 17:28, 30; 1 Thessalonians 5:2–3; Revelation 3:3; 16:15
16. —a flash of lightning, Matthew 24:27; Luke 17:24
17. —the snap of a snare/trap, Luke 21:34–36
18. —the appearance of vultures over a carcass, Matthew 24:28; Luke 17:37
19. —the arrival of summer (a blossoming fig tree), Matthew 24:32–33
20. —the flood in the days of Noah, Matthew 24:37–39; Luke 17:26–27
21. —the judgment in the days of Lot, Luke 17:28–30
22. —working people suddenly taken from their tasks or sleep, Matthew 24:40–41; Luke 17:34–36
23. —the burglary of a household by a thief, Matthew 24:43; Luke 12:39–40; 17:30; 1 Thessalonians 5:2–7; 2 Peter 3:10; Revelation 3:3; 16:15
24. —a master checking up on slaves, Matthew 24:45–51; Luke 12:42–48
25. —an owner inspecting his slaves' activities, Mark 13: 35–36; Luke 12:35–37
26. —a returning nobleman, Luke 19:12–27
27. —a bridegroom's arrival, Matthew 25:1–13
28. —a returning slaveholder who appears and demands an accounting, Matthew 25:14–30

29.—the sudden pains and joy of childbirth.	John 16:21
30. **It will not happen until [after] the apostasy begins and the man of lawlessness [*the anarchist,* MESSAGE] is revealed.**	2 Thessalonians 2:3
31. It will happen at the sounding of the seventh angel.	Revelation 10:7; 11:15
32. The whole world will have heard the Gospel witness,	Matthew 24:14; Mark 13:10
33. and Jerusalem (the Jews) will wish to bless Him.	Matthew 23:39; Luke 13:35
34. It will climax the time of restoration spoken of by all the prophets,	Acts 3:20–21
35. taking place after astronomical signs (the sun is darkened, the moon is turned to blood and stars fall)	Matthew 24:29–30; Mark 13:24–25; Luke 21:25–26; Acts 2:20; Revelation 6:12–13
36. and perplexing earthly signs,	Luke 21:25
37. which will cause believers to know that their redemption draws close.	Luke 21:28
38. **The Lord Jesus Christ—the Lord Himself—**	John 14:3; Philippians 3:20; 1 Thessalonians 2:19; 3:13; 4:16; 2 Thessalonians 2:1; 1 Timothy 6:14–15
39.—the same Jesus raised from the dead—	Acts 1:11; 1 Thessalonians 1:10; Revelation 1:4, 7–8; 4:8; 11:17
40. will be revealed descending from heaven	Philippians 3:20; 1 Thessalonians 1:10; 4:16; 2 Thessalonians 1:7; Revelation 19:11
41. accompanied by all His holy, mighty angels	Matthew 16:27; 24:31; 25:31; Mark 8:38; Luke 9:26; John 1:51; 2 Thessalonians 1:7; Revelation 19:14
42. and ten thousands	Jude 14
43. of all His saints	1 Thessalonians 3:13; 4:14; Revelation 19:14
44. in, on and with the clouds of heaven.	Matthew 24:30; 26:64; Mark 13:26; 14:62; Luke 21:27; 1 Thessalonians 4:17; Revelation 1:7; 14:14–20
45. Every eye shall see Him (that is, He will be visible to all human beings on earth),	Matthew 24:30; Luke 17:24; Revelation 1:7

46. including those who pierced Him. Revelation 1:7
47. **He will come in the same physical body He had when He left.** Acts 1:11
48. **He will come with power and great glory,** Matthew 6:13; 24:27; Mark 13:26; Luke 21:27; 2 Thessalonians 1:9; Titus 2:13; 1 Peter 5:1
49. clothed in the great glory of His Father, Matthew 16:27; 24:30; Mark 8:38; Luke 21:27; 1 Peter 4:13
50. and in His own glory, Matthew 25:31; Luke 9:26; 21:27
51. "sitting on the right hand of the Power." Matthew 26:64; Mark 14:62; Luke 22:69
52. **He will come with a shout.** 1 Thessalonians 4:16; John 5:25, 28
53. **He will come with the trumpet of God,** Matthew 24:31; 1 Thessalonians 4:16
54. the last trump, 1 Corinthians 15:52
55. **He will come with the voice of an archangel.** 1 Thessalonians 4:16
56. He will send forth His angels, Matthew 24:31; Mark 13:27
57. who will gather His elect "from the farthest part of earth." Matthew 24:31; Mark 13:27; Luke 13:28–30
58. The angels will separate the wicked from the just. Matthew 13:39–42, 49–50
59. **He will appear sinless, and as our salvation,** Hebrews 9:28; 1 Peter 1:5
60. to those who look for Him. Hebrews 9:28; 2 Peter 3:12
61. He comes as our Chief Shepherd 1 Peter 5:4
62. and the Judge of unbelievers and the disobedient. Matthew 7:23; 12:32, 41–42; 24:37–41; 2 Thessalonians 1:8–9; James 5:9; 1 Peter 4:5; Jude 15
63. **He will appear in flaming fire,** 2 Thessalonians 1:8
64. slaying the man of lawlessness with the breath of His mouth and bright appearance, 2 Thessalonians 2:8
65. bringing sudden destruction with no escape. 1 Thessalonians 5:3
66. **At the same time the heavens will pass away with a roar and fire,** Hebrews 12:26–27; 2 Peter 3:10, 12
67. the elements will melt with fervent heat, 2 Peter 3:10, 12

68. and the earth and its works will be burned up. — 2 Peter 3:7, 10
69. The creation itself will be delivered. — Romans 8:21
70. **When He comes, the bodies of the deceased Christians will be raised from the dead (resurrected)—** — John 5:25–29; 6:39–40, 44, 54; 11:23–26; Philippians 3:10–11, 14; 1 Thessalonians 4:15–16; 5:10; 1 Corinthians 15:22–23, 52; 2 Corinthians 4:14
71. their bodies to be joined to their living spirits— — 1 Thessalonians 3:13; 4:14
72. and the saints still alive on the earth will be caught up ("raptured") with the other saints to meet the Lord in the air and the clouds. — 1 Thessalonians 4:15, 17; Revelation 20:5–6
73. This first resurrection will involve God's elect people from everywhere. — Matthew 22:28, 30–32; 24:31; Mark 12:25–26; Luke 20:33–38; 1 Corinthians 6:14; 1 Thessalonians 3:13
74. So we will ever (permanently) be with the Lord and live together with Him. — 1 Thessalonians 4:17; 5:10
75. God's people hope in the resurrection. — Acts 23:6; 24:15, 21; 26:6–8; 28:20
76. **The bodies of all of us will be instantly changed (redeemed) to be like His glorious body,** — Romans 8:23; 1 Corinthians 15:51–53; Ephesians 1:14; Colossians 3:4
77. an act accomplished by the powerful working of the Holy Spirit — 2 Corinthians 4:14; 5:1–5; Philippians 3:21
78. as we see Christ as He is. — 1 John 3:2
79. Our change will happen as fast as the blinking of an eye. — 1 Corinthians 15:52
80. **The saints who have walked in this life with blameless hearts of holiness,** — 1 Thessalonians 3:13; 5:23; 1 Timothy 6:14
81. with great joy — 1 Peter 4:13
82. will gather in His presence, — John 14:3; 1 Corinthians 15:23; 1 Thessalonians 2:19; 3:13; 2 Thessalonians 2:1

83. and the Lord will be glorified in His saints — Romans 8:18–19; 2 Thessalonians 1:10; 2:14; 1 Peter 1:7
84. and be marveled at among all who believe — 2 Thessalonians 1:10
85. as they find final relief from earth's afflictions. — Romans 8:18; 2 Thessalonians 1:7
86. There will be a remnant of believing Israel saved. — Romans 9:27–28; 11:15, 25–26
87. **When He comes He will bring to light things hidden in darkness, as well as the counsels of hearts,** — 1 Corinthians 4:5
88. and all partial (incomplete) things will be done away. — 1 Corinthians 13:10
89. We believers shall appear with Him in glory, — Ephesians 5:27; Colossians 3:4
90. and be granted great peace, — 1 Peter 1:13
91. as well as God's complete and final salvation. — 1 Thessalonians 5:9
92. We will be established blameless in holiness before God. — 1 Thessalonians 3:13
93. **The Second Coming will fulfill and climax Scripture,** — Acts 3:20–21
94. while declaring the absolute authority of Christ as supreme Ruler, King and Lord of all the universe. — Acts 2:35–36; 1 Timothy 6:14–15; Revelation 14:14–20; 19:11–16
95. **The Second Coming will be the great and notable Day of the Lord,** — Acts 2:20; 1 Thessalonians 5:2; 2 Peter 3:10
96.—"in that day," — Matthew 7:22; Luke 10:12; 2 Thessalonians 1:10; 2 Timothy 1:18
97.— "on that day," — 2 Timothy 4:8
98.— "until that day," — Matthew 26:29; Mark 14:25; 2 Timothy 1:12
99. —"that day," — Matthew 24:36; Mark 13:32; Luke 21:34; 2 Thessalonians 2:3
100.— "the day of visitation," — 1 Peter 2:12

101.— "the day," Matthew 25:13; Luke 17:30; Romans 13:11–12; 1 Corinthians 3:13–15; 1 Thessalonians 5:5, 8; Hebrews 10:25

102.— "day of judgment," Matthew 10:15; 11:22, 24; 12:36; Mark 6:11; Acts 17:31; 2 Peter 2:9; 3:7; Romans 2:16; 1 John 4:17; Jude 6

103.— "the last day," John 6:39–40, 44, 54; 11:24; 12:48

104.— "in the day of wrath," Romans 2:5–10; Revelation 6:16–17; 14:14–20

105.— "the day of our Lord Jesus Christ," "the Son of Man in His day," Luke 17:24; Romans 2:16; 1 Corinthians 1:8; 5:5; 2 Corinthians 1:14; Philippians 1:6, 10; 2:16; 2 Thessalonians 2:2

106.— "the day of redemption," Ephesians 4:30

107.— "the day of God." 2 Peter 3:12

108. **He will come as King of kings and Lord of lords.** Matthew 6:13; 24:3, 30; 1 Timothy 6:14–15; Revelation 17:14; 19:11–16

109. **He will sit on His glorious throne** Matthew 19:28; 25:31

110. and He will judge cities and nations Matthew 12:18, 20; 25:31–46 Luke 10:12–14

111. and the generations. Luke 10:14; 11:31–32, 51

112. This will initiate the "regeneration." Matthew 19:28

113. All tribes of the earth shall mourn. Matthew 24:30; Luke 21:35; Revelation 1:7

114. The apostles will sit on twelve thrones and judge the twelve tribes of Israel and the Church will judge the world and angels. Matthew 8:12; 19:28; 1 Corinthians 6:2–3

115. Christ's reign will be initiated Revelation 11:15

116. and we shall reign with Him. Matthew 8:11; 2 Timothy 2:12; Revelation 20:6

117. **He shall reward every man according to his works.** Matthew 15:13; 16:27; 25:19; Mark 10:30–31; Luke 6:35; Romans 2:6–9; 1 Corinthians 3:8; Ephesians 6:8; Colossians 3:24–25; Revelation 2:23; 21:7–8; 22:12

118. All will stand before the Judgment Seat of Christ. Romans 14:10–12; 1 Corinthians 3:8; 2 Corinthians 5:10

119. We will be judged by Jesus' words. John 12:48
120. Nothing is secret that will not be revealed. Matthew 18:35; Luke 8:17
121. We shall be "repaid" at the resurrection of the just. Luke 14:14
122. Judgment will be brought (for the living and dead), Acts 10:42; 17:31; 24:25; Romans 2:16; 2 Timothy 4:1; Jude 15; Revelation 11:17–18; 20:11–14
123. and rewards dispensed (unfading crowns of righteousness and glory given to all who love His appearing), 2 Timothy 4:8; James 1:12; 1 Peter 1:13; 5:4
124. and we will be exceedingly joyful that we once suffered with Him and underwent trials. Acts 14:22; Hebrews 10:36–38; 11:35; James 5:8; 1 Peter 1:7, 13; 4:13
125. **He has prepared a place and He will receive us.** John 14:3
126. He will come and serve His followers, Luke 12:37–40
127. and drink the fruit of the new vine with us and eat the Passover. Matthew 26:29; Luke 22:16, 18, 29–30
128. **It is important to keep God's commandment until Christ comes.** 1 Timothy 6:14
129. Three of the seven churches of Asia Minor were spiritually challenged to improve in the light of His coming. Revelation 2:25; 3:3, 11
130. We are to wake up and repent of permitting false teachings. Revelation 2:16
131. We are to hold fast to our faith (what we have), for fear of losing our crowns. Revelation 2:25; 3:11
132. We are to heed the prophetic words of this book [Revelation]. Revelation 22:7
133. We are to be bold in conduct and goodness, 2 Peter 3:11
134. being diligent to be found by Him in peace, without spot and blameless. 2 Peter 3:14
135. As often as we partake of Communion, we remind ourselves of Christ's death until He comes. 1 Corinthians 11:26

136. We must possess the righteousness that is from God by faith. — Philippians 3:9
137. The Church is to participate in spiritual gifts until He comes. — 1 Corinthians 1:7
138. Christ will confirm/sustain His people until the end, that we may be blameless at the Second Coming. — 1 Corinthians 1:8
139. **Your participation in this event will be our greatest joy.** — 1 Thessalonians 2:19
140. Wait patiently and expectantly for Him. — 1 Thessalonians 1:10; 2 Thessalonians 3:5
141. Be at peace and believe our testimony, — 2 Thessalonians 1:10
142. for He will bring it to pass. — 1 Thessalonians 5:24
143. **Christ is waiting patiently for the right time to come so He will get the full harvest.** — Mark 4:29; James 5:7–8; 2 Peter 3:9; Revelation 14:14
144. We, too, must be patient, — Hebrews 10:36–38; James 5:7
145. looking for and hastening His coming— — 2 Peter 3:12
146. establishing our hearts, — James 5:8
147. being sober and hoping to the end, — 1 Peter 1:13
148. abiding in Him so that we may have confidence and not be ashamed. — 1 John 2:28
149. He will keep what I have committed to Him until that Day. — 2 Timothy 1:12; 4:18
150. And in that Day we will boast of each other. — 2 Corinthians 1:14
151. **Jesus' question: When He comes, will He find faith on the earth?** — Matthew 28:20; Luke 18:8
152. We are not to be worried about the dedication of others, but serve Him until He comes. — John 21:22–23
153. Believers will be received by Him. — John 14:3, 18, 28–29; 16:16–22
154. We are to be prayerful in our waiting for Him. — Luke 12:36

***Note:** The following three references received special attention in chapters 5 and 7 because of their bewildering nature*

155. Some then living would not die until they saw the Son of Man coming in His Kingdom. — Matthew 16:28; Mark 9:1; Luke 9:27; 2 Peter 1:16
156. Disciples would not finish going through the cities of Israel before He came. — Matthew 10:23
157. This generation would not pass away until all things took place. — Matthew 24:34; Mark 13:30; Luke 21:32

The apostolic prayers:
158. By Paul: "O Lord, come!" — 1 Corinthians 16:22
159. By John: "Amen. Even so, come, Lord Jesus!" — Revelation 22:20

One Supreme Consideration

What a magnificent job our seven experts—Jesus, Luke, Paul, Peter, John, James and Jude—have done in presenting their information! A beautiful harmony and unity run throughout the New Testament on this subject, in spite of the different styles and perspectives of the authors, and despite the communication problems inherent in that long-ago society.

The valuable information in the four appendixes will greatly aid your understanding of this subject. (It seemed best to place the material there rather than in our chapters. Some of this text will serve well for future reference.) My desire has been to present the overall story of Jesus' return in a readable fashion for the average person, yet supply the kind of information that will enhance in-depth study. In this book you have a truly unique approach to a vital subject, with all available Scripture and basic insights put into your hands.

We tend to get bogged down in the mechanics of spirituality. Jesus and the writers of the New Testament gave us many principles to consider in that regard. But they concentrated on one supremely important aspect of Jesus' Second Coming: *readiness*. Join me in a renewed effort to serve the Lord faithfully until He comes, ever watchful and ever dedicated to the task set before us.

APPENDIX A

THE FOUR BIG QUESTIONS ABOUT CHRIST'S RETURN

This summary uses 29 Scripture thoughts to answer four fundamental questions about the Second Coming of Christ:

1. *Why* must Jesus come again?
2. *In what manner* will He come again?
3. *What will happen* when He comes again?
4. *When* will He come again?

I have provided both the scriptural answers and the references where these answers may be found. The following summary comprises 29 significant facts about the Second Coming of Christ arranged under the four major questions.

Why Must Jesus Come Again?

- *To fulfill and climax all Scripture* (Acts 3:20–21; 2 Peter 1:16).
- *To show finally and conclusively that Jesus is King of kings and Lord of lords* (1 Timothy 6:14; Revelation 19:16).

- *To gather in the earth's harvest* (James 5:7; Revelation 14:14).
- *To execute judgment and dispense rewards; to fulfill justice* (Jude 15; Revelation 22:12).
- *To gather the Church to Himself and be glorified in her* (2 Thessalonians 1:10; John 14:3, 18).

In What Manner Will Jesus Come Again?

- *Quickly and unexpectedly* (Luke 21:35; 1 Thessalonians 5:2; 2 Peter 3:10; Revelation 22:20).
- *In the same physical body He had when He left* (Acts 1:11).
- *In the glory of His Father, in flaming fire* (Matthew 16:27; 24:30; 25:31; 2 Thessalonians 1:7).
- *Accompanied by angels with ten thousands of His saints* (Matthew 16:27; 24:31; 2 Thessalonians 1:7; Jude 14).
- *In the clouds of heaven* (Matthew 24:30; 26:64; Mark 14:62; Luke 21:27; Revelation 1:7).
- *Beheld by every eye* (Matthew 24:27; Revelation 1:7; Matthew 24:30).
- *With shout, angelic voice and seventh trump* (1 Thessalonians 4:16; Revelation 10:7).
- *As the sinless One, the acme of perfection* (Hebrews 9:28).

What Will Happen When Jesus Comes Again?

- *The first resurrection, that of the righteous, will take place* (John 5:28; 1 Corinthians 15:52; 1 Thessalonians 4:16).
- *Our bodies will be glorified* (1 Corinthians 15:51; Philippians 3:21; Colossians 3:4).
- *Christ will wreak vengeance on the ungodly and destruction of the wicked one* (Matthew 24:37–39; 2 Thessalonians 1:8; 2:8).
- *The angels will gather the redeemed* (Matthew 24:31; Mark 13:27).

- *The Church will make an accounting to her Lord* (Matthew 16:27; Luke 9:26; 12:37; 19:15; 1 Corinthians 4:5; 2 Timothy 4:1, 8; 1 Peter 4:13).
- *We shall be like Him* (1 John 3:2).
- *We will be personally received by Him* (John 14:3).
- *The creation shall undergo violent, cleansing upheaval* (2 Peter 3:7–13).

When Will Jesus Come Again?

- *Very soon!* (Revelation 22:20).
- *Exact time unknown, but the Church may know the approximate time and season* (Matthew 23:39; 24:42; 25:13; Mark 13:32; Luke 21:30).
- *When the Jews (Jerusalem) are willing to bless Him* (Matthew 23:39).
- *After the whole world hears the Gospel* (Matthew 24:14).
- *After the sun is darkened and the moon turned to blood* (Matthew 24:29; Luke 21:25; Revelation 6:12).
- *After the Antichrist system of last days is revealed* (2 Thessalonians 2:3; Revelation 19:20).
- *When the seventh angel sounds his trumpet* (1 Corinthians 15:2; 1 Thessalonians 4:16; Revelation 10:7).
- *At the last day* (John 6:39–40, 44, 54).

APPENDIX B

ALL THE NEW TESTAMENT REFERENCES ON THE SECOND COMING

Have you ever purchased a book because it contained information so significant that it was worth more to you than the price of the book? I have done that many times. As a teenage Christian I searched in vain for a book that could give me all the basic references on the Second Coming of Christ. I have continued to look for that book. Now you hold it in your hands! Since I could not find such a book, I have written it myself.

This Appendix B puts the 453 Second Coming verses of the New Testament squarely before you. It is the backbone of the body of this book—and easily worth more than the price of the volume!

I realize, of course, that some sincere Christians will not agree with all the verses I have chosen. This does not trouble me; I merely want to bring you the information as best I can, hoping you will be provoked to serious contemplation on the subject. I do think, based on my research, that most sincere Bible students will agree with most, if not all, my choices. Do keep in mind that a belief about the Second Coming, even if beautifully constructed, should not deliberately leave out, sidestep or ignore troublesome verses. All the pieces of the puzzle are made to fit!

Note: The following 453 verses speak of the Lord's Second Coming, the Day arriving, the dead being raised and changed, and the time of judgment and redemption.

Matthew

(106 verses)	6:13	"Yours is the kingdom and the power and the glory."
	7:22–23	"Many will say to Me in that day, 'Lord, Lord, have we not. . . ?' And then I will declare to them, 'I never knew you.'"
	8:11–12	"Many will come . . . and sit down with Abraham, Isaac, and Jacob in the kingdom of heaven. But the sons of the kingdom will be cast out into outer darkness."
	10:15	"It will be more tolerable for the land of Sodom and Gomorrah in the day of judgement than for that city!"
	:23	"You will not have gone through the cities of Israel before the Son of Man comes."
	11:22	"It will be more tolerable for Tyre and Sidon in the day of judgment than for you."
	:24	"It shall be more tolerable for the land of Sodom in the day of judgment than for you."
	12:18	"He will declare justice to the Gentiles. . . ."
	:32	"It will not be forgiven him, either in this age or in the age to come."
	:36	"For every idle word men may speak, they will give account of it in the day of judgment."
	:41–42	"The men of Nineveh will rise up in the Judgment with this generation and condemn it. . . .The queen of the South will rise up in the judgment with this generation and condemn it."
	13:30	"At the time of harvest I will say to the reapers, 'First gather together the tares . . . to burn them, but gather the wheat into my barn.'"
	:39–42	"The harvest is the end of the age, and the reapers are the angels. . . . The Son of Man will send out His angels, and they will gather out of His kingdom all things that offend . . . and will cast them into the furnace of fire."

:49–50	"So it will be at the end of the age. The angels will come forth, separate the wicked from among the just. . . ."
15:13	"Every plant which My heavenly Father has not planted will be uprooted."
16:27	"The Son of Man will come . . . then He will reward each. . . ."
:28	"Some standing here . . . shall not taste death till they see the Son of Man coming in His kingdom."
18:35	"So My heavenly Father also will do to you if each of you, from his heart, does not forgive."
19:28	"In the regeneration, when the Son of Man sits on the throne of His glory, you who have followed Me will also sit on twelve thrones, judging the twelve tribes of Israel."
22:28	"In the resurrection, whose wife of the seven will she be?"
:30–32	"In the resurrection they neither marry nor are given in marriage. . . . But concerning the resurrection . . . God is not the God of the dead, but of the living."
23:39	"You shall see Me no more till you say, 'Blessed is He who comes in the name of the Lord!'"
24:3	"And what will be the sign of Your coming, and of the end of the age?"
:14	"This gospel of the kingdom will be preached in all the world . . . and then the end will come."
:27	"As the lightning comes . . . so also will the coming of the Son of Man be."
:28	"Wherever the carcass is . . . there the eagles [vultures] will be gathered."
:29–31	"The sign of the Son of Man will appear in heaven, and . . . they will see the Son of Man coming. . . . And He will send His angels."
:32–33	". . . when you see all these things, know that it is near."
:34	This generation will by no means pass away till all these things are fulfilled."
:36	"But of that day and hour no one knows."
:37–39	"As the days of Noah were, so also will the coming of the Son of Man be."

	:40–42	"One will be taken and the other left. . . . you do not know what hour your Lord is coming."
	:43–44	"If the master . . . had known what hour the thief would come. . . . You also be ready, for the Son of Man is coming at an hour when you do not expect."
	:45–51	". . . The master of that servant will come on a day when he is not looking for him. . . ."
	25:1–13	". . . The bridegroom is coming. . . . You know neither the day nor the hour in which the Son of Man is coming."
	:14–30	". . . The lord of those servants came and settled accounts with them. . . ."
	:31–46	"When the Son of Man comes in His glory . . . then He will sit on the throne of His glory. . . . The nations will be gathered before Him. . . ."
	26:29	". . . until that day when I drink it new with you in My Father's kingdom."
	:64	"You will see the Son of Man . . . coming on the clouds of heaven."
	28:20	"I am with you always, even to the end of the age."
Mark		
(22 verses)	4:29	"The harvest has come."
	6:11	"It will be more tolerable for Sodom and Gomorrah in the day of judgement than for that city!"
	8:38	". . . when He comes in the glory of His Father."
	9:1	"Some . . . will not taste death till they see the kingdom of God present with power."
	10:30–31	". . . and in the age to come, eternal life. But many who are first will be last, and the last first."
	12:25–26	"When they rise from the dead, they neither marry nor are given in marriage. . . ."
	13:10	"The gospel must first be preached to all the nations."
	:24–25	"The sun will be darkened, and the moon will not give its light; the stars will fall. . . ."
	:26–27	"They will see the Son of Man coming in the clouds with great power and glory. And then He will send His angels."
	:30	"This generation will by no means pass away till all those things take place."
	:32–33	"Of that day and hour no one knows. . . . You do not know when the time is."
	:34–37	". . . Watch therefore, for you do not know when the master of the house is coming. . . ."

	14:25	". . . until that day when I drink it new in the kingdom of God."
	:62	"You will see the Son of Man . . . coming with the clouds."
Luke		
(82 verses)	6:35	"Your reward will be great."
	8:17	"Nothing is secret that will not be revealed."
	9:26	". . . when He comes in His own glory."
	:27	"There are some . . . who shall not taste death till they see the kingdom of God."
	10:12	"It will be more tolerable in that Day for Sodom."
	:14	"It will be more tolerable for Tyre and Sidon at the judgment."
	11:31	"The queen of the South will rise up in the judgment with the men of this generation."
	:32	"The men of Nineveh will rise up in the judgment."
	:51	"[Blood] shall be required of this generation."
	12:35–38	". . . You . . . be like men who wait for their master. . . ."
	:39–40	". . . You also be ready, for the Son of Man is coming [like a thief] at an hour you do not expect."
	:42–48	". . . Blessed is that servant whom his master will find so doing when he comes. . . ."
	13:28	"There will be weeping . . . when you see Abraham and Isaac and Jacob and all the prophets in the kingdom of God, and yourselves thrust out."
	:29	"They will come from the east and the west, from the north and the south, and sit down in the kingdom of God."
	:30	"There are last who will be first, and there are first who will be last."
	:35	"You shall not see Me until the time comes when you say, 'Blessed is He who comes in the name of the Lord!'"
	14:14	"You shall be repaid at the resurrection of the just."
	17:22–37	". . . As the lightning . . . flashes . . . as it was in the days of Noah . . . as it was also in the days of Lot . . . so will it be. . . . Remember Lot's wife. . . . One will be taken and the other will be left. . . . Wherever the body is, there the eagles will be gathered."

	18:8	"When the Son of Man comes, will He really find faith on the earth?"
	19:12–27	"A certain nobleman went into a far country to receive for himself a kingdom and to return. . . ."
	20:33–38	"In the resurrection, whose wife does she become?" . . . "Those who are counted worthy to attain that age, and the resurrection from the dead, neither marry nor are given in marriage. . . ."
	21:25–28	"There will be signs. . . . Then they will see the Son of Man coming. . . ."
	:29–31	"When you see these things happening, know that the kingdom of God is near."
	:32	"This generation will by no means pass away till all things are fulfilled."
	:34–36	". . . Watch . . . pray always that you may be counted worthy . . . to stand before the Son of Man."
	22:16, 18	"I will no longer eat of it [this Passover]. . . . I will not drink of the fruit of the vine until the kingdom of God comes."
	:29–30	". . . You may eat and drink at My table in My kingdom."
	:69	"Hereafter the Son of Man will sit on the right hand of the power of God."
John		
(28 verses)	1:51	"You shall see heaven open, and the angels of God ascending and descending upon the Son of Man."
	5:25–29	". . . The dead will hear the voice of the Son of God. . . . All who are in the graves will hear His voice and come forth . . . to the resurrection."
	6:39, 40, 44, 54	"I will raise him up at the last day."
	11:23–26	"Your brother will rise again. . . . I am the resurrection. . . ."
	12:48	"The word that I have spoken will judge him in the last day."
	14:3	"I will come again and receive you to Myself."
	:18	"I will come to you."
	:28–29	"I am going away and coming back to you. . . ."
	16:16–18	"A little while, and you will not see Me. . . ."
	:19	"Again a little while, and you will see Me."

	:20–21	"Your sorrow will be turned into joy. . . ."
	:22	"I will see you again."
	21:22–23	"If I will that he remain till I come, what is that to you? . . ."
Acts		
(16 verses)	1:11	"This same Jesus . . . will so come in like manner."
	2:20	". . . the coming of the great and awesome day of the Lord."
	:35	". . . till I make Your enemies Your footstool."
	3:20–21	". . . that He may send Jesus. . . ."
	10:42	". . . Judge of the living and the dead."
	14:22	"We must through many tribulations enter the kingdom of God."
	17:31	"He will judge the world . . . by the Man whom He has ordained."
	23:6	"Concerning the hope and resurrection of the dead I am being judged!"
	24:15	"I have hope in God . . . that there will be a resurrection of the dead, both of the just and the unjust."
	:21	"Concerning the resurrection of the dead I am being judged."
	:25	. . . and the judgment to come.
	26:6–8	"I stand . . . for the hope of the promise . . . our twelve tribes . . . hope to attain. . . ."
	28:20	"For the hope of Israel I am bound with this chain."
Romans		
(23 verses)	2:5–10	In the day of wrath . . . God . . . "will render to each one according to his deeds." . . .
	:16	In the day when God will judge the secrets of men by Jesus Christ. . . .
	8:18–19	. . . the glory which shall be revealed in us. . . . the revealing of the sons of God.
	:21	The creation itself also will be delivered.
	:23–25	We ourselves groan. . . eagerly waiting for . . . the redemption of our body. . . . We eagerly wait for it.
	9:27–28	". . . The remnant will be saved. . . ."
	11:15	What will their acceptance be but life from the dead?
	:25–26	". . . Hardening . . . has happened to Israel until the fullness of the Gentiles. . . ."

	13:11–12	It is high time to awake out of sleep; for now our salvation is nearer. . . . The day is at hand.
	14:10–12	We shall all stand before the judgment seat of Christ. . . . Each of us shall give account.
1 Corinthians		
(23 verses)	1:7–8	Come short in no gift, eagerly waiting for the revelation of our Lord Jesus Christ . . . blameless in the day of our Lord Jesus Christ [*when our Lord Jesus Christ returns*, nlt].
	3:8	Each one will receive his own reward.
	:13–15	Each one's work will become manifest; for the Day will declare it. . . . The fire will test each one's work.
	4:5	Judge nothing . . . until the Lord comes.
	5:5	. . . that his spirit may be saved in the day of the Lord Jesus [*when the Lord returns*, nlt].
	6:2–3	The saints will judge the world. . . . We shall judge angels.
	:14	God both raised up the Lord and will also raise us up.
	11:26	Proclaim the Lord's death till He comes.
	13:10	When that which is perfect has come, then that which is in part will be done away.
	15:22–23	In Christ all shall be made alive. . . . Afterward those who are Christ's at His coming.
	:42–44	The body is sown in corruption, . . . raised in incorruption . . . in glory . . . in power . . . a spiritual body.
	:51–54	. . . The dead will be raised incorruptible, and we shall be changed.
	16:22	O Lord, come!
2 Corinthians		
(8 verses)	1:14	We are your boast . . . in the day of the Lord Jesus.
	4:14	He . . . will also raise us up with Jesus, and will present us with you.
	5:1–5	. . . We groan, earnestly desiring to be clothed with our habitation which is from heaven. . . .
	:10	We must all appear before the judgment seat of Christ. . . .
Galatians		
(1 verse)	5:5	We . . . eagerly wait for the hope of righteousness by faith.

Ephesians		
(4 verses)	1:14	[The Holy Spirit is] the guarantee of our inheritance until the redemption of the purchased possession.
	4:30	You were sealed for the day of redemption.
	5:27	[Christ loved the church] that He might present it to Himself a glorious church.
	6:8	Whatever good anyone does, he will receive the same from the Lord.
Philippians		
(10 verses)	1:6	. . . until the day of Jesus Christ.
	:10	Be sincere and without offense till the day of Christ.
	2:16	[Hold] fast the word of life, so that I may rejoice in the day of Christ.
	3:9	[I count all things loss that I may] be found in Him, . . . the righteousness which is from God by faith.
	:10–11	[I count all things loss that I may] know . . . the power of His resurrection . . . if . . . I may attain to the resurrection from the dead.
	:14	I press toward the goal for the prize of the upward call of God in Christ Jesus.
	:20–21	We also eagerly wait for the Savior, the Lord Jesus Christ, who will transform our lowly body.
	4:5	The Lord is at hand.
Colossians		
(3 verses)	3:4	When Christ who is our life appears, then you also will appear with Him.
	:24–25	From the Lord you will receive the reward.
1 Thess-alonians		
(19 verses)	1:10	Wait for His Son from heaven.
	2:19	. . . our Lord Jesus Christ at His coming.
	3:13	. . . the coming of our Lord Jesus Christ with all His saints.
	4:14–18	. . . the coming of the Lord. . . . The Lord Himself will descend. . . . Then we . . . shall . . . meet the Lord in the air. . . .
	5:2–7	The day of the Lord . . . comes as a thief in the night. . . .
	:8	Let us who are of the day be sober.
	:9	. . . to obtain salvation through our Lord Jesus Christ.
	:10	Whether we wake or sleep, we should live together with Him.

	:23	. . . the coming of our Lord Jesus Christ.
	:24	He. . . will do it.
2 Thess-alonians		
(10 verses)	1:7–10	. . . when the Lord Jesus is revealed from heaven . . . when He comes, in that day.
	2:1–3	Concerning the coming of our Lord Jesus Christ . . . that Day will not come unless the falling away comes first.
	:8	. . .. the brightness of His coming.
	:14	. . . the obtaining of the glory of our Lord Jesus Christ.
	3:5	. . . the patience of Christ.
1 Timothy		
(3 verses)	1:1	. . . the Lord Jesus Christ, our hope.
	6:14–15	. . . our Lord Jesus Christ's appearing. . . .
2 Timothy		
(6 verses)	1:12	He is able to keep what I have committed to Him until that Day.
	:18	. . . mercy from the Lord in that Day.
	2:12	If we endure, we shall also reign with Him.
	4:1	The Lord . . . will judge the living and the dead at His appearing.
	:8	There is laid up for me the crown of righteousness . . . on that Day, . . . but also to all who have loved His appearing.
	:18	. . . preserve me for His heavenly kingdom.
Titus		
(3 verses)	2:11–13	. . . . the blessed hope and glorious appearing of our great God and Savior Jesus Christ.
Hebrews		
(9 verses)	6:2	. . . the doctrine . . . of resurrection . . . and of eternal judgment.
	9:28	He will appear a second time.
	10:25	. . . as you see the Day approaching.
	:36–38	. . . He who is coming will come. . . .
	11:35	. . . that they might obtain a better resurrection.
	12:26–27	"Yet once more I shake not only the earth, but also heaven." . . .

James		
(4 verses)	1:12	He will receive the crown of life.
	5:7	Be patient, brethren, until the coming of the Lord.
	:8	The coming of the Lord is at hand.
	:9	The Judge is standing at the door!
1 Peter		
(9 verses)	1:5	. . . for salvation ready to be revealed in the last time.
	:7	. . . at the revelation of Jesus Christ.
	:13	. . . at the revelation of Jesus Christ.
	2:12	. . . in the day of visitation.
	4:5	They will give an account to Him who is ready to judge the living and dead.
	:7	The end of all things is at hand.
	:13	When His glory is revealed. . . .
	5:1	. . . the glory that will be revealed.
	:4	When the Chief Shepherd appears. . . .
2 Peter		
(10 verses)	1:16	. . . the power and coming of our Lord Jesus Christ.
	2:9	The day of Judgement
	3:3–4	Scoffers will come in the last days . . . saying, "Where is the promise of His coming?"
	:7	. . . reserved for fire until the day of judgment.
	:9	"The Lord is not slack concerning His promise. . . ."
	:10	The day of the Lord will come as a thief.
	:11	". . . since all these things will be dissolved. . . ."
	:12	[We ought to be] looking for and hastening the coming of the day of God.
	:14	". . . looking forward to these things, be diligent. . . ."
1 John		
(5 verses)	2:18	It is the last hour.
	:28	. . . when He appears . . . at His coming.
	3:2–3	When He is revealed, we shall be like Him. . . . This hope in Him purifies.
	4:17	. . . boldness in the day of judgment.
Jude		
(5 verses)	6	. . . for the judgment of the great day.
	14–15	"Behold, the Lord comes."
	21	Keep . . . looking for the mercy of our Lord Jesus Christ unto eternal life.
	24	. . . to present you faultless before the presence of His glory with exceeding joy.

Revelation	1:4	. . . from Him . . . who is to come.
(44 verses)	:7	Behold, He is coming with clouds.
	:8	. . . says the Lord, "who . . . is to come."
	2:16	"Repent, or else I will come to you quickly. . . ."
	:23	"And I will give to each one of you according to your works."
	:25	"But hold fast what you have till I come."
	:26	"He who overcomes, and keeps My works until the end. . . ."
	3:3	"I will come upon you as a thief, and you will not know what hour."
	:11	"Behold I come quickly! Hold fast what you have."
	4:8	". . . who was and is and is to come!"
	6:12–13	". . . the sun became black . . . and the moon became like blood."
	:16–17	". . . For the great day of His wrath has come."
	10:7	"In the days of the sounding of the seventh angel . . . the mystery of God would be finished."
	11:15	The seventh angel sounded: And . . . "He shall reign forever and ever!"
	:17	". . . who is to come."
	:18	"Your wrath has come, and the time of the dead, that they should be judged."
	14:14–20	On the cloud sat One like the Son of Man, having on His head a golden crown, and in His hand a sharp sickle. . . . And the earth was reaped. . . .
	16:15	"I am coming as a thief."
	17:14	"He is Lord of lords and King of kings."
	19:11–16	And behold, a white horse. And He who sat on him was called Faithful and True. . . . His name is called The Word of God. . . .
	20:5–6	. . . Blessed and holy is he who has part in the first resurrection.
	:11–14	Then I saw a great white throne. . . . And they were judged.
	21:7	"He who overcomes shall inherit all things."
	:8	". . . their part in the lake which burns with fire and brimstone."
	22:7	"I am coming quickly!"
	:12	"I am coming quickly."
	:20	"I am coming quickly." Amen. Even so, come, Lord Jesus!

APPENDIX C

DANIEL'S SEVENTY-WEEKS PROPHECY

Daniel 9:24–27 is the most comprehensive prophecy of the Bible. Confined within the 490 years of its prophetic boundaries are six of the greatest divine objectives of all time. In addition God's angel predicts the anointing of the Messiah *to the exact year,* as well as His sacrificial crucifixion. The advent of the messianic Kingdom is indicated, and the strange period of three and a half years (mentioned five times in Revelation) clearly identified. This prophecy supplies the key to the proper interpretation of the last book of the Bible as well as the events of the last days.

The word translated "weeks" is more accurately rendered "sevens"; thus the prophecy could be called "The Seventy of Sevens"—that is, seventy weeks or 490 days. Most Bible scholars recognize that, in this prophecy, one day equals one year (Genesis 29:27–28; Leviticus 25:8; Numbers 14:34; Ezekiel 4:6), which makes it a prophecy spanning 490 years.

Objective of the Prophecy

Right from the beginning the prophecy sharpens its focus: "Seventy weeks are determined for *your people* and for *your holy city"* (Daniel 9:24, emphasis added). The subjects are natural Israel (God's people at that time) and the holy city of Jerusalem. Six actions are to be fulfilled during this period, according to this verse. Seventy weeks (or 490 years) have been "determined" in order to

- Finish the transgression
- Make an end of sins
- Make reconciliation for iniquity
- Bring in everlasting righteousness
- Seal up the vision and prophecy
- Anoint the Most Holy

These expressions, as we will soon see, involve both Jews and Gentiles. Although the six actions involve the Jews and their city, Daniel will reveal a redemption intended for the whole world, which is the heart of his prophecy. I like this comment by Kevin J. Conner:

> Messiah's ministry, though to Judah and Jerusalem first, actually opens up redemption for the whole world. For this reason, the fulfilment of the clauses involved both Jews and Gentiles in the fullest sense. . . . For, a consideration of the six clauses shows that *judicially* and *provisionally,* all were fulfilled at Calvary by Messiah in His first coming, but *possessionally* and *experientially* all find absolute fulfilment at Messiah's second coming. The clauses involve not only Judah and Jerusalem, though the prophecy centered there, but ultimately involves the whole world. Therefore, we may say, the clauses are fulfilled to be fulfilled![1]

Two historical events will occur during this time frame of 490 years, which will facilitate the fulfillment of the six statements: the crucifixion of Christ and His Second Coming. For this to be true, however, the 490 years cannot run continuously, since the cross and Second Coming are separated (as we know) by more than two thousand years. There must be a breach or break that will disengage the prophetic running time on Israel and Jerusalem.

An opening or gap is to be made in God's program—a window of opportunity, you might say, a time slot for the Gentiles to be brought into His purposes. Like a set of parentheses in a sentence, marvelously provided by God, a breach will be provided for the ingathering of the Gentiles.

The Division of the Weeks

The seventy weeks are divided into *three* parts:

1. Seven weeks = 49 years
2. Sixty-two weeks = 434 years
3. One week = seven years

There shall be seven weeks. . . . The prophecy is to begin "from the going forth of the command to restore and build Jerusalem" (Daniel 9:25). It is generally accepted that there were three decrees issued by Persian kings for this purpose: in 536 B.C., 457 B.C. and 444 B.C. The most logical date for the decree would be 457 B.C., but disagreement exists about which king made the decree. It was probably made by either Artaxerxes (Queen Esther's stepson) in the seventh year of his reign, or by Cyrus.[2]

Ezra was chosen to fulfill the decree (Ezra 7). During the first "seven weeks" (or 49 years), the city of Jerusalem was actually rebuilt "in troublesome times" (Daniel 9:25). The book of Nehemiah records the exciting story.

The following chart covers the 174-year chronology from the beginning of captivity until Nehemiah returned to Babylon.

Overview from Captivity to Return

70 years	606 B.C.: Beginning of captivity in Babylon
	536 B.C.: End of captivity, edict of Cyrus of Persia
20 years	536 B.C.: 49,897 Jews return with Zerubbabel
	536 B.C.: Seventh month, altar built, sacrifices resumed
	535 B.C.: Work on Temple begun and stopped
	520 B.C.: Work renewed; prophets Haggai and Zechariah arrive

	516 B.C.: Temple completed
60 years	478 B.C.: Esther becomes queen of Persia
25 years	457 B.C.: Ezra (with 7,000 others) goes to Jerusalem
	444 B.C.: Nehemiah rebuilds the wall (in 52 days)
	432 B.C.: Nehemiah returns to Babylon

The fall of Babylon at the hands of the Medes and Persians occurred in 538 B.C. Two years later Cyrus, king of Persia, issued a decree allowing the Jews to return to Jerusalem and rebuild the Temple. Note that Isaiah prophesied that Cyrus would be used by the Lord in the restoration of the Temple (Isaiah 44:28; 45:1–4, 13; 46:11), the dating of the seventy-weeks prophecy actually begins with the decree issued in 457 B.C.

An interesting side thought: The captivity began in 606 B.C. and ended in 536 B.C., so the length of the exile was seventy years—a remarkable fulfillment of Jeremiah 25:11–12.

Ezra 7 shows us the fulfillment of Daniel's prophecy. Approximately 59 years after the completion of the Temple, Ezra arrived in Jerusalem and began his work of spiritual restoration. About thirteen years later Nehemiah arrived in the capacity of governor. Thus Ezra and Nehemiah, two of the great personalities of the Bible, were brought together in the work of fulfilling God's Word.

. . . And sixty-two weeks. The "seven weeks and sixty-two weeks" (or 483 years) were to reach from Artaxerxes' decree "until the Messiah the Prince" (Daniel 9:25). Adding 483 years to 457 B.C. would bring us to A.D. 26, the year scholars believe Jesus was anointed Messiah by the Holy Spirit at the river Jordan. Jesus was anointed at age thirty (Numbers 4; Luke 3:23), which would make it the year A.D. 30. So when the known error of four years in our present calendar is accounted for, Daniel's prophecy finds dramatic fulfillment, pinpointing the exact year in history when Jesus would be anointed Messiah!

A final week, or seven years, finishes out the prophecy (Daniel 9:27). Seven years—now where does that fit in?[3] Two key thoughts will guide us. One has to do with the Prince Messiah, and the other with "the prince who is to come" (verse 26).

After the sixty-two weeks Messiah shall be cut off. This "cutting off" (verse 26) refers to the Messiah's death by crucifixion (Isaiah 53:8). This event was to take place sometime during the last week of the prophecy. When would it happen? (*After sixty-two weeks* does not mean "right at the end of," but rather "at some time after.") The answer is given in Daniel 9:27, where we find that the Messiah would be cut off "in the middle of the week"—that is, after three and a half years.

What would the Messiah be doing for three and a half years? The answer is so simple that it is missed. Jesus' earthly ministry, from anointing in the Jordan to death on the cross, was three and a half years! How do we know this? That time span is a generally acknowledged fact, computed from the gospel passages (especially in John) that refer to the Passover feasts occurring during His earthly ministry. Also, Jesus' parable of the fig tree in Luke 13:6–9 has definite chronological overtones that verify His three-and-a-half-year ministry.

The people of the prince who is to come. This is the second prince mentioned in Daniel's prophecy. The first is Jesus, "Messiah the Prince" (verse 25). "The prince who is to come" (verse 26) was Titus, the son of the Roman emperor Vespasian, who came in A.D. 70 and, it was prophesied, "shall destroy the city and the sanctuary" (9:26), which he did.

An interesting note by David Sell:

> What is particularly amazing about this prophecy is that it says it would be the "people" of the prince who would destroy the sanctuary. Josephus, the famous Jewish historian, gives us a written account of this grizzly event. According to his writings, as the Roman armies began to destroy the city of Jerusalem, a great number of Jews barricaded themselves inside the temple while the Romans continued to destroy the rest of the city. Many of these Jews were wounded and dying. Finally, as starvation set in and more Jews continued to die, the stench of decaying bodies coming from the temple was so bad that the soldiers, *"the people of the prince,"* insisted upon igniting the temple on fire to kill the rest and eliminate the smell.
>
> When the Romans finally entered the temple after the fire was out, they soon realized that abundant quantities of gold had melted

> and seeped underneath the massive stones which made up the temple wall. When they realized there was gold under the stones, they removed them all one by one, thus fulfilling the words of Jesus who said, *"there will not be left one stone upon another"* (Mt. 24:1–2).[4]

Not only did Jesus prophesy the coming destruction of Jerusalem, but He used Daniel's prophecy as a basis for His prediction (Matthew 24:15; Luke 21:20–24).

He shall confirm a covenant with many for one week. Verse 27 is the pivotal verse of the entire prophecy, with the interpretation dependent on who *he* refers to! There are only two real choices: "Messiah the Prince" (verse 25) and Prince Titus (verse 26). The use of a pronoun like *he* implies that the subject has already been identified. For instance, if I were to say, "He just walked into the room," you would not have enough information to identify who *he* is. But if I said, "John arrived about an hour ago, and he just walked into the room," you would know immediately that *he* is John. Pronouns need a referent.

Some suggest that the mysterious *he* is the Antichrist of the last days. But grammatically this is hardly possible, since there has been no previous mention of the Antichrist throughout the prophecy. No, the choice is definitely between Jesus Christ and Prince Titus.

Notice the clarity of the verse when *he* is interpreted as the Messiah:

- Messiah is "he" who is to come (verse 25).
- Messiah is "he" who is cut off (verse 26).
- Messiah is "he" who establishes covenants (verse 27).
- Messiah is "he" who "shall bring an end to sacrifice and offering" (verse 27).

Only Jesus Messiah could "confirm a covenant" (Isaiah 42:6; Romans 15:8; Hebrews 13:20). This was done when He "[brought] an end to sacrifice and offering" (verse 27) through the shedding of His own precious blood. Covenants are confirmed or ratified by the shedding of blood. And according to Hebrews 9:16: "Where there is a testament, there must also of necessity be the death of the testator." This was done "not for Himself" (verse 26), but for the people (see Mark 16:20; Hebrews 7:27; 8:6, 10; 9:14–15; 10:10, 29.) God's acceptance of blood sacrifice ceased when Jesus died on the cross. Isaiah 66:1–4 clearly shows us the divine attitude toward blood shed *after* Calvary. Jesus shed His precious blood to confirm the covenant. Now bulls and goats are no longer acceptable.

But in the middle of the week.... Through the sacrifice of Himself as the perfect and lasting sacrifice, Jesus the Messiah ended sacrifice and offering. It happened "in the middle of the week" (verse 27). This was dramatically fulfilled by Jesus' death in two ways.

First, Jesus was crucified after three and a half years of earthly ministry, or in the middle of the last seven-year week of Daniel's prophecy.

Secondly, strong evidence indicates that Jesus died in the middle of the literal seven-day Passion Week. This means he was crucified not on Friday, but rather on Wednesday. If you are unaware of the debate on when crucifixion day occurred, this statement could be quite a shock. The key to the controversy is Matthew 12:40: "As Jonah was three days and three nights in the belly of the great fish, so will the Son of Man be three days and three nights in the heart of the earth." This clear statement of actual days and nights requires a reappraisal of traditional ideas. See my footnote for additional information.[5]

Where is the other half-week? The prophecy of Daniel requires both the cross and the Second Coming to "confirm a covenant with many for one week" (verse 27). This last verse of the prophecy uses the expression *even until the consummation,* which ties it to the book of Revelation. The final three and a half years, then, must be at the end of the age! They are not mentioned in the gospels, the Acts or the epistles, but they are mentioned *five times* in the book of Revelation.

Here are the five verses that describe this specific period of three and a half years:

- 42 months: Jerusalem trodden down by the Gentiles (Revelation 11:2)
- 1,260 days: The prophetic ministry of the two witnesses (Revelation 11:3)
- 1,260 days: The woman nourished in the wilderness (Revelation 12:6)
- Time, times, half a time: The woman protected from the serpent (Revelation 12:14)
- 42 months: The Antichrist world government, the Beast, continues (Revelation 13:5)

The angel Gabriel did not instruct Daniel concerning the last half, or the seventieth week, because this period of time belonged to another dispensation. Now, however, we approach the fulfillment of this great prophecy. Notice that the three-and-a-half-year period is mentioned to Daniel both *before* and *after* he received the seventy-week prophecy (Daniel 7:25; 12:7).

On the wing of abominations shall be one who makes desolate. The KJV says *for the overspreading of abominations.* David Sell explains: "The Hebrew word for 'wing' means overspreading, which indicates an abomination on one end and an abomination on the other end. . . . The final abomination butts right up against the consummation, or the very end."[6]

Jesus mentioned the first abomination in Matthew 24:15: "'Therefore when you see the *"abomination of desolation,"* spoken of by Daniel the prophet, standing in the holy place' (whoever reads, let him understand)." Luke 21:20 clearly identifies the meaning: "When you see Jerusalem surrounded by armies, then know that its desolation is near." That is why some of the disciples would live to see the fulfillment—the Romans actually standing in the Temple sanctuary. (We discussed this in chapter 7.) Titus and his troops became God's instrument in desolating Temple, city and people. They did so in a manner obnoxious to the Jews, and this was the religious abomination Jesus referred to. The abomination and desolation by the Romans was the natural outcome of the Jews' rejection of Christ's atonement, so Jesus told them, "Your house is left to you desolate" (Matthew 23:38).

This present age has also seen the "overspreading" of this religious abomination, which is hostile to the Kingdom of God. It will reach its outer limit in the Antichrist of Revelation 13. Paul describes this "lawless one" in 2 Thessalonians 2:3–4 as "the man of sin . . . the son of perdition, who opposes and exalts himself above all that is called God or that is worshiped, so that he sits as God in the temple of God, showing himself that he is God." This is decreed to take place until "the consummation"—that is, the Second Coming of Christ—when judgment is poured out on this desolator.

Paul assures us how it will end: "The lawless one will be revealed, whom the Lord will consume with the breath of His mouth and destroy with the brightness of His coming" (2 Thessalonians 2:8).

The Length of the Tribulation

Some commentators insist on a seven-year Tribulation at the end of this age, and that the Antichrist breaks a covenant with the Jews in the middle of this seventh week. There are four critical problems with this approach:

1. The cross is essential if there is to be reconciliation for iniquity, an end of transgression and the beginning of everlasting righteousness. To put the whole seventh week at the end eliminates the cross from the 490 years, since the 62 weeks come to an end *three years before the crucifixion*.
2. To infer that the *he* of Daniel 9:27 refers to the Antichrist requires the breaking of a grammatical rule about pronouns—that the subject of the pronoun must already be introduced, and in this case it has not been.
3. We must not disregard how Jesus the Messiah was cut off in the middle of the week, bringing an end to sacrifice and offerings. This third problem is critical.
4. There is no seven-year Tribulation to be found in the book of Revelation! There are, however, five mentions of a three-and-a-half-year Tribulation (which we identified in

> the last section). Some suggest adding two of the three-and-a-half-year references together, thereby coming up with the needed seven years. What, then, prevents us from adding up three periods, or all the five periods? We have no precedent to do this.[7]

See more on the Tribulation in chapter 9.

"The Times of the Gentiles"

This expression, found in Luke 21:24 and Romans 11:25, refers to a parenthetical period of time, the Church age, set between the first and second halves of Daniel's seventieth week. During this period God extends His mercy and covenant to all the heathen (Gentile) peoples of the world (Luke 2:32; Acts 9:15; 13:46–47; 15:14; Romans 11:11; Ephesians 3:6).

Daniel's great message to Israel and Jerusalem is set in a galaxy of prophecies about Gentile nations. God used the first great "universal empire" of Babylon to captivate His people and cure them of their idolatry. Medo-Persia, the second universal empire, was used by God to bring about their restoration. Rome, the third universal empire, subjugated the Jews, destroyed Jerusalem and slaughtered the Christians.

Daniel 2 prerecords the history of the Gentile nations, including those of our own day. Finally the great world powers will be brought to naught as God's Kingdom breaks them into pieces (Daniel 2:44).

APPENDIX D

THE MILLENNIUM: WHAT WILL WE DO FOR A THOUSAND YEARS?

Then I saw an angel coming down from heaven, having the key to the bottomless pit and a great chain in his hand. He laid hold of the dragon, that serpent of old, who is the Devil and Satan, and bound him for *a thousand years;* and he cast him into the bottomless pit, and shut him up, and set a seal on him, so that he should deceive the nations no more till the *thousand years* were finished. But after these things he must be released for a little while.

And I saw thrones, and they sat on them, and judgment was committed to them. And I saw the souls of those who had been beheaded for their witness to Jesus and for the word of God, who had not worshiped the beast or his image, and had not received his mark on their foreheads or on their hands. And they lived and reigned with Christ for a *thousand years.* But the rest of the dead did not live again until the *thousand years* were finished. This is the first resurrection. Blessed and holy is he who has part in the first resurrection. Over such the second death has no power, but they

> shall be priests of God and of Christ, and shall reign with Him a *thousand years*.
>
> Now when the *thousand years* have expired, Satan will be released from his prison and will go out to deceive the nations which are in the four corners of the earth, Gog and Magog, to gather them together to battle, whose number is as the sand of the sea.
>
> Revelation 20:1–8 (emphasis added)

Joy glanced at the strange title with a quizzical look. "What's that all about?"

Her reaction was understandable, given the unusual title of the book I was researching: *The Dark Side of the Millennium: The Problem of Evil in Rev. 20:1–10.* The author, Arthur H. Lewis, an amillennialist, first presented his thoughts at the 1977 annual meeting of the Evangelical Theological Society. Based on certain assumptions, he argued against a literal, thousand-year millennial Kingdom.

Unfortunately the book lumps all literal millennialists together as believing that evil men and nations will populate the messianic Kingdom. Many of us who believe in a literal Millennium, however, cannot agree that sinners, evil and rebellion will exist in the Millennium. (My arguments will appear later.) Consider the gist of Lewis' approach:

> Revelation 20 presents the millennial society as a mixture of saints and sinners. The Gog and Magog nations revolt against the King at the end of the thousand years, but they exist as groups of wicked people throughout the entire course of the age. This aspect immediately raises a doubt about the correlation of the millennium with the other kingdom passages in the Bible, which invariably speak of its glory and perfection. So serious is this darker side of the picture that it may prove to be the "Achilles heel" of the entire millennarian [sic] system of interpretation.[1]

Lewis' study aims to demonstrate "that evil is indeed an integral part of the thousand-year period described in Revelation 20 . . . [and] sufficient reason to deny the identification of the millennium with the glorious future kingdom of Christ."[2]

More Arguments Against a Literal Millennium

Charles R. Erdman, in his book *The Revelation of John*, mentions two big reasons he has difficulty accepting a literal Millennium. First, he says, "no such Millennium is mentioned in any other part of the Bible. . . . No limited period of ten centuries of peace, with a tragic ending in universal war, can be discovered on any other page of inspired prophecy."

Erdman's second objection is to the additions attached to the framework of Revelation 20. He lists seven beliefs common in the dispensational approach that he finds unacceptable:

- Two comings of Christ
- Two resurrections of believers
- Changes in nature to fulfill Old Testament prophecies
- The conversion of Israel, which then forms a body distinct from the Christian Church
- An enlarged Jerusalem to be capital of the Jewish people
- A rebuilt Temple with animal sacrifices reestablished
- Christians of all ages appearing on earth in glorified bodies who, with Christ and Israel, will reign over all the world[3]

I, too, find all seven of the above points unacceptable. But a literal Millennium need not include all this unwarranted baggage.

What About a Literal Millennium?

Every school of interpretation believes in a Millennium. The bottom-line questions are these: *What is the nature of this period? Is it a literal thousand years or does it symbolize a spiritual truth? Is it happening now or is it yet to come? Is it a Jewish period or a Christian era?*

The following nine questions are the questions most asked. Following these answers, we will examine "the dark side" of the Millennium.

1. What Is the Millennium?

The actual word does not appear in our English Bible. A Latin word meaning "a thousand years," it refers to a period of time mentioned six times in Revelation 20. The period begins with the Second Coming of Christ and the binding of Satan (verse 2) and ends with Satan's release for a short time at the conclusion of the thousand years (verses 3, 7). The *first resurrection* (that of the righteous) takes place at the beginning of the thousand years. The *second resurrection* (the general resurrection of the rest of the dead) occurs at the end of the thousand years. Both are announced in Revelation 20.

2. Is the Thousand Years Merely Symbolic?

Since the Millennium is unique to the book of Revelation, some feel it must automatically be interpreted symbolically. Not necessarily; the context must indicate the need for such interpretation.

I am convinced that Revelation 20 indicates a *literal* time period. It would then run consistently with the other subjects mentioned. For instance:

The angel is to be taken literally.

Heaven is to be taken literally.

The key, the chain and the seal could be symbolic—but what do they symbolize? An actual binding is taking place.

"Dragon" is symbolic, but it is quickly identified as "that serpent of old, who is the Devil and Satan" (verse 2). (A symbol imparts insight for some condition or aspect not apparent without additional help.)

The bottomless pit (*abusson*) is a literal place. The demons begged Jesus not to send them there (Luke 8:31); and Paul contrasts heaven and the abyss as real places (Romans 10:7). The other seven references in Revelation also indicate that the bottomless pit is a real place.

The souls of the martyrs are real.

The fire coming down from heaven is real.

The lake of fire is surely literal—or does it represent something even worse than our imaginations can conceive?

Since seven of the above eight references are clearly to be taken literally, why should it seem farfetched to accept a literal one thousand years?

The time statements in Revelation seem to relate best to literal time periods: three and a half years; 42 months; time, times and a half a time; and ten days. The "silence in heaven for about half an hour" (Revelation 8:1) is certainly open to question.

But the monotonous repetition—*six times!*—of "thousand years" (sometimes with the article "a" and sometimes "the") is significant. John seems obsessed with this phrase. If he meant to convey an indefinite time period, he could have used other words. The plain appearance and open-faced presentation in this text makes it appear literal.[4]

3. Why Is a Literal Millennium Needed?

If you can explain why our physical bodies must be changed and undergo resurrection, then you can answer why the earth must also undergo a mighty change and be inhabited by the righteous. The same reason applies. Our bodies are part of our whole salvation, and the purification of the earth is part of God's total redemptive program. See our discussion of Romans 8 in chapter 10 and 2 Peter 3 in chapter 11.

Mankind and his redemption are linked to the earth and its redemption, and the program of God will be incomplete until both are set free of the curse. ". . . The creation eagerly waits for the revealing of the sons of God. For the creation was subjected to futility, not willingly, but because of Him who subjected it in hope; because the creation itself also will be delivered from the bondage of corruption into the glorious liberty of the children of God" (Romans 8:19–21). The completion of God's redemptive plan will find a righteous, redeemed people living happily with Christ on a purified, redeemed earth.

The first man, Adam, was given the authority to govern the earth (although God knew he would fail). Once having failed, Adam and Eve and their descendants were driven in shame from the cursed Garden. The earth is destined, however, for restoration to pristine glory and beauty—to serve joyfully the man who was made in God's image and to glorify God. When Christ and His followers rule the earth, it is man reinstated, which will be accomplished through Christ and His Church. The new, curse-less earth is the ideal habitation for all the redeemed, glorified, sinless followers of Jesus Christ. As Charles Spurgeon said, "In the place where he fought the battle he desires to celebrate the victory."[5] This will happen at the final triumph, when Jesus Christ returns. What a climax for human history!

A final reason for belief in a literal Millennium: God's principle of the seventh day as Sabbath also needs fulfillment. God, mankind and the earth must complete natural history with a rest of God in which righteousness prevails and sin no longer exists. The Millennium will be a time of rejoicing and jubilee as all God's people celebrate the victory of the Lamb over the dragon.

Here are eight compelling, summary reasons to believe in a literal Millennium:

1. **Closure.** It is a fitting conclusion for God's plan of the ages.
2. **Transformation.** By lifting the curse on the earth through purging with fire, the entire physical order is restored to God's original intention.
3. **Redemption.** A humanity free from death and sin will live on an earth released from corruption and decay.
4. **Perfection.** The people of God will remain in immediate communion with God on the earth.
5. **Vindication.** The establishment of the Kingdom of God on earth will be tangible and convincing proof of the victory of righteousness over evil.
6. **Consolation.** One united people of God (Jews and Gentiles) will live at last under the new covenant on earth. There is a purpose in God's restoration of believing Israelites into the olive tree.

7. **Exaltation.** The martyrs and those who suffered most will be exalted and rewarded with respect.
8. **Sabbath.** There is a holy purpose in such a Sabbath—living and ruling with Christ, ceasing from worldly endeavors and simply resting in Him.

4. Did the Prophets Foretell This Time?

Yes, the "day of the Lord" prophecies find meaningful fulfillment in this thousand-year period. The "whole earth" prophecies describe the Millennium of Revelation 20, although the actual chronological time of one thousand years is not revealed, apparently because such an exact time frame would prove more confusing than helpful.

> Let the whole earth be filled with His glory. Amen and Amen (Psalm 72:19).
>
> "Truly, as I live, all the earth shall be filled with the glory of the LORD" (Numbers 14:21).
>
> "The whole earth is full of His glory [literally, *fullness of the whole earth is His glory*]!" (Isaiah 6:3).
>
> The earth shall be full of the knowledge of the LORD as the waters cover the sea (Isaiah 11:9)
>
> The earth will be filled with the knowledge of the glory of the LORD (Habakkuk 2:14).
>
> The LORD shall be King over all the earth. In that day it shall be—"The LORD is one," and His name one (Zechariah 14:9).

5. Did Jesus Foretell This Time?

Yes, but when talking to a Jewish audience, He did not use the Latin term *millennium* to describe this period. He used terms that would be meaningful to Jewish minds. During His earthly ministry, Jesus introduced the subject; but disclosing a specific length of time would have been premature and inappropriate.[6]

What terms did He use? In Matthew 19:28 the Greek word *palingenesia* (*palin*, again; *genesis*, birth) is translated *regeneration*: "Assuredly I say unto you, that in the regeneration when the Son of Man sits on the throne of His glory, you who have followed Me will also sit on twelve thrones, judging the twelve tribes of Israel" (emphasis added). Because the Jews eagerly anticipated the end of the existing order and the beginning of a new one, this is what they understood Jesus to mean. And this, in my estimation, is a clear reference to the Millennium. See my more complete explanations in chapter 5 ("Judea Beyond the Jordan"), chapter 8 ("Times of Refreshing, Restoration and Regeneration") and chapter 10 ("Transformation of the Creation").

Jesus also used *this age* and also *the age to come* (Matthew 12:32). He taught that there would be a definite end to this age (Matthew 13:39, 49). Twenty verses testify to this concept, using *aion* (age) in the Greek text.[7] We live in "this present evil age." When Jesus referred to "the age to come," He meant the Millennium. Eternity is our English word that translates into "the ages of the ages" (that is, unending ages).[8]

Jesus taught much on the Kingdom of God and its present spiritual expression, and how it will find dramatic literal fulfillment in the future. The Kingdom really belongs to the age to come and is set in sharp contrast to our present age. At this time we see death, but in the Kingdom we will enjoy life eternal. We now see a mixing of the righteous and the wicked, but in the coming Kingdom all wickedness and sin will be destroyed. Satan is now considered "the god of this age," but in the future God's rule will not only have destroyed Satan, but will have replaced evil with righteousness. The Millennium on earth is the ideal place for the literal, total fulfillment of Jesus' teaching on the Kingdom of God. It is the age of His manifested rule, the expression of an absolute Kingdom that illustrates justice and righteousness, peace among people, harmony within the creation and mankind being allowed to share in what the Lord does.

Finally, although Jesus did not refer specifically to the Millennium, He used millennial terminology. He talked of resurrection, thrones and judgment, which connects directly with Revelation 20 (Matthew 19:28–29).

6. Did the Epistles Foretell This Time?

Yes. Paul referred to creation groaning, waiting to be delivered into the liberty of the sons of God (Romans 8).

Peter described the cleansing of the earth by fire (2 Peter 3). The transformed earth (described in chapter 11) is one that has been redeemed and prepared for righteousness. "Do not forget this one thing," he wrote, "that with the Lord one day is as a thousand years, and a thousand years as one day" (2 Peter 3:8). Probably he quoted Psalm 90:4: "A thousand years in Your sight are like yesterday when it is past, and like a watch in the night." Undoubtedly Peter was indicating that God does not operate according to our clock. But isn't it interesting that "one day of the Lord" is said to equal one thousand years?!

7. Isn't Satan Already Bound?

To a certain degree he is. Satan is hindered but not annihilated or rendered inoperative (Hebrews 2:14). We are forced to one inescapable conclusion: He is presently active on planet earth, even if the messianic Kingdom has already been inaugurated in the hearts of men and women. It is essential to keep in mind that there are actually *three* stages in the triumph of divine power over the devil. See my comments in chapter 12, "The Book of Revelation: The Final Triumph."[9] The devil's demise is settled: First, the cross renders him ineffective; next, the Second Coming binds him for a thousand years; and third, the Great White Throne consigns him to the lake of fire.

8. Who Will Inhabit This New Millennial Earth?

The inhabitants will be the redeemed of all ages, their original physical bodies changed and glorified in the first resurrection. They will live lives dedicated fully to God and His glorification. The resurrection introduces this coming age, the Millennium, and changes God's people to their glorified state.

After the resurrection, according to Jesus, "they neither marry nor are given in marriage, but are like angels of God in heaven"

(Matthew 22:30). The time of childbearing and marriage will be past, as well as that of trying to convert the unsaved. The lifestyle that formerly characterized planet earth will be over. "Flesh and blood cannot inherit the kingdom of God; nor does corruption inherit incorruption" (1 Corinthians 15:50). The earth and the people of God will enjoy their Sabbath rest.

9. Will Israel Enjoy a Special Status During the Millennium?

Many premillennialists see a special status for Israel during the Millennium, though they disagree concerning its exact nature. Let's do a quick review of the dispensational approach to the Millennium. It anticipates:

- A virtual restoration of the Old Testament economy
- Renewal of God's relations with Israel
- Israel's restoration to the land of Palestine
- Jesus on David's literal throne and ruling the world from Jerusalem
- Restoration of Temple worship, the priestly order and the sacrificial system
- The fulfillment of virtually all Old Testament prophecies not fulfilled by the time of Christ[10]

Although a millennialist, I cannot see the Kingdom of God on earth finding expression as described above. It simply is not taught in the New Testament.

It is good to be aware of all Old Testament information, but apply it only as Jesus and His apostles did. They taught that the Kingdom of God would find dynamic expression in the age to come. The disciples believed that Jesus was already seated on David's throne and that He would reign in the age to come (Mark 16:19; Luke 1:32; Acts 2:33–36; 13:34; Colossians 3:1). But the idea of a Jewish kingdom on earth with a reinstituted Jewish economy and worship system was simply not part of the faith of the early Church.

Literal Israel is given no promise in the New Testament that she will replace the Church as God's primary interest. Paul taught that there is one olive tree representing the true people of God (Romans 11). Both unbelieving Jews and Gentiles can be grafted in through faith in Jesus Christ. There is no salvation for Jew or Gentile who does not have faith in Christ. Whether called Israel or the Church, there is now only one people of God, who will live and reign with Christ for a thousand years (Galatians 3:26–29). See my explanation in chapter 6 of eight Scriptures that teach why Jerusalem was forsaken.

Is There a Darker Side to the Millennium?

Arthur Lewis suggested in *The Dark Side of the Millennium* that a literal millennial society would be "a mixture of saints and sinners." There would have to be "groups of wicked people throughout the entire course of the age." Finally, "evil is indeed an integral part of the thousand-year period."

Unfortunately, this *is* the belief held by some millennialists. John Walvoord, for instance:

> The millennial period therefore begins with a society in which both Jews and Gentiles are saved. As children are born into their homes, however, even though they are in the favorable circumstances of the millennial scene, it seems obvious that some of these will not actually be born again, and of these the company of those who rebel against Christ in Revelation 20:8–9 is formed.[11]

Arthur Katterjohn of Wheaton College says, drawing on Zechariah 14:16: "Evidently certain peoples of the world will survive the second coming judgment, since they will have been relatively untouched by Antichrist."[12] Bob Gundry also follows this line of thinking.[13]

To explain the rebellious Gog and Magog "nations" of Revelation 20, both pretribulational and posttribulational dispensationalists must tell us how these sinners will get into the Millennium. Some will ostensibly be born to Christians; others are sinners who survived the Tribulation and Second Coming judgment. But both of these ideas are easily challenged.

First, there will be no children born to the glorified saints who occupy the Millennium. Jesus plainly taught that people who have been resurrected do not reproduce (Matthew 22:30). Second, no sinners will survive the Second Coming. All will die, their souls to await the second resurrection. Recall that Jesus will be "revealed from heaven with His mighty angels, in flaming fire taking vengeance on those who do not know God, and on those who do not obey the gospel of our Lord Jesus Christ. These shall be punished with everlasting destruction from the presence of the Lord and from the glory of His power" (2 Thessalonians 1:7–9).

Here is why the citizens of the Millennium must be only glorified saints:

1. The seventy-weeks prophecy ended at the Second Coming. The Millennium comes *after* the Second Coming. Sin, sinners, transgression and iniquity will have been judged and done away with.
2. Antichrist physically perishes at the Second Coming, and that same brightness does away with all sinners. Their souls are then imprisoned, along with the devil, to await their final judgment at the second resurrection.
3. If resurrected, glorified saints, natural men and women and unconverted children all occupied the Millennium together, a tragic incompatibility would spoil the divine objective for this period. God wants a perfect people, living on a perfect earth, with a perfect government, living in perfect relationship with Him.
4. Those who live during the millennial reign of Christ on earth are the godly resurrected. In that state they are married to God, not to one another.
5. The parables of Jesus indicate there will be no mixture of good and bad peoples (Matthew 13 and 25).

So who are the nations mentioned in Revelation 20? The nations who follow Satan at the end of the Millennium are the ungodly raised in the second resurrection who were not alive on earth during the Millennium. At the Second Coming all who died in Christ will connect with their original bodies. In a blink of an eye they will be changed and will take on incorruption. But nothing will happen to the ungodly. Their bodies will remain dead and their spirits in torment.

At the end of the Millennium, all the ungodly are called to stand in the White Throne Judgment to account for their deeds. This is the time of their physical resurrection (note Matthew 10:28). They have been residing in Hades or hell—other names for the bottomless pit (Luke 8:31; Romans 10:7). Satan has also been held captive in this abyss for one thousand years.

According to Revelation 20:9, "they went up on the breadth of the earth." This "going up" is a translation of *anabaino*, which means literally "to ascend upward" (as the prayers of the saints ascend in Revelation 8:4, and as Jesus went up onto a mountain in Matthew 5:1, and as He came up out of the waters of baptism in Matthew 3:16). The ungodly dead will be raised and come up (ascend out of death) onto the breadth of the earth—which means they are all over the earth. Satan rushes to deceive them for the last time, gathering them from the "four quarters of the earth" to surround the gathering of the saints.

In response to this final rebellion of Satan and the ungodly, God will send His fire to devour them.[14] Then, in the presence of all the godly standing before His throne in shining garments, God almighty will bring judgment on the ungodly and on Satan himself. (See my comments on the White Throne in chapter 12.)

APPENDIX E

A MAJOR PARADIGM SHIFT

We cannot begin to understand the depth of love and emotion God has sustained for His people Israel throughout the centuries. Nor can we comprehend the measures He has taken to bring correction and direction to them. The destruction of Jerusalem and the harsh statements of Jesus do not seem to be in divine character, but those actions were truly in the best interests of God and His people.

From time to time a happening takes place that acts as "a hinge of history," completely changing the direction of a man, family, nation or even the world. The dramatic shift in God's dealings with the Jews is such an event, and it is foreshadowed in a remarkable Old Testament story. After a thousand years of developing Israel, God was willing to split His beloved nation. This traumatic action was a prophetic shadow of what was to come in the Church age.

The Division of Ancient Israel

One day Jeroboam, a valiant warrior King Solomon put in charge of all his forced labor, was walking alone on a country road outside Jerusalem. There he was confronted by the prophet Ahijah wearing a new cloak. Suddenly the prophet grasped the garment and tore it into twelve pieces.

"Take for yourself ten pieces," Ahijah declared, "for thus says the LORD, the God of Israel: 'Behold, I will tear the kingdom out of the hand of Solomon and will give ten tribes to you'" (1 Kings 11:31).

This tragic judgment resulted from Israel's idolatry, rebellion and disobedience against the ways of the Lord. The breakup occurred within a few years, during the reign of Solomon's son Rehoboam.

King Rehoboam treated his laborers with undue harshness, so they rebelled, with ten tribes going north to form the Northern Kingdom of Israel under Jeroboam, in fulfillment of Ahijah's prophecy. An unusual expression describes this seemingly tragic development: "The turn of affairs was from the LORD" (1 Kings 12:15).

God had high objectives in mind, and when His people cooperated, those objectives were obtainable. He was willing to sacrifice His whole program, however, for principle. Other examples: Adam driven from the Garden of Eden; the scattering of the people at the Tower of Babel; God's using the sin of Jeroboam to destroy the northern tribes.

This division of the nation would be followed, nearly a thousand years later, by a division within Judaism itself.

The Split in Judaism

No other world religion has been challenged by such a major shift in emphasis as Judaism. The long-awaited arrival of the predicted Messiah finally occurred, and with His advent, an unexpectedly *spiritual* Kingdom of God.

Jesus the Messiah brought salvation and healing to many, but He did nothing about taxes or political change. He was concerned with changing human hearts, not governments. He introduced spiritual principles that upgraded the laws of Moses and introduced concepts of faith, affording new appreciation for Abraham.

Jesus arrived as the King-Priest of the line of David, but He died for His efforts to cleanse the Judaism of His day from the corruption that had sucked out its spiritual life. His death, however, was more than retaliation. Jesus died as the Lamb of God to make atonement for and bring redemption to His people.

Jesus concentrated His three-and-a-half-year ministry on the Jewish people who lived in Palestine. His disciples were instructed to reach only Jews. He traveled the land with His message, and from time to time boldly entered the great Temple of Jerusalem, the seat of Judaism, to bring His message to common folk and religious authorities alike.

But they rejected Him. The Jews and Romans, hardly friends before, joined forces to crucify the Lord of heaven. "He came to His own, and His own did not receive Him" (John 1:11). In fact, they killed Him.

No one was prepared for what happened after the rabbi from Nazareth had been buried three days. The sealed, Roman-guarded tomb burst open. Jesus, Lord and Christ, arose from the dead!

The resurrected Christ met with His disciples several times in Galilee, and finally gave His last words at Olivet. To the awe and wonderment of His friends, Jesus began bodily to ascend before their very eyes. Still they persisted with political questions, which Jesus brushed aside. Instead He emphatically called to them to wait in Jerusalem. He would send the mighty Helper, the Holy Spirit, who would enable them to herald His message beyond Judaism to the whole world.

As Jesus vanished in a bright cloud, two heavenly beings in white garments appeared, promising that He would return to earth just as they had seen Him depart. (Apparently, as we have seen, His return is directly connected with the fulfillment of His Great Commission.)

A Brand-New Life Form

Out of the dead stump of a decadent Judaism, a sprig of life sprouted. Drawing on the virtue of their magnificent heritage,

Jesus and His Way became the new expression of the Kingdom of God and the olive tree that was Israel. The root of the past was not lost; rather, it found expression in a new, Spirit-inspired life form. As always there remained a faithful remnant. Those who followed Jesus were now that group.

Jesus not only opened the door for Israel's redemption; He sent forth the Good News to all nations. At first His followers who made up the newly formed Church were ethnic Jews. Soon, however, the Gentiles throughout the Roman Empire began to hear of this Christ for all nations who gave hope to the poor and downtrodden. The Jewish Messiah became known as the benevolent Savior of the whole world.

Although Roman leaders and government responded no better than their Jewish counterparts, the common people throughout the realm received His message with joy. Held together by fear of Rome's iron fist, the empire was sustained by a tragic system of slave labor. The news—hope for now and even beyond the grave!—swept through the dark caverns of captivity, and multitudes of the earth's downcast responded in faith to the light that burst on their souls.

The Jewish Christian Church was suddenly inundated with Gentiles, heathen of every description. Some of the Jewish Christian leaders found this unclean, spiritual menagerie hard to accept. The apostle Paul, in contrast—and others as well, empowered by the Spirit and by fresh insights from the Hebrew Scriptures—declared that old Israel had been replaced by the new Israel of God, composed not only of Jews but of believing people from every kindred, tribe and tongue.

Suddenly physical circumcision, kosher foods, special ordinances and all other accouterments of Jewish religion were replaced by good, basic, godly living through the power of the Holy Spirit. Paul and the other apostles, inspired by the Holy Spirit, drafted informative letters and sent them to the congregations meeting throughout the nations of that time. These epistles were granted the same status as the ancient Hebrew Scriptures, and carefully explained the new way of life and how the old Scriptures were now fulfilled in the new.

Redemption had come to all nations. Anyone in any ethnic group who responded in faith to the message of salvation in Christ could be saved. As old Simeon the prophet said over the infant Jesus: "He is a light to reveal God to the nations, and he is the glory of your people Israel" (Luke 2:32, NLT).

So now both Jew and Gentile who believe in the Lord Jesus, the Messiah, are baptized by the Holy Spirit into the one people of God. And now, as every generation before us, we, the Church of today, together await the glorious return of Jesus the Messiah.

NOTES

Chapter 1: It's Later Than You Think!

1. Differences of opinion are bound to exist. James Montgomery Boice, for instance, in his *Foundations of the Christian Faith* (Downers Grove: InterVarsity, 1986), p. 705, says the Second Coming is mentioned 318 times in the New Testament. *The International Standard Bible Encyclopedia* also mentions 318 verses, but neither source lists the verses. In contrast, some postmillennialists believe there are fewer than a dozen verses that actually apply to the Second Coming (because passages such as the Olivet Discourse and the book of Revelation are already fulfilled). William Edward Biederwolf took what he considered to be the important Old and New Testament references and made commentary on them, also quoting comments from older sources in *The Second Coming Bible Commentary* (Grand Rapids: Baker, 1985 [1924]). My choice and tabulation of New Testament verses is different from his.

2. Jesus spoke these words while living humbly among mankind as the Son of Man. Now, in His glorified state with the Father, He surely knows this information.

3. Charles H. Spurgeon, *12 Sermons on the Second Coming of Christ* (Grand Rapids: Baker, 1995 reprint), pp. 116–17.

4. Lazarus had a physical resurrection; he was restored to physical life and then died, having lived out his life span. The resurrection of the saints does not merely return them to physical life, but rather introduces them to a new dimension of life in which the power and life of the Holy Spirit totally redeems our bodies from all weakness, pain, decay and death.

5. Similar to Noah and family in the Ark, waiting for the waters to subside and the new earth to appear.

Chapter 2: Why All These Strange Words?

1. F. F. Bruce, *Answers to Questions* (Grand Rapids: Zondervan, 1972), p. 199.

2. W. E. Vine, *Expository Dictionary of New Testament Words* (Westwood, N.J.: Revell, 1966), p. 208.

3. D. E. Hiebert, "Parousia," Merrill C. Tenney, gen. ed., *The Zondervan Pictorial Encyclopedia of the Bible*, Vol. 4 (Grand Rapids: Zondervan, 1975), p. 601.

4. W. Bauer, William F. Arndt and F. Wilbur Gingrich, eds., *A Greek-English Lexicon of the New Testament and Other Early Christian Literature* (Chicago: University of Chicago Press, 1957), p. 635.

5. James Hope Moulton and George Milligan, *The Vocabulary of the Greek Testament: Illustrated from the Papyri and Other Non-Literary Sources* (Grand Rapids: Zondervan, 1976), p. 497.

6. Ibid., p. 62. *Apokalypsis* is composed from two Greek words: 1) the preposition *apo*, meaning "away from" or "off," and 2) the verb *kalyptein*, "to cover."

7. J. Rodman Williams, *Renewal Theology: Systematic Theology from a Charismatic Perspective*, Vol. 3 (Grand Rapids: Zondervan, 1992), p. 304.

8. See the subhead "Reading that Critically Investigates the Origin of Dispensationalism," chapter 3. This approach was crystallized by John Nelson Darby around 1830 and was then propagated by *The Scofield Reference Bible*.

9. George Eldon Ladd, *The Blessed Hope* (Grand Rapids: Eerdmans, 1956), pp. 77–80.

10. David L. Cooper, *Future Events Revealed According to Matthew 24 and 25* (Los Angeles: David L. Cooper, 1935), p. 110.

11. Ladd, *Hope*, p. 105.

12. Douglas J. Moo, "The Case for the Posttribulation Rapture Position," G. L. Archer Jr., Paul D. Feinberg, Douglas J. Moo and Richard R. Reiter, *Three Views on the Rapture: Pre-, Mid-, or Post-Tribulation?* (Grand Rapids: Zondervan, 1984), p. 208.

13. See Ladd, *Hope*, chapter 6.

14. This will be considered in chapter 6.

15. Some contend that *departure* in Acts 20:29 does not refer to Paul's death. Admittedly the Greek word on its own does not automatically give that meaning, but I maintain that the context warrants this interpretation.

16. Leading dispensationalist John F. Walvoord, former president of Dallas Theological Seminary, feels that it is not justifiable to deny imminency by using "these temporary problems in the first century." He argues that most of the Church on a given day would not know "whether Paul or Peter was still alive, and most of them were not informed about the predictions." *The Blessed Hope and the Tribulation* (Grand Rapids: Zondervan, 1976), p. 73. It seems to me that the people would pretty much follow the beliefs of their leaders.

17. William G. Moorehead, "Millennium," James Orr, gen. ed., *The New International Standard Bible Encyclopaedia*, Vol. 3 (Grand Rapids: Eerdmans, 1974 reprint), p. 2054.

18. Williams, *Renewal Theology*, p. 395.

19. See the review of major millennial views by Millard J. Erickson, *A Basic Guide to Eschatology: Making Sense of the Millennium* (Grand Rapids: Baker, 1977, 1998), chapters 3–5, pp. 55–106.

20. See Marvin Rosenthal, *The Pre-Wrath Rapture of the Church* (Nashville: Thomas Nelson, 1990). Also, Robert Van Kampen, *The Rapture Question Answered: Plain & Simple* (Grand Rapids: Revell, 1997).

21. The most satisfying premillennial (nondispensational) treatment of the seventy weeks prophecy of Daniel 9 that I have seen is that by Restoration theologian Kevin J. Conner, *The Seventy Weeks Prophecy: An Exposition of Daniel 9* (Blackburn, Victoria, Australia: Acacia, 1981). He sees the first half of the seventieth week fulfilled in Jesus' earthly ministry of three and a half years and the last half fulfilled in the three-and-a-half-year Tribulation. See my comments in Appendix C.

Chapter 3: What Do the Interpreters Say?

1. Bruce, *Answers*, p. 228.

2. The initial definitions of the four positions are taken from "Christian History Timelines: The End," *Christian History*, 61 (Vol. XVIII, No. 1): 26, 27.

3. Ladd, *Hope*, p. 162.

4. "Christian History Timelines," *Christian History*, p. 27.

5. Anthony A. Hoekema, "Amillennialism," Robert G. Clouse, ed., *The Meaning of the Millennium: Four Views* (Downers Grove, Ill.: InterVarsity, 1977), chapter 4.

6. St. Augustine, *The City of God*, Book XX, chapters 7–9. Robert Maynard Hutchins, ed. in chief, *Great Books of the Western World* (Chicago: Encyclopaedia Britannica, 1952), pp. 535–40. It has been suggested that Augustine, other scholars and even the reformers had their theology of the thousand years greatly affected by their strong reaction against a materialistic chiliasm (focused on sensual gratification) that sought to take root in the Church; as, Robert H. Mounce, *The Book of Revelation: The New International Commentary on the New Testament* (Grand Rapids: Eerdmans, 1977), p. 358.

7. William E. Cox, *Amillennialism Today* (Phillipsburg, N.J.: Presbyterian and Reformed, 1966), p. 1. Quote from Walvoord, *The Millennial Kingdom* (Findlay, Ohio: Dunham, 1959; reprint, Grand Rapids: Zondervan, 1974), p. 6.

8. This position presented by Hoekema, *The Meaning of the Millennium*, pp. 160–64. Also, see the presentation of William E. Cox, *Biblical Studies in Final Things* (Philadelphia: Presbyterian and Reformed, 1967), pp. 160–64.

9. "Christian History Timelines," *Christian History*, p. 26.

10. *The Scofield Reference Bible* lists these dispensations on page 5: innocency, conscience, human government, promise, law, grace, and kingdom.

11. Walvoord, *Millennial Kingdom*, p. 16.

12. See the presentation of Herman A. Hoyt, "Dispensational Premillennialism," *The Meaning of the Millennium*, chapter 2.

13. Erickson, *Basic Guide*, p. 103.

14. This attitude does not reflect the beliefs of the historic premillennialist. Less emphasis is placed on national Israel, and in some places no emphasis whatsoever. Some feel the Church, as spiritual Israel, has replaced natural Israel, and many Old Testament prophecies and promises are now fulfilled in the Church rather than in natural Israel. Generally there is a belief that natural Israel will yet be saved when she turns to Christ (Romans 11:15–16).

15. Charles C. Ryrie, *Dispensationalism Today* (Chicago: Moody, 1965), p. 45. Ryrie says on p. 140: "Use of the words Israel and Church shows clearly that in the New Testament national Israel continues with her own promises and the Church is never equated with a so-called 'new Israel' but is carefully and continually distinguished as a separate work of God in this age."

16. See John F. Walvoord, *The Rapture Question* (Findlay, Ohio: Dunham, 1957), pp. 23–27.

17. Zola Levitt, *Broken Branches: Has the Church Replaced Israel?* (Dallas: Zola Levitt, 1995), p. 34.

18. M. R. DeHaan, *The Second Coming of Jesus* (Grand Rapids: Zondervan, 1974, nineteenth printing), pp. 16–17.

19. Charles C. Ryrie, *The Basis of the Premillennial Faith* (New York: Loizeaux, 1953), p. 12.

20. Erickson, *Basic Guide*, p. 120.

21. The above thoughts were gleaned from Clouse, *The New Millennium Manual;* Erickson, *Basic Guide;* and Blaising, *Progressive Dispensationalism.* Craig A. Blaising and Darrell L. Bock comment: "Progressive dispensationalists understand the dispensations not simply as different arrangements between God and humankind, but as successive arrangements in the progressive revelation and accomplishment of redemption. . . . All these dispensations point to a future culmination in which God will both politically administer Israel and Gentile nations and indwell all of them equally (without ethnic distinctions) by the Holy Spirit." *Progressive Dispensationalism* (Wheaton: Victor/BridgePoint, 1993), p. 48.

22. I like the way they restructure redemptive history, allowing "flow" to God's program rather than the tight compartments of the traditional dispensations. Also, I am pleased to see a reappraisal of what has been a very radical distinction between Old Testament Israel and the New Testament Church. These changes, however, could signal a departure from classical dispensationalism.

23. "Christian History Timelines," *Christian History,* p. 27.

24. Keith A. Mathison, *Postmillennialism: An Eschatology of Hope* (Phillipsburg, N.J.: Presbyterian and Reformed, 1999), p. 263, endnote 6.

25. Ibid., p. 190. Also note these two statements from J. Marcellus Kik: "The millennium, in other words, is the period of the gospel dispensation, the Messianic kingdom, the new heavens and new earth, the regeneration, etc. The millennium commenced either with the ascension of Christ or with the day of Pentecost and will remain until the second coming of Christ." And, "The thousand years . . . make up the gospel dispensation from the first coming of Christ till that brief period of apostasy expressed in the words 'and after that he must be loosed a little season.'" *An Eschatology of Victory* (Phillipsburg, N.J.: Presbyterian and Reformed Publishing Co., 1971), pp. 17, 41.

26. Kenneth L. Gentry Jr., *He Shall Have Dominion: A Postmillennial Eschatology* (Tyler, Tex.: Institute for Christian Economics, 1992), p. 79.

27. Clouse, *The New Millennium Manual,* p. 48.

28. Kik, *Eschatology,* p. 4.

29. Loraine Boettner, "Postmillennialism," *The Meaning of the Millennium,* p. 117, a revised essay (with more recent figures) taken from Boettner's well-known book *The Millennium* (Philadelphia: Presbyterian and Reformed, 1957).

30. See the impressive book by Iain H. Murray, *The Puritan Hope: Revival and the Interpretation of Prophecy* (Edinburgh: Banner of Truth, 1971).

31. R. C. Sproul, *The Last Days according to Jesus* (Grand Rapids: Baker, 1998), pp. 200–201. Based on the material of Kenneth L. Gentry Jr., *He Shall Have Dominion.*

Chapter 4: Jesus Talked a Lot About His Coming Back

1. Based on material from J. Sidlow Baxter, *Explore the Book* (Grand Rapids: Zondervan, 1966), pp. 218–19. I know there are various interpretations for John 14:3, but this simple approach has great appeal to me. Baxter makes this interesting statement, after sharing his amazement that some believe in a two-phase return of Christ: "Mark well the parallels here—angels, voice, trumpet, congregating, clouds. All are agreed that Matthew XXIV teaches the splendid, outward, public coming. Then what kind of Bible interpretation is it which can take *exactly the same phrases and symbols* in I Thessalonians IV.15–18 and say that *there* they teach a *secret* coming!" (p. 219).

2. Not all agree that this refers to the Second Coming. Postmillenarian J. Marcellus Kik, for instance, argues convincingly that this text refers to "the coronation scene of Christ, which took place after the ascension. . . . He made that cloud His chariot, entered

the presence of the Ancient of Days and gave evidence of the sacrifice He had made at Calvary. *Eschatology*, p. 37.

3. My book *Awaken the Dawn!* explains the close connection between Jesus' prayer life and the understanding of His ministerial calling (Portland: Bible Temple, 1990).

4. George A. Buttrick, "The Gospel According to St. Matthew," *The Interpreter's Bible*, Vol. VII (New York/Nashville: Abingdon, 1951), p. 541.

5. George Eldon Ladd, "Matthew," *The Biblical Expositor*, Vol. 3 (Philadelphia: A. J. Holman, 1960), p. 64.

6. David Hill, *The Gospel of Matthew (New Century Bible)* (London: [Oliphants] Marshall, Morgan and Scott, 1972), p. 327.

7. Various versions help us visualize these talents by suggesting: "five bags of gold" (NEB); "five thousand dollars" (Williams); "$10,000" (Beck).

8. Hill, *Matthew*, p. 325.

Chapter 5: How Jesus Described His Second Coming

1. Sproul, *Last Days*, p. 14. Also, see Williams' discussion, *Renewal Theology*, pp. 309–14.

2. Sproul's entire book, *The Last Days according to Jesus*, addresses the main questions that preterists must answer. He distinguishes between "moderate preterism" (many future prophecies in the NT have already been fulfilled; some crucial prophecies have not yet been fulfilled) and "radical preterism" (all future prophecies in the NT have already been fulfilled). See also John F. MacArthur's discussion on what he calls "hyper-preterism" with its extreme positions. *The Second Coming* (Wheaton: Crossway, 1999), pp. 9–13.

3. The late George Eldon Ladd of Fuller Seminary, a historic premillennialist, pioneered this concept and has been its most articulate spokesman. See his book *The Gospel of the Kingdom* (Grand Rapids: Eerdmans, 1959).

4. George M. Lamsa, *Gospel Light: Comments on the Teachings of Jesus from Aramaic and Unchanged Eastern Customs* (Philadelphia: A. J. Holman, 1936), pp. 79–81.

5. A. T. Robertson, *Word Pictures in the New Testament*, Vol. I (Nashville: Broadman, 1930), p. 82.

6. Albert Schweitzer, *The Quest of the Historical Jesus* (New York: Macmillan, 1957 reprint), pp. 358–60. Schweitzer maintained that Jesus believed Himself to be Israel's Messiah of the end times but embraced death because the consummation did not arrive when He expected it.

7. R. V. G. Tasker, *The Gospel According to St. Matthew: Tyndale New Testament Commentaries* (Grand Rapids: Eerdmans, 1979), p. 108.

8. Alfred Edersheim, *The Life and Times of Jesus the Messiah*, Vol. I (Grand Rapids: Eerdmans, 1950), pp. 646–47. Also note this statement by G. Campbell Morgan: "This was the first reference that Christ ever made to His coming in any other sense than that of His presence with them in the world at that time. It was an incidental word, and I personally feel that there can be no escape from the conviction that upon that occasion His reference was not to the coming with which He dealt at a later period, but to His visitation of Jerusalem in judgment at her destruction a generation after His Cross." Quoted by Biederwolf, *Second Coming Bible Commentary*, p. 315.

9. David Chilton, *Paradise Restored: A Biblical Theology of Dominion* (Tyler, Tex.: Dominion, 1987), chapters 8 and 10.

10. D. A. Carson, "Matthew," Frank E. Gaebelein, gen. ed., *The Expositor's Bible Commentary*, Vol. 8 (Grand Rapids: Zondervan, 1984), p. 253.

11. Cox, *Biblical Studies*, p. 117.

12. George Eldon Ladd, *A Theology of the New Testament* (Grand Rapids: Eerdmans, 1974), p. 200.

13. F. F. Bruce, *The Hard Sayings of Jesus* (Downers Grove, Ill.: InterVarsity, 1983), p. 109.

14. See the discussion of *doxa* in Geoffrey W. Bromiley's abridged one-volume *Theological Dictionary of the New Testament*, Gerhard Kittel and Gerhard Friedrich, eds. (Grand Rapids: Eerdmans, 1985), pp. 178–81.

15. Charles H. Spurgeon, "An Awful Premonition," *12 Sermons*, pp. 3–6.

16. Chilton, *Paradise*, pp. 69–70.

17. William A. Cox, noted amillennial writer, agrees with this interpretation. *Biblical Studies*, p. 117.

18. Chilton, *Paradise*, p. 85. Chilton gives a good explanation about the proper approach to Bible interpretation.

19. F. F. Bruce, *The Gospel of John* (Grand Rapids: Eerdmans, 1983), p. 62.

20. James Bryant Rotherham, *The Emphasized Bible* (Grand Rapids: Kregel, 1974 reprint), p. 93.

21. Wilbur M. Smith comments: "In the Olivet Discourse four things are said to accompany our Lord in His return: power (Matt. 24:30); great glory (24:30; 26:31; Mark 13:26; Luke 21:27); angels (Matt. 24:31; 25:31); and clouds (Matt. 24:30). These factors are also present in other references to Christ's return, as in Matthew 16:27; 19:28; 24:64, and always accompany any epochal manifestations of deity (see Ex. 19:16; 34:5; 40:34–36; II Pet. 1:16, 17; Acts 1:8–11; Rev. 19)." "In the Study" ("The Olivet Discourse"), *Moody Monthly* (September 1957): 49.

22. Matthew 28:3 describes the countenance of the angel of the Lord as "like lightning."

23. Angels have always fascinated humans. Recently in a used bookstore I counted 23 books on the subject, and later in a new bookstore I counted 30. In spite of the great interest, however, our biblical sources remain rather limited. Key references: Hebrews 1:14; Matthew 18:10; Acts 12:7; 27:23.

24. T. W. Manson, *The Sayings of Jesus* (Grand Rapids: Eerdmans, 1957), pp. 216–17.

25. Vine, *Expository Dictionary*, p. 267.

26. Carson, "Matthew," *Expositor's Bible Commentary*, pp. 425–26.

27. Friedrich Büchsel, "*Palingenesia* in the NT," Gerhard Kittel, ed., *Theological Dictionary of the New Testament*, Vol. 1 (Grand Rapids: Eerdmans, 1964), p. 688.

28. Chilton, *Paradise*, p. 199.

29. Manson, *Sayings of Jesus*, p. 217.

Chapter 6: Birth Pangs Coming

1. Beasley-Murray, *Last Days*, p. 383.

2. Edersheim, *Life and Times*, Vol. II, p. 431.

3. Giovanni Papini, "The Life of Christ," in *A Reader's Digest Family Treasury of Great Biographies*, Dorothy Canfield Fisher, trans., Vol. III (Pleasantville, N.Y.: Reader's Digest, 1970), p. 102.

4. Josephus, *Jewish Wars*, 7:1:1. John F. MacArthur makes this interesting statement on the Temple stones: "The Western Wall, which remains standing even today, was part of the retaining wall built when the temple mount was expanded to make room for the immense structure Herod wanted to build. As such, it held up the temple's outer court, but it was not part of the temple building per-se; so it is no exception to Christ's prophecy that not one stone of the temple would be left standing." *Second Coming*, p. 225.

5. Beasley-Murray, *Last Days*, p. 386.

6. This significant statement by Jesus raises the question of whether or not the long-continued hardness of the Jews as a nation toward the Gospel will one day end. The Puritan writers particularly addressed this question, making Romans 11:25–26 their chief authority. Is the salvation of the Jews something to be realized progressively through the ages, or will there be a definite move of the Spirit to bring this to pass? See the presentation of Iain H. Murray, *The Puritan Hope*, chapter IV, in which a strong, persuasive argument is given for a national conversion.

7. I find it impossible to substantiate that the Bible actually teaches a future Temple. Tim LaHaye and Jerry Jenkins say: "All prophecy teachers who interpret the Scriptures literally agree that the Jewish temple in Israel will be rebuilt. . . . That there will be a third temple is predicted by the prophet Daniel, the apostles Paul and John, and none other than the Lord Jesus Himself. They all taught that Israel's third temple will be rebuilt either before the Tribulation begins or soon thereafter, for it is seen in complete operation by the middle of the Tribulation, when it will be desecrated. Obviously, since Israel does not now have a temple, the third temple must be rebuilt for such an event to occur." *Are We Living in the End Times?* (Wheaton: Tyndale, 1999), p. 122.

8. Kik, *Eschatology*, p. 88.

9. The discourses are identified by a similar formula that ends each one (see 5:28; 11:1; 13:53; 19:1; 26:1).

10. Smith, "Olivet Discourse," p. 46.

11. Sproul, *Last Days*, p. 32.

12. I like Robert L. Thomas and Stanley N. Gundry, *A Harmony of the Gospels* (Chicago: Moody, 1978), which uses the New American Standard Bible.

13. Two good sources for such critical study are I. Howard Marshall, *Commentary on Luke: New International Greek Testament Commentary* (Grand Rapids: Eerdmans, 1978), pp. 752–83; and, for Mark's gospel, George R. Beasley-Murray, *Jesus and the Last Days: The Interpretation of the Olivet Discourse* (Peabody, Mass.: Hendrickson, 1993).

14. Johnston M. Cheney, *The Life of Christ in Stereo*, Stanley A. Ellisen, ed. (Portland: Western Baptist Seminary, 1969), p. ix.

15. Jesus used this teaching tool of the "coming-yet-present" in regard to: 1) the resurrection (John 5:25); 2) the scattering of the disciples because of persecution (John 16:32); and 3) the present-yet-future appearance of the Kingdom of God (Matthew 25:31; Luke 11:20). As it applies to the Kingdom, see *The Presence of the Future* by George Eldon Ladd (Grand Rapids: Eerdmans, 1974).

16. See also 1 Corinthians 6:9; 15:33; Galatians 6:7; James 1:16; Revelation 2:20; 12:9; 13:14.

17. Beasley-Murray, *Last Days*, pp. 389–90.

18. Wilbur M. Smith, *You Can Know the Future* (Glendale, Calif.: G/L Regal, 1971), p. 59.

19. Papini, "Life of Christ," p. 106.

20. Information taken from David Sell, *Understanding End Times* (Pleasanton, Calif.: Northern California Bible College, 1999), pp. 12–13.

21. I. Howard Marshall, *Luke*, p. 765.

22. Some maintain that these "birth pangs" refer to the time leading up to the destruction of Jerusalem in A.D. 70 (such as postmillennialist J. Stuart Russell, *The Parousia: The New Testament Doctrine of Our Lord's Second Coming* (Grand Rapids: Baker, 1999 reprint). Others believe just as strongly that these events refer to the Tribulation period (such as dispensationalist John F. MacArthur, *Second Coming*). Why not a dual application—the period leading up to the destruction of Jerusalem and also the whole Church age? Perhaps

we have more than an either-or choice. Why not use the both-and method? Keep open to the possibility that for us some things are already past and some are yet future. With an open mind it is possible to reconcile the otherwise difficult-to-understand verses. The text itself, in spite of difficulties, remains intact and authentic.

23. Marshall, *Luke*, p. 766.

24. John Foxe (rewritten and updated by Harold J. Chadwick), *The New Foxe's Book of Martyrs* (North Brunswick, N.J.: Bridge-Logos, 1997).

25. Each of us must face the end of our individual lives, which can come at any time. Hebrews 3:14: "We have become partakers of Christ if we hold the beginning of our confidence steadfast to the end." The New Testament does teach that there is "this age" and that it will have an end (Matthew 13:22, 39, 49; 28:20; Luke 16:8; 20:34; Romans 12:2; 1 Corinthians 1:20; 2:6, 8; 3:18; 2 Corinthians 4:4; Galatians 1:4; Ephesians 1:21; 2:2; 1 Timothy 6:17; 2 Timothy 4:10; Titus 2:12). Also, there is an "age to come," which is, I feel, the literal millennial reign of Christ here on earth (Matthew 12:32; Mark 10:30; Luke 18:30; 20:35; Ephesians 1:21; Hebrews 6:5).

26. This is possibly the most controversial point made by preterist interpreters. Curtis Vaughan's article "Colossians" comments on the expression *proclaimed to every creature under heaven*: "Its universality is a mark of its authenticity. C. F. D. Moule suggests that the statement does not mean that the gospel had been preached to every individual, but that it had been 'heard in all the great centers of the Empire (cf. Rom. 15:19–23). . . .' [F. F.] Bruce suggests that Paul was 'perhaps indulging in a prophetic prolepsis.' . . . Obviously there is an element of hyperbole in the statement." Frank E. Gaebelein, gen. ed., *The Expositor's Bible Commentary*, Vol. 11 (Grand Rapids: Zondervan, 1978), p. 188.

27. Ladd, *Gospel of the Kingdom*, p. 139.

28. Sell, *End Times*, p. 8.

29. As told by Sue Curran, *I Saw Satan Fall Like Lightning* (Orlando, Fla.: Creation House, 1998), pp. 82–83.

30. Philip Schaff, *History of the Christian Church*, Vol. VII (Grand Rapids: Eerdmans, 1950), p. 305.

31. Ibid., p. 1.

32. Fascinating witness of this phenomenon in China is given by Danyun, trans. by Brother Dennis Balcombe, in *Lilies Amongst Thorns* (Kent, U.K.: Sovereign World, 1991). One amazing testimonial among many involves Yun, a man who miraculously fasted without food or water for 74 days and, in spite of unbelievable torture and mistreatment in a Chinese prison, gave Spirit-inspired words to his tormentors. See also Jane Rumph, *Stories from the Front Lines* (Grand Rapids: Chosen, 1996).

33. Bruce, *Hard Sayings*, pp. 208–09.

Chapter 7: Judgment and Glory

1. I believe this refers to Jesus the Messiah, who alone can make covenant and who was indeed "cut off" (verse 26) "in the middle of the week" (after three and a half years of ministry, and also literally in the middle of Passion Week). See Kevin Conner's excellent study, *The Seventy Weeks Prophecy*.

2. See Appendix C for the author's understanding of Daniel's seventy-week prophecy.

3. MacArthur, *Second Coming*, p. 79.

4. Wilbur M. Smith comments: "The word rendered 'abomination' is *bdelugma*, meaning 'a foul thing,' often used in LXX in passages referring to idolatry (e.g., I Kings 11:5; 21:26; II Kings 21:2; and, similarly, in Rev. 17:4, 5; 21:27). The word translated 'desola-

tion' is *eremosis*, in this form only in the Olivet Discourse, but as a verb *eremoo* in Matthew 12:25; Luke 11:17; Revelation 17:16; 18:17, 19." "Olivet Discourse," p. 49.

5. R. V. G. Tasker argues—rightly, I think—that this does not refer to the desecration of the Temple by Antiochus Epiphanes, who set up a heathen altar within the sacred precincts in 168 B.C., or to Caligula in A.D. 38, who attempted to erect a statue of himself in the Temple. Tasker says that "some idol or statue erected in the Temple does not seem to be in keeping with the present context, where the appearance of *the abomination of desolation* is regarded as the *first* indication that an attack upon Jerusalem is imminent. . . ." *The Gospel According to St. Matthew*, p. 229.

6. Sproul, *Last Days*, p. 40.

7. Flavius Josephus, *Wars of the Jews*, 7:9:3, *The Works of Josephus: Complete and Unabridged*, translated by William Whiston (Lynn, Mass.: Hendrickson, 1980), p. 587.

8. Ibid., 6:5:1.

9. William E. Cox rightly says that this "great tribulation" (verse 21) is not to be confused with a last-days Tribulation. He says, "Jesus referred to this as the greatest tribulation ever known or ever to be. Bible scholars generally agree that our Lord meant this was to be the greatest tribulation ever to come upon Israel *as a nation*. Since the Jewish state came to its prophesied end in A.D. 70, an even greater tribulation could come to pass—involving not Israel, but the church—and still not be contradictory to the words of our Lord." *Biblical Studies in Final Things*, p. 102.

10. See, for example, George Eldon Ladd, "Matthew," *The Biblical Expositor*, Carl F. H. Henry, consulting ed., Vol. 3 (Philadelphia: A. J. Holman, 1960), p. 64.

11. Perhaps the most outstanding presentation of the preterist view of the Olivet Discourse is that by J. Stuart Russell, *The Parousia*. I am delighted that this 1887 classic was reprinted in 1999. I do not agree with all Russell says, but the material is original and thought-provoking and should be considered. As R. C. Sproul says in the foreword: "Russell's book has forced me to take the events surrounding the destruction of Jerusalem far more seriously than before, to open my eyes to the radical significance of this event in redemptive history" (p. x).

12. Smith, *You Can Know*, p. 33.

13. The KJV use of *eagle* instead of *vulture* tends to glorify the parable. Actually the Greek word *aetos* can mean "eagle," "kite" or "vulture." D. A. Carson comments: "Here Jesus quotes a proverb (cf. Job 39:30; Luke 17:37). 'Eagle' (KJV) is wrong: 'vulture' (NIV) is correct. . . . Eagles are not normally carrion eaters." "Matthew," *Expositor's Bible Commentary*, p. 503.

14. I am intrigued by the possibility that Jerusalem was the carcass that would be surrounded by Rome's imperial eagles [vultures].

15. Marshall, *Luke*, p. 774.

16. Sproul mentions reports, some by Josephus and some by Tacitus, that involved heavenly phenomena—a star resembling a sword, a comet around A.D. 60 (Halley's Comet also appeared in A.D. 66), a bright light shining around the altar and the Temple, and a vision of chariots and soldiers running around among the clouds and surrounding cities; and earthly phenomena reported by priests—a quaking, a great noise and the sound of a great multitude saying, "Let us remove hence." *Last Days*, pp. 121–27.

17. Isaiah 13:10; 34:4; Ezekiel 32:7; Joel 2:10, 31; Amos 8:9; Haggai 2:6, 21; Acts 2:19, 20; Revelation 6:12.

18. Ayer's Rock (2,845 feet high, six miles around) is probably an asteroid since its composition is so dissimilar to the surrounding earth. Scientists have kept an eye on the asteroid belt region between Mars and Jupiter, where a large number of flying rocks exist.

Presently some two hundred asteroids have been identified and are being tracked. But scientists do not know all that exist!

19. David Chilton in *Paradise Restored* says: "The word *tribes* here has primary reference to *the tribes of the land of Israel;* and the 'mourning' is probably meant in two senses. First, they would mourn in sorrow over their suffering and the loss of their land; second, they would ultimately mourn in repentance for their sins, when they are converted from their apostasy." But I disagree that this applies to the time of A.D. 70. Jesus made this statement after Israel's house had already been left desolate (Matthew 23:38). He was now dealing with the second great event of the Olivet Discourse—His glorious return. This will be visible to all tribes of peoples everywhere. Christ's concern was now the whole world (including Israel).

20. Beasley-Murray, *Last Days*, p. 429.

21. Ibid., p. 425.

22. Cheney, *Life of Christ*, pp. 259–60.

23. A good discussion of whether this word means "generation" or "race" is given by F. F. Bruce in *The Hard Sayings of Jesus*, pp. 225–27. He says: "'This generation' is a recurring phrase in the Bible, and each time it is used it bears the ordinary sense of the people belonging, as we say, to one fairly comprehensive age-group. . . . Jesus's hearers could have understood him to mean only that 'all these things' would take place within *their* generation."

24. Ibid., p. 228.

25. Russell, *Parousia*, pp. 84–85.

26. Marshall, *Luke*, p. 753.

27. See Ladd's discussion, *Hope*, chapter 6.

28. John E. Hartley, "1994 *qawa*," R. Laird Harris, ed., *Theological Wordbook of the Old Testament*, Vol. 2 (Chicago: Moody, 1980), p. 791.

29. Max Lucado, *When Christ Comes* (Nashville: Word, 1999), pp. 15–16.

Chapter 8: What Acts Says About the Second Coming

1. G. Campbell Morgan, *The Acts of the Apostles* (New York: Revell, 1924), p. 22.

2. 1 Timothy 3:16: "received up in glory." This quotation of Alford by Biederwolf is interesting: "There was a manifest propriety in the last withdrawal of the Lord while ascending; not consisting in a *disappearance* of His body as on former occasions since the Resurrection; for thus might His abiding humanity have been called into question. As it was He went up in human form, and so we think and pray to Him." *Second Coming Bible Commentary*, p. 402.

3. Daniel describes Jesus' ascension *into* heaven rather than His Second Coming *from* heaven. He did not move toward earth but "came to the Ancient of Days, and they brought Him near before Him." Luke 1:32 says, "The Lord God will give Him the throne of His father David," and Acts 2:33 says, "Having been exalted to the right hand of God, and having received from the Father the promise of the Holy Spirit, He has poured forth this which you both see and hear." According to Acts 2:34–35 this is to fulfill Psalm 110:1: "The LORD said to my Lord, 'Sit at My right hand, till I make Your enemies Your footstool.'"

4. About verse 10—"While they looked steadfastly"—R. J. Knowling says: "[It] denotes a fixed, steadfast, protracted gaze. . . . The verb . . . is frequently employed by medical writers to denote a peculiar fixed look." *The Expositor's Greek Testament*, Vol. 2 (Grand Rapids: Eerdmans, 1951), pp. 57–58.

5. Were they men or angels? We do not know, but it is intriguing to consider that it could have been Moses and Elijah. As in Luke 9:30–31: "Behold, two men talked with Him, who were Moses and Elijah, who appeared in glory and spoke of His decease [lit., *exodus*, "departure," NASB], which He was about to accomplish at Jerusalem."

6. Robertson, *Word Pictures*, Vol. III, p. 12.

7. The theme of the Day of the Lord runs throughout the prophetic books. A few examples: Isaiah 2:12; 13:6; Ezekiel 7:7–8; 13:5; Zephaniah 1:14–18.

8. The Greek word *dei* ("it is necessary") indicates urgent necessity. The Williams translation uses *retained*. The *Interlinear Greek-English New Testament* gives the translation "It behoves heaven to receive."

9. Many places in the Psalms (for example, 117:1) exhort the nations to praise the Lord. Jesus' great desire to reach all the nations was fueled by the prophetic psalms. These psalms are destined for fulfillment in that all nations will hear the message of Christ and be given opportunity before the end to worship the true and living God.

10. Robertson, *Word Pictures*, Vol. III, p. 46.

11. Vine, *Expository Dictionary*, p. 333.

12. Colin Brown, gen. ed., *Dictionary of New Testament Theology*, Vol. 3 (Grand Rapids: Zondervan, 1971), p. 837.

13. Bromiley, *Theological Dictionary* (abridged), p. 389. Thayer's *Lexicon* defines *kairos* as "a definitely limited portion of time, with the added notion of suitableness. . . . changeableness," and the Greek word *Cr. (chronos)* as "time in general . . . .duration." Joseph Henry Thayer, *A Greek-English Lexicon of the New Testament* (New York: American Book, 1889), p. 391.

14. This is borne out by Peter's use of the verb form of *apostolos*, indicating that Christ is the representative of Him who sent Him.

15. Consider these examples from John's gospel: chapter 2—water is made into wine to declare the new is better than the old; chapter 5—healing on the Sabbath to explain the deeper meaning of the Sabbath; chapter 6—bread is multiplied to introduce the Bread of Life; chapter 9—a blind man is healed to explain spiritual darkness; chapter 11—Lazarus is raised from the dead to emphasize eternal life.

16. An interesting word with two prefixes, a double compound ("double whammy"), giving it an extra punch.

17. "All His holy prophets." Note "prophets" mentioned in verses 18, 21, 22, 23, 24, 25. Prophets spoke to their own generations, but also to those who live now: 1 Peter 1:10–12; 2 Peter 1:16–21.

18. Carson, "Matthew," *Expositor's Bible Commentary*, p. 425.

19. See Lucado, *When Christ Comes*, chapter 11, "Love's Caution: A Day of Ultimate Justice."

20. Resurrection of the just: see 1 Corinthians 15:12–23; Luke 14:14; 20:35–38; for the resurrection of unjust as well as just cf. Daniel 12:2; John 5:28–29; Revelation 20:12–14.

21. F. F. Bruce, *The Acts of the Apostles: The Greek Text with Introduction and Commentary* (Grand Rapids: Eerdmans, 1970 reprint), p. 426.

Chapter 9: Assurance for the Mystified Thessalonians

1. The premillennial dispensationalist feels strongly not only about the protection of the Church; he is also concerned with the proper interpretation of Daniel's seventy-week prophecy (Daniel 9). This would include time for the rise of the Antichrist, the building of a Jewish Temple, etc. See my Appendix C.

2. Gundry, *First the Antichrist* (Grand Rapids: Baker, 1997), pp. 67–68. Gundry agrees with Ladd in attacking the doctrine of imminency. As a dispensationalist he differs from Ladd by suggesting that Israel and the Church are separate entities. Gundry does, however, believe that during the Tribulation God still views the Jew and the Gentile as together making up the Church. After the Tribulation the distinction between Jew and Gentile resumes.

3. MacArthur, *Second Coming*, p. 87. Arthur Katterjohn, a dispensational posttribulationist, states his view: "The notion that Jesus will come *for* His saints is often taught to the exclusion of the grander theme that He will be coming *with* His saints. These are not two separate comings, but one and the same. Believers alive at that time will be caught up to meet Christ in the air and proceed to accompany Him to the earth. . . . The pretribulational distinction between *for* His saints and *with* His saints is not proof of two returns, but evidence that when He comes, we will be with Him." *The Tribulation People* (Carol Stream, Ill.: Creation House, 1975), p. 101.

4. William Hendriksen, "Thessalonians," *Thessalonians, the Pastorals and Hebrews: New Testament Commentary* (Grand Rapids: Baker, 1995), p. 116.

5. Ladd, *Hope*, p. 79.

6. M. R. Vincent, *Word Studies in the New Testament* (Wilmington: Associated Publishers and Authors, 1972 reprint), p. 953.

7. Werner Forester, "Harpazo," Kittel, ed. *Theological Dictionary*, Vol. I, p. 472. Gives one of the best succinct discussions of *harpazo*.

8. J. B. Smith, *Greek-English Concordance* (Scottdale, Pa.: Herald, 1955), p. 41.

9. Moulton and Milligan, *Vocabulary*, p. 53.

10. Gundry: ". . . to distinguish the Day of Christ from the Day of the Lord overlooks the fact that Paul uses a much wider variety of expressions than these two. . . . In wording, 'Day of the Lord Jesus' is just as different from 'Day of Christ' as 'Day of the Lord' is. And so on with regard to all the variations. It makes no more sense to refer the various expressions to different events than it does to refer 'Jesus,' 'Christ,' 'Lord,' 'Lord Jesus,' 'Lord Christ,' and 'Lord Jesus Christ' to different persons. To top it off, none of the variations on 'Day of the Lord' occur in passages that provide an argument for pretribulationism." *First the Antichrist*, pp. 42–43.

11. Mathison, *Postmillennialism*, p. 225.

12. Ibid., p. 226.

13. Hendriksen, "Thessalonians," p. 159.

14. Ibid., p. 165.

15. Gundry says: ". . . Since Paul gives no indication that the man of lawlessness, the Antichrist, will ever have professed allegiance to God and Christ, 'rebellion' seems a better translation than 'apostasy,' which would imply an earlier such allegiance." *Antichrist*, p. 21.

16. The KJV reads "man of sin," and the RSV, NIV and NASB have "the man of lawlessness." Williams feels that "the man of sin" is preferable to "lawlessness," because it better signifies the concentration of evil he represents. The word includes the meaning of wickedness or iniquity as well. *Renewal Theology*, p. 334, footnote #72.

17. Arthur H. Lewis, *The Dark Side of the Millennium: The Problem of Evil in Rev. 20:1–10* (Grand Rapids: Baker, 1980), p. 52.

18. Williams, *Renewal Theology*, p. 304.

19. Ladd, *A Commentary on the Revelation of John* (Grand Rapids: Eerdmans, 1972), p. 178. See also Charles R. Erdman, *The Revelation of John* (Philadelphia: Westminster, 1936), pp. 110–15.

20. Smith, *You Can Know*, p. 57.

Chapter 10: Here Comes the Judge

1. F. F. Bruce, *The Letter of Paul to the Romans: An Introduction and Commentary: The Tyndale New Testament Commentaries,* Leon Morris, gen. ed. (Grand Rapids: Eerdmans, 1985), p. 160.

2. Quoted by Biederwolf, *The Second Coming Bible Commentary,* pp. 414, 416.

3. C. K. Barrett, *A Commentary on the Epistle to the Romans* (New York: Harper & Row, 1957), p. 165.

4. Ibid., p. 166.

5. Bruce, *Romans,* p. 161.

6. Murray J. Harris, "2 Corinthians," *Expositor's Bible Commentary,* Vol. 10 (Grand Rapids: Zondervan, 1976), p. 349.

7. Bauer, *Lexicon,* p. 139.

8. Thayer, *Lexicon,* p. 101.

9. The five crowns are based on the material by Rick Howard, *The Judgment Seat of Christ* (Woodside, Calif.: Naioth Sound and Publishing, 1990), pp. 45–57.

10. Ibid., p. 47.

11. W. C. G. Proctor, "II Corinthians," *The New Bible Commentary,* F. Davidson, ed. (Grand Rapids: Eerdmans, 1953), pp. 993–94.

Chapter 11: Our World Will Burst into Flame

1. Simon J. Kistemaker, *New Testament Commentary: Exposition of the Epistles of Peter and of the Epistle of Jude* (Grand Rapids: Baker, 1987), p. 338. Some commentators connect this thought with: 1) 1 Corinthians 7:29, "the time is short[ened]"—i.e., "contracted, compressed, brought within narrow limits" (Biederwolf, *Second Coming Bible Commentary,* p. 433). 2) Matthew 24:22, "unless those days were shortened" (i.e., the number of days, not the length of the days).

2. Ibid. Some corroborating Scriptures might be the early prayers (Matthew 6:10; Luke 11:2; 1 Corinthians 16:22; Revelation 22:20). See also Matthew 24:14; Acts 3:19–21.

3. Biederwolf, *Second Coming Bible Commentary,* p. 532.

4. Ladd, *New Testament,* p. 557.

5. Robertson, *Word Pictures,* Vol. VI, p. 176. Vincent comments that "the kindred noun *rhoidzos* is used in classical Greek of the whistling of an arrow; the sound of a shepherd's pipe; the rush of wings; the plash of water; the hissing of a serpent; and the sound of filing." *Word Studies,* p. 336.

6. Biederwolf, *Second Coming Bible Commentary,* p. 531.

7. Kistemaker, *New Testament Commentary,* p. 336.

8. Vincent says: "The elements (stoicheia). Derived from stoichos, a row, and meaning originally one of a row or series; hence a component or element. The name for the letters of the alphabet, as being set in rows. Applied to the four elements—fire, air, earth, water—and in later times to the planets and signs of the zodiac. . . . The kindred verb stoicheo, to walk, carries the idea of keeping in line, according to the radical sense. Thus, walk according to rule (Gal. 6:16); walkest orderly (Acts 21:24). . . . Here the word is of course used in a physical sense, meaning the parts of which this system of things is composed." *Word Studies,* p. 337.

9. Biederwolf, *Second Coming Bible Commentary,* p. 533.

10. Kistemaker, *New Testament Commentary,* p. 337.

11. Henry Alford, *Alford's Greek Testament: An Exegetical and Critical Commentary*, Vol. 4, Part 2 (Grand Rapids: Guardian, 1976, 5th ed. [1857]), p. 418.

12. Robertson, *Word Pictures*, Vol. VI, p. 180.

13. Biederwolf, *Second Coming Bible Commentary*, p. 534.

Chapter 12: The Book of Revelation: The Final Triumph

1. Curran, *Fall Like Lightning*, pp. 30–31. Also see the fine presentation by Charles H. Kraft, *I Give You Authority* (Grand Rapids: Chosen, 1997).

2. Alford, "Apocalypse of John," *Greek Testament*, Vol. 4, p. 732.

3. Other references on the resurrection: Matthew 22:31–32; John 11:24; 1 Corinthians 15:12, 22–23, 26, 42–43, 54; Philippians 3:21; 1 Thessalonians 4:14–16.

4. Also, see the discussion by Erickson, *Basic Guide*, pp. 97–101.

5. The parable of Jesus in Matthew 25:31–46 can fit this description. Jesus comes and sits on His throne of glory. It is possible that "all the nations gathered unto Him" occurs at the end of the thousand years and is just another way of describing the scenario in Revelation 20. The key is found in verses 41 and 46: "Then he will also say to those on the left, 'Depart from Me, you cursed, into the everlasting fire prepared for the devil and his angels.' . . . And these will go away into everlasting punishment, but the righteous into eternal life." Every description brings some aspect of God's dealings, and we are not to be confused by conflicting approaches and try to press them into one mold.

Appendix C: Daniel's Seventy-Weeks Prophecy

1. Kevin J. Conner, *The Seventy Weeks Prophecy: An Exposition of Daniel 9* (Blackburn, Victoria, Australia: Acacia, 1981), p. 28. In my estimation this is the best book available on the subject. Conner has left no stone unturned in his effort to present a solid case.

2. According to Bishop Ussher, this command was given by King Artaxerxes in 457 B.C. (Ezra 7). *The Zondervan NIV Bible Commentary* also accepts this date: "The most likely fulfillment is the decree issued to Ezra in the seventh year of Artaxerxes I (i.e., 457 B.C.)." Richard Polcyn with consulting editors, Kenneth L. Barker and John R. Kohlenberger III, *The Zondervan NIV Bible Commentary* (Grand Rapids: Zondervan, 1994), p. 1389. *The Pulpit Commentary* marks the date at 458 B.C. *The Pulpit Commentary* (Grand Rapids: Eerdmans, 1962), Vol. 13, p. 269. Since these dates are so close, we will use the 457 B.C. date to serve as the beginning point of the prophecy, with the understanding that it could be one year earlier. These are lunar years rather than 360-day calendar years.

Conner presents a convincing argument that it was actually the decree of Cyrus that was given in 457 B.C. (see Chapter 7, "The Seventy Weeks"). He bases his conclusion on the thorough work of Martin Anstey's *Chronology of the Old Testament* (Grand Rapids: Kregel Publications, 1973) and also a careful analysis of what God said concerning Cyrus (Isaiah 44:26–28; 45:1–13).

3. *The dispensational premillennialist* believes that the seven years will be at the end of the age, just before Christ's Second Coming. *The amillennialist* believes that the seventy-weeks prophecy was meant to be continuous and unbroken, so the seven years is already fulfilled. The *postmillennialist* also believes that the prophecy has already been fulfilled. Our presentation here is an alternative to the usual interpretations.

4. Sell, *End Times*, p. 19.

5. The clear statement of Matthew 12:40 ("three days and three nights") can be harmonized with the more than a dozen idiomatic references to "the third day" or "three

days." Jesus' statement in Matthew 12:40 is not an idiom because He clearly states the number of nights as well as days; we must interpret the burial time, therefore, in the light of His literal statement.

The three days must be interpreted as the Jews interpreted their days—that is, from sundown to sundown (or, 6 P.M. to 6 P.M.). Thus Jesus was crucified on Wednesday, buried just before sundown, and was in the tomb three full days. First day: Wednesday 6 P.M. to Thursday 6 P.M. Second day: Thursday 6 P.M. to Friday 6 P.M. Third day: Friday 6 P.M. to Saturday 6 P.M. Jesus arose from the dead on the first day of the week, Sunday, anytime after Saturday sundown (our time). This also means that He did not necessarily rise from the dead as the sun rose on Sunday morning.

Also note that during the Passion Week there were two Sabbaths: the regular Jewish Sabbath on Saturday, but also Thursday, which was considered a high Sabbath since it was the first day of a Jewish convocation (John 19:31).

Since this subject could take a chapter in itself, I refer you to the best coverage (with charts) that I know: Kevin J. Conner, *The Three Days and Three Nights* (Blackburn, Victoria, Australia: Acacia, 1988), available from City Bible Publishing, Portland, Oregon.

6. Sell, *End Times,* p. 21.

7. Ibid., p. 22. I have reworded Sell's four questions.

Appendix D: The Millennium: What Will We Do for a Thousand Years?

1. Lewis, *Dark Side,* p. 5.

2. Ibid., p. 12.

3. Erdman, *Revelation,* pp. 155–56.

4. The symbolical is usually apparent because it uses figures, characters and situations that are not common to our thinking. For instance, the Lamb of God (Revelation 5:5) is pictured as having seven horns and seven eyes. Since no such creature exists, we must assume a spiritual application for these bizarre attributes. (The eyes and horns connote omniscience and omnipotence.)

5. Charles Spurgeon, "He Cometh with Clouds," *12 Sermons,* p. 115.

6. George Ladd's much quoted statement: "I can find no trace of the idea of either an interim earthly kingdom or of a millennium in the Gospels." Robert G. Clouse, ed., *The Meaning of the Millennium,* p. 38. I must respectfully disagree with my former seminary professor, for the reasons I list.

7. See note #25 in chapter 6 for references.

8. As a historical premillennialist, Ladd gives one of the best discussions of "this age" and "the age to come." But, although he notes that the Millennium is to follow the Parousia (with its attendant two stages in the resurrection and two stages in the defeat of Satan), he feels that "the age to come" must be pushed farther off—and "the Millennium ends in failure so far as the full achievement of God's reign is concerned." *Gospel of the Kingdom,* p. 38. This approach, I feel, dilutes the grand triumph of the Second Coming and the very purpose for Christ's reign on earth!

9. Ibid., p. 46.

10. See the discussion by Erickson, *Basic Guide,* pp. 103–6.

11. Walvoord, *Millennial Kingdom,* p. 317.

12. Katterjohn, *Tribulation People,* p. 124.

13. Gundry, *Antichrist,* p. 128.

14. See Sell's explanation, *End Times,* p. 98.

BIBLIOGRAPHY

Alford, Henry. *Alford's Greek Testament: An Exegetical and Critical Commentary.* Grand Rapids: Guardian, 1857 (1976 5th edition). Vol. 4.

Allis, Oswald T. *Prophecy and the Church.* Philadelphia: Presbyterian and Reformed, 1945.

Anstey, Martin. *Chronology of the Old Testament.* Grand Rapids: Kregel Publications, 1973.

Archer, G. L. Jr., Paul D. Feinberg, Douglas J. Moo and Richard R. Reiter. *Three Views on the Rapture: Pre-, Mid-, or Post-Tribulation?* Grand Rapids: Zondervan, 1984.

Augustine, Saint. *The City of God.* Robert Maynard Hutchins, ed. in chief. *Great Books of the Western World.* Chicago: Encyclopaedia Britannica, 1952.

Barrett, C. K. *A Commentary on the Epistle to the Romans.* New York: Harper & Row, 1957.

Bauer, W., William F. Arndt and F. Wilbur Gingrich, eds. *A Greek-English Lexicon of the New Testament and Other Early Christian Literature.* Chicago: University of Chicago Bauer Press, 1957.

Bavinck, Herman, ed. John Bolt, trans. by John Vriend. *The Last Things: Hope for This World and the Next.* Grand Rapids: Baker, 1996.

Baxter, J. Sidlow. *Explore the Book.* Grand Rapids: Zondervan, 1966.

Beasley-Murray, George R. *Jesus and the Last Days: The Interpretation of the Olivet Discourse.* Peabody, Mass.: Hendrickson, 1993.

Berkhof, Louis. *Systematic Theology.* Grand Rapids: Eerdmans, 1941.

Berknouwer, G. C. *The Return of Christ.* Grand Rapids: Eerdmans, 1972.

Biederwolf, William Edward. *The Second Coming Bible Commentary.* Grand Rapids: Baker, 1985 (1924 original printing).

Blaising, Craig A., and Darrell L. Bock. *Progressive Dispensationalism: An Up-to-Date Handbook of Contemporary Dispensational Thought.* Wheaton: Victor/BridgePoint, 1993.

Blummer, Alfred. *A Critical and Exegetical Commentary on the Gospel According to S. Luke (The International Critical Commentary*). Edinburgh: T. and T. Clark, 1951 reprint.

Boettner, Loraine. *The Millennium.* Philadelphia: Presbyterian and Reformed, 1957.

Boice, James Montgomery. *Foundations of the Christian Faith.* Downers Grove, Ill.: Inter-Varsity, 1986.

Bromiley, Geoffrey. *Theological Dictionary of the New Testament.* One-volume abridgement. Grand Rapids: Eerdmans, 1985.

Brown, Colin, gen. ed. *Dictionary of New Testament Theology.* Grand Rapids: Zondervan, 1971. Vol. 3.

Bruce, F. F. *The Letter of Paul to the Romans: An Introduction and Commentary (Tyndale New Testament Commentaries).* Leon Morris, gen. ed. Grand Rapids: Eerdmans, 1985.

———. *The Hard Sayings of Jesus.* Downers Grove, Ill.: InterVarsity, 1983.

———. *The Gospel of John.* Grand Rapids: Eerdmans, 1983.

———. *Answers to Questions.* Grand Rapids: Zondervan, 1972.

———. *The Acts of the Apostles: The Greek Text with Introduction and Commentary.* Grand Rapids: Eerdmans, 1970 reprint.

Büchsel, Friedrich. "*Palingenesia* in the NT." Gerhard Kittel, ed. *Theological Dictionary of the New Testament.* Grand Rapids: Eerdmans, 1964. Vol. 1, p. 688.

Buttrick, George A. "The Gospel According to St. Matthew." *The Interpreter's Bible.* New York/Nashville: Abingdon, 1951. Vol. VII.

Campbell, Roderick. *Israel and the New Covenant.* Tyler, Tex.: Geneva Ministries, 1983 (1954).

Carson, D. A. "Matthew." Frank E. Gaebelein, gen. ed. *The Expositor's Bible Commentary.* Grand Rapids: Zondervan, 1984. Vol. 8.

Chafer, Lewis Sperry. *Dispensationalism.* Dallas: Dallas Theological Seminary, 1936.

Cheney, Johnson M., ed. Stanley A. Ellisen. *The Life of Christ in Stereo.* Portland, Ore.: Western Baptist Seminary, 1969.

Chilton, David. *Paradise Restored: A Biblical Theology of Dominion.* Tyler, Tex.: Dominion, 1987.

Clouse, Robert G., ed. George E. Ladd, Herman A. Hoyt, Loraine Boettner and Anthony A. Hoekema. *The Meaning of the Millennium: Four Views.* Downers Grove, Ill.: InterVarsity, 1977.

Clouse, Robert G., Robert N. Hosack and Richard V. Pierard. *The New Millennium Manual.* Grand Rapids: Baker, 1999.

Conner, Kevin J. *The Foundations of Christian Doctrine.* Portland: Bible Temple, 1980.

———. *The Seventy Weeks Prophecy: An Exposition of Daniel 9.* Blackburn, Victoria, Australia: Acacia, 1981.

———. *The Three Days and Three Nights.* Blackburn, Victoria, Australia: Acacia, 1988.

Cooper, David L. *Future Events Revealed According to Matthew 24 and 25.* Los Angeles: David L. Cooper, 1935.

Cox, William E. *An Examination of Dispensationalism.* Philadelphia: Presbyterian and Reformed, 1971.

———. *Amillennialism Today.* Phillipsburg, N.J.: Presbyterian and Reformed, 1966.

———. *Biblical Studies in Final Things.* Philadelphia: Presbyterian and Reformed, 1967.

Curran, Sue. *I Saw Satan Fall Like Lightning: A Divine Revelation of How to Take New Authority Over the Devil.* Orlando, Fla.: Creation House, 1998.

Danyun, trans. by Brother Dennis [Balcom]. *Lilies Amongst Thorns.* Kent, England: Sovereign World, 1991.

DeHaan, M. R. *The Second Coming of Jesus.* Grand Rapids: Zondervan, 1974.

Edersheim, Alfred. *The Life and Times of Jesus the Messiah.* Grand Rapids: Eerdmans, 1950.

Erdman, Charles R. *The Revelation of John.* Philadelphia: Westminster, 1936.

Erickson, Millard J. *A Basic Guide to Eschatology: Making Sense of the Millennium.* Grand Rapids: Baker, 1999 reprint.

Forester, Werner. "Harpazo." Gerhard Kittel, ed. *Theological Dictionary of the New Testament.* Grand Rapids: Eerdmans, 1964. Vol. 1.

Foxe, John. *The New Foxe's Book of Martyrs*. Rewritten and updated by Harold J. Chadwick. North Brunswick, N.J.: Bridge-Logos, 1997.

Gali, Mark, ed. "A History of the Second Coming" (issue theme). *Christian History,* 61 (Vol. XVIII, No. 1).

Gentile, Ernest B. *Awaken the Dawn!* Portland: Bible Temple, 1990.

Gentry, Kenneth L. Jr. *He Shall Have Dominion: A Postmillennial Eschatology.* Tyler, Tex.: Institute for Christian Economics, 1992.

Gundry, Robert H. *First the Antichrist.* Grand Rapids: Baker, 1997.

———. *The Church and the Tribulation*. Grand Rapids: Zondervan, 1973.

Harris, Murray J. "2 Corinthians." Frank E. Gaebelein, gen. ed. *The Expositor's Bible Commentary.* Grand Rapids: Zondervan, 1976. Vol. 10.

Hartley, John E. "1994 *qawa.*" R. Laird Harris, ed. *Theological Wordbook of the Old Testament.* Chicago: Moody, 1980. Vol. 2, p. 791.

Hendriksen, William. "Thessalonians." *Thessalonians, the Pastorals and Hebrews (New Testament Commentary).* Grand Rapids: Baker, 1995.

Hiebert, D. E. "Parousia." Merrill C. Tenney, gen. ed., *The Zondervan Pictorial Encyclopedia of the Bible*. Grand Rapids: Zondervan, 1975. Vol. 4, p. 601.

Hill, David. *The Gospel of Matthew (New Century Bible).* London: (Oliphants) Marshall, Morgan and Scott, 1972.

Hodge, Charles. *Systematic Theology.* New York: Scribner's, 1871. Vol. IV.

Hoekema, Anthony A. *The Bible and the Future*. Grand Rapids: Eerdmans, 1979.

Howard, Rick. *The Judgment Seat of Christ.* Woodside, Calif.: Naioth Sound and Publishing, 1990.

Josephus, Flavius, trans. by William Whiston. *Wars of the Jews. The Works of Josephus: Complete and Unabridged.* Lynn, Mass.: Hendrickson, 1980.

Katterjohn, Arthur. *The Tribulation People.* Carol Stream, Ill.: Creation House, 1975.

Kik, J. Marcellus. *An Eschatology of Victory*. Phillipsburg, N.J.: Presbyterian and Reformed, 1971.

Kistemaker, Simon J. *New Testament Commentary: Exposition of the Epistles of Peter and of the Epistle of Jude.* Grand Rapids: Baker, 1987.

Knowling, R. J. "The Acts of the Apostles." W. Robinson Nicoll, ed. *The Expositor's Greek Testament.* Grand Rapids: Eerdmans, 1951. Vol. 2.

Kraft, Charles H. *I Give You Authority.* Grand Rapids: Chosen, 1997.

Ladd, George E. *A Theology of the New Testament.* Grand Rapids: Eerdmans, 1974.

———. *The Presence of the Future*. Grand Rapids: Eerdmans, 1974.

———. *A Commentary on the Revelation of John.* Grand Rapids: Eerdmans, 1972.

———. "Matthew." *The Biblical Expositor.* Philadelphia: A. J. Holman, 1960. Vol. 3.

———. *The Gospel of the Kingdom*. Grand Rapids: Eerdmans, 1959.

———. *The Blessed Hope*. Grand Rapids: Eerdmans, 1956.

———. *Crucial Questions about the Kingdom of God.* Grand Rapids: Eerdmans, 1952.

LaHaye, Tim, and Jerry B. Jenkins. *Are We Living in the End Times?* Wheaton: Tyndale, 1999.

Lamsa, George M. *Gospel Light: Comments on the Teachings of Jesus from Aramaic and Unchanged Eastern Customs*. Philadelphia: A. J. Holman, 1936.

Larkin, Clarence. *Dispensational Truth*. Philadelphia: Clarence Larkin, c. 1920.

Levitt, Zola. *Broken Branches: Has the Church Replaced Israel*? Dallas: Zola Levitt, 1995.

Lewis, Arthur H. *The Dark Side of the Millennium: The Problem of Evil in Rev. 20:1–10.* Grand Rapids: Baker, 1980.

Lindsey, Hal. *The Late Great Planet Earth.* Grand Rapids: Zondervan, 1970.

Lucado, Max. *When Christ Comes.* Nashville: Word, 1999.

MacArthur, John F. *The Second Coming*. Wheaton: Crossway, 1999.

MacPherson, Dave. *The Incredible Cover-Up: The True Story of the Pre-Trib Rapture*. Plainfield, N.J.: Logos, 1975.

Manson, T. W. *The Sayings of Jesus*. Grand Rapids: Eerdmans, 1957.

Marshall, I. Howard. *Commentary on Luke (New International Greek Testament Commentary)*. Grand Rapids: Eerdmans, 1978.

Mathison, Keith A. *Postmillennialism: An Eschatology of Hope*. Phillipsburg, N.J.: Presbyterian and Reformed, 1999.

Mauro, Philip. *The Gospel of the Kingdom*. Sterling, Va.: Grace Abounding, 1988.

———. *The Seventy Weeks and the Great Tribulation*. Swengel, Pa.: Bible Truth, 1944.

Moorehead, William G. "Millennium." James Orr, gen. ed. *The New International Standard Bible Encyclopaedia*. Grand Rapids: Eerdmans, 1974 reprint. Vol. 3, p. 2054.

Morgan, G. Campbell. *The Acts of the Apostles*. No city: Revell, 1924.

Moulton, James Hope, and George Milligan. *The Vocabulary of the Greek Testament: Illustrated from the Papyri and Other Non-Literary Sources*. Grand Rapids: Zondervan, 1976.

Mounce, Robert H. *The Book of Revelation (The New International Commentary on the New Testament)*. Grand Rapids: Eerdmans, 1977.

Murray, Iain H. *The Puritan Hope: Revival and the Interpretation of Prophecy*. Edinburgh: Banner of Truth, 1971.

Papini, Giovanni, trans. by Dorothy Canfield Fisher. "The Life of Christ" in *A Reader's Digest Family Treasury of Great Biographies*. Pleasantville, N.Y.: Reader's Digest, 1970. Vol. III.

Payne, J. Barton. *Encyclopedia of Biblical Prophecy*. New York: Harper & Row, 1973.

Polcyn, Richard. *The Zondervan NIV Bible Commentary*. Grand Rapids: Zondervan, 1994.

Proctor, W. C. G. "II Corinthians." F. Davidson, ed. *The New Bible Commentary*. Grand Rapids: Eerdmans, 1953.

Reese, Alexander. *The Approaching Advent of Christ*. London: Marshall, Morgan & Scott, 1937.

Robertson, A. T. *Word Pictures in the New Testament*. Nashville: Broadman, 1930. Vols. I, III, IV and VI.

Rosenthal, Marvin. *The Pre-Wrath Rapture of the Church*. Nashville: Thomas Nelson, 1990.

Rotherham, Joseph Bryant. *The Emphasized Bible*. Grand Rapids: Kregel, 1974 reprint.

Rumph, Jane. *Stories from the Front Lines: Power Evangelism in Today's World*. Grand Rapids: Chosen, 1996.

Russell, J. Stuart. *The Parousia: The New Testament Doctrine of Our Lord's Second Coming*. Grand Rapids: Baker, 1999 reprint (1887).

Ryrie, Charles Caldwell. *Dispensationalism Today*. Chicago: Moody, 1965.

———. *The Basis of the Premillennial Faith*. New York: Loizeaux, 1953.

Saucy, Robert L. *The Case for Progressive Dispensationalism*. Grand Rapids: Zondervan, 1993.

Schaff, Philip. *History of the Christian Church*. Grand Rapids: Eerdmans, 1950. Vol. VII.

Schweitzer, Albert. *The Quest of the Historical Jesus*. New York: Macmillan, 1957 reprint.

Scofield, C. I., ed. *The Scofield Reference Bible*. New York: Oxford University Press, 1967.

Sell, David. *Understanding End Times*. Pleasanton, Calif.: Northern California Bible College, 1999.

Smith, J. B. *Greek-English Concordance*. Scottdale, Pa.: Herald, 1955.

Smith, Wilbur M. "In the Study" ("The Olivet Discourse"). *Moody Monthly*, September 1957.

———. *You Can Know the Future*. Glendale, Calif.: G/L Regal, 1971.

Sproul, R. C. *The Last Days according to Jesus*. Grand Rapids: Baker, 1998.

Spurgeon, Charles H. *12 Sermons on the Second Coming of Christ*. Grand Rapids: Baker, 1995 reprint.

Strong, Augustus H. *Systematic Theology.* Philadelphia: Griffith and Roland, 1907.

Tasker, R. V. G. *The Gospel According to St. Matthew: Tyndale New Testament Commentaries.* Grand Rapids: Eerdmans, 1979 (eighth reprinting).

Thayer, Joseph Henry. *A Greek-English Lexicon of the New Testament.* New York: American Book, 1889.

Thomas, Robert L., and Stanley N. Gundry. *A Harmony of the Gospels.* Chicago: Moody, 1978.

Van Kampen, Robert. *The Rapture Question Answered: Plain & Simple.* Grand Rapids: Revell, 1997.

Vaughan, Curtis. "Colossians." Frank E. Gaebelein, gen. ed. *The Expositor's Bible Commentary.* Grand Rapids: Zondervan, 1978. Vol. 11.

Vincent, M. R. *Word Studies in the New Testament.* Wilmington, Del.: Associated Publishers and Authors, 1972 reprint.

Vine, W. E. *Expository Dictionary of New Testament Words.* Westwood, N.J.: Revell, 1966.

Walvoord, John F. *The Millennial Kingdom.* Grand Rapids: Zondervan, 1959.

———. *The Rapture Question.* Findlay, Ohio: Dunham, 1957.

———. *The Blessed Hope and the Tribulation.* Grand Rapids: Zondervan, 1976.

———. "Second Coming." Merrill C. Tenney, gen. ed. *The Zondervan Pictorial Encyclopedia of the Bible.* Grand Rapids: Zondervan, 1975. Vol. 5, pp. 325–28.

Williams, J. Rodman. *Renewal Theology: Systematic Theology from a Charismatic Perspective.* Three volumes in one. Grand Rapids: Zondervan, 1992. Vol. 3.

SUBJECT INDEX